# What Happened to Recess and Why Are Our Children Struggling in Kindergarten

# What Happened to Recess and Why Are Our Children Struggling in Kindergarten

Susan Ohanian

McGraw-Hill
New York   Chicago   San Francisco   Lisbon
London   Madrid   Mexico City   Milan   New Delhi
San Juan   Seoul   Singapore   Sydney   Toronto

Library of Congress Cataloging-in-Publication Data applied for.

# Mcgraw-Hill

A Division of The McGraw·Hill Companies

1 2 3 4 5 6 7 8 9 10 DOC/DOC 0 9 8 7 6 5 4 3 2

ISBN 0-07-138326-3

Product or brand names used in this book may be trade names or trademarks. Where we believe that there may be proprietary claims to such trade names or trademarks, the name has be used with an Initial capital or it has be capitalized in the style used by the name claimant. Regardless of the capitalization used, all such names have been used in an editorial manner without any intent to convey endorsement of or other affiliation with the name claimant. Neither the author nor the publisher intends to express any judgment as to the validity or legal status of any such proprietary claims.

KeyLinks: The Connection Between Instruction & Assessment is a registered trademark of Harcourt.
PowerPoint and AutoContent Wizard are registered trademarks of Microsoft Corporation.
Pee-Chee is a registered trademark.
BAND-AID is a registered trademark.

*The sponsoring editor for this book was Barbara Gilson, the editing supervisor was Maureen B. Walker, and the production supervisor was Peter McCurdy. It was set in Janson Text by TypeWriting.*

*Printed and bound by R. R. Donnelley & Sons, Inc.*

McGraw-Hill books are available at special quantity discounts to use as premiums and sales promotions, or for use in corporate training programs. For more information, please write to the Director of Special Sales, Professional Publishing, McGraw-Hill, Two Penn Plaza, New York, NY 10121-2298. Or contact your local bookstore.

This book is printed on recycled, acid-free paper containing a minimum of 50% recycled, de-inked fiber.

# Contents

# Foreword

ALFIE KOHN

**O**f all the chasms that separate one world from another, none is greater than the gap between the people who make policy and the people who suffer the consequences. There are those who reside comfortably on Mount Olympus, issuing edicts and rhetoric, and then there are those down on the ground who come to know the concrete reality behind the words. It's the difference between a legislator who casually runs his pen through a budget item (perhaps smiling to himself about reducing the size of government) and a struggling single mom who learns that there will be no help with heating-oil expenses this winter. It's the difference between a man with a chest full of ribbons who pokes a pin into a map (perhaps muttering about the need to push back the enemy's perimeter) and a young man on the scene whose liver is suddenly punctured by a sniper's bullet.

And it's the difference between important grown-ups who piously exhort us to hold our educational system "accountable" and a nine-year-old who has come to detest school because the days are now full of practice tests in place of projects and puzzles. Up there: people pounding the pulpits about the need for World-Class Standards. Down here: little kids weeping, big kids denied diplomas on the basis of a single exam score, wonderful teachers reduced to poring over the want ads.

There is a lot to be said about the spurious logic of the Tougher Standards movement and about the way standardized tests measure what matters least. The arguments and evidence are there, for anyone who cares to peer behind the sanctimonious rhetoric, or investigate the way exams are designed and used. My file cabinets are bulging with arresting arguments and damning data.

But you hold in your hands a book by a longtime teacher whom I once described as defiantly anecdotal. Susan Ohanian, who coined the much-needed word *Standardista* to describe those denizens of Mount Olympus, is an existentialist. Widespread misinterpretations of that philosophical movement notwithstanding, existentialism starts with the fact that each of us is a center of experience, the one who perceives and acts in and reflects on a world. It rebels against the systems and practices that crush or deny your subjectivity by reducing you to a part of a crowd, a scientific datum, or a pale approximation of some transcendent reality.

Once, the existentialists rebelled against Hegelian essentialism or Platonic forms. Today, they—we—are called upon to rebel against people who don't think about children "except as they distribute themselves across deciles," as Paul Hogan, former director of the National Council of Teachers of English, once put it. Susan, our archivist of educational absurdities, fearlessly clipping newspapers and trawling the Internet, insists that we think about children as children. She refuses to relinquish her sense of outrage or to become inured to what has become commonplace in our schools. Some books leave the reader with greater insight into the intellectual architecture of problematic practices, perhaps more data to build a case against them. This book is more likely to leave you wondering: "Are we out of our *minds*? What in the hell have we been letting them do to our kids?"

A couple of hundred years ago, Kant told us that the one thing we're not permitted to do, morally speaking, is to treat people as means to an end, as tools or instruments to achieve other objectives. It's been a while since I've read him, but I don't recall that he made an exception for really short people who don't eat their vegetables. Thus, it will not do to sacrifice children on the altar of accountability, to use them in a giant high-stakes experiment and ignore the very real harm.

About a year ago, Deborah Meier and I were having one of those dinners where we try to figure out the fundamental nature of the

Tougher Standards movement before the check arrives. On that particular night we stumbled upon a very dark possibility, one that is perhaps best communicated in the form of a thought experiment. Suppose that next year almost all the students in your state met the standards and passed the tests. What do you suppose would be the reaction from the politicians, businesspeople, and newspaper editorialists? Would these folks shake their heads in frank admiration and say, "Damn, those teachers are good"? That possibility, of course, is improbable to the point of hilarity. Every time I've laid out this hypothetical scenario, audiences tell me that across-the-board student success would immediately be taken as evidence that the tests were too easy.

So what does that mean? The inescapable implication, as Meier points out, is that the phrase "high standards" *by definition* refers to standards that everyone won't be able to meet. If everyone could meet them, that would be taken as prima facie proof that the standards were too low, and they would then be ratcheted upward—*until failures were created.* Despite its sugarcoated public-relations rhetoric, the whole standards-and-accountability movement is not about helping all children to become better learners. It is not committed to leaving no child behind. Just the opposite: it is an elaborate sorting device, separating wheat from chaff. And don't ask what happens to the chaff.

It's one thing to justify this heartless enterprise in the name of capital-letter abstractions, like Excellence or Higher Expectations. That leaves one with a bad taste. But when the process of flunking vast numbers of children, or forcing them to drop out, or turning whole schools into giant test-prep factories is rationalized as being in the best interest of poor and minority students—the ones who actually suffer most from high-stakes testing—then one staggers backward at the sickening paradox, the sheer Orwellian audacity of the Standardistas.

Often, of course, they can succeed in raising average test scores. You deprive kids of recess, eliminate music and the arts, cut back the class meetings and discussions of current events, offer less time to read books for pleasure, squeeze out the field trips and interdisciplinary projects and high-quality electives, spend enough time teaching test-taking tricks, and, you bet, it's possible to raise the scores. But that result is meaningless at best. When a school or district reports better test results this year than last, knowledgeable parents and other observers respond by saying, "So what?" (because higher test scores do not necessarily reflect higher quality teaching and learning)—or even "Uh oh" (because higher test scores may indicate *lower* quality teaching and learning).

And once you realize that the tests are, at best, unreliable indicators of quality, then what possible reason would there be to subject kids—usually African American and Latino kids—to those mind-numbing, spirit-killing, regimented instructional programs that were designed principally to raise test scores? If your only argument in favor of such a program is that it improves results on deeply flawed tests, you haven't offered any real argument at all. Knock out the artificial supports propping up "Success for All," "Open Court," "Reading Mastery," and other prefabricated exercises in drilling kids to produce right answers (often without any understanding), and these programs will then collapse of their own dead weight.

To knock out those supports, though, we must offer a sustained critique that embraces both data and experience. Not to sound like Ecclesiastes, but there is a time for studies and a time for stories, a place for both heated outrage and for cool analysis. Similarly, there is room for a range of strategies, from mild letters to the editor all the way to civil disobedience. The last chapter of this book, with its examples of what other people already are doing to derail this juggernaut, will offer hope, inspiration, and practical ideas. Every parent in North America who doubts that a standardized test score accurately reflects the proficiencies and possibilities of his or her child, every parent who worries about the educational consequences of this testing fad, should realize that there is no earthly reason why that child should be sent to school on the days the tests are given.

That's the enduring lesson of the civil rights movement: bad practices or unjust laws can continue only with our cooperation and consent. If, having educated and mobilized our neighbors, we withhold that consent and refuse to cooperate in what is being done to (all) our kids, then we can restore sanity to the schools—and, while we're at it, bring back recess.

Alfie Kohn's eight books on human behavior and education include *The Schools Our Children Deserve: Moving Beyond Traditional Classrooms and "Tougher Standards"* (Houghton Mifflin, 1999) and *The Case Against Standardized Testing* (Heinemann, 2000). His Web site, www.alfiekohn.org, includes a list of practical strategies for fighting the Standardistas, as well as resources, references, and contact information for grassroots groups around the U.S.

# What Happened to Recess and Why Are Our Children Struggling in Kindergarten

..THIS WEEK WE TOOK A TEST TO SEE IF WE'RE READY FOR THE TEST THAT TESTS OUR TEST SKILLS...

.. WAIT UNTIL KINDERGARTEN!..

Used with permission, Walt Handelsman © 2001 Newsday.

*Chapter 1*

# Training the National Guard Way

When Hollywood makes a movie, the American Humane Association (no relation to the Humane Society of America) watches out for animals and insects that appear in the film. Even maggots. In the movie *L.A. Confidential*, when a detective discovered a reeking corpse under a house, an observer from the American Humane Association was on hand to make sure the maggots were not mistreated.

Compared to kindergartners, apes live a life of luxury. According to the specific rules regarding the treatment of apes making movie appearances, if an ape works for more than three days in a row, then "a play area, empty room or private park where the ape may exercise and relax must be provided." Obviously, what America's schoolchildren need is a Childhood Humane Association, an association to make sure they are given equal protection with apes. In the name of standards, of making sure young children acquire what are billed as "skills for the global economy," schoolchildren across the country have no playtime. Atlanta made front-page headlines by building an elementary school with no playground. In 1998, a front-page story in the *New York Times* featured a picture of an appealing little kindergartner in Atlanta, Toya Gray, who confided to the reporter that she'd like "to sit on the grass and look for ladybugs."

Not a likely subject for front-page news in the newspaper of record? The *Times* zeroed in on the fact that in the name of standards and excellence, Toya's school, a new structure, was built very deliberately—without a playground. Eliminating playgrounds from the blueprints is the new fad in school construction. In this way school personnel prove they are devoted to high standards. Lollygagging over ladybugs is not permitted for children being trained for the global economy. The then Atlanta superintendent of schools, Benjamin O. Canada, explained the policy, "We are intent on improving academic performance. You don't do that by having kids hanging on the monkey bars." Funny thing. The U.S. Army acknowledges the need for a ten-minute break every hour during training sessions. Those in charge have determined that they get greater results in their training sessions when these short rest periods are inserted.

From California to Chicago to Virginia, school districts have abolished recess. And even in districts where recess is still on the books, increasingly, children who score poorly on standardized tests are forced to forgo the play break. While their better-scoring peers play games outside, the low scorers must stay in the classroom to practice their skills. Distressed teachers have told me about this phenomenon in New York City, in rural upstate New York, in Florida, Texas, California, Illinois, Pennsylvania, Michigan, and Idaho. The kids who do well on tests get a play break. Those who don't test well get more skill drill, frequently referred to as kill drill. Ironically, as plenty of experts will testify, by taking away children's free time, schools are making it more difficult for them to pay attention. Particularly with the stress of test prep muzzling them in class, children need some free time. But Tom Walker, director of school management for Manatee County, Florida, expresses a view that has taken hold across the country, telling the *Sarasota Herald-Tribune*, "We're in school basically for instruction, and recess, in most cases, does not provide instruction."

Maybe the schoolchildren of America should unionize. Children unite: You have nothing to lose but your workbooks. Think about it: The Agreement between Continental Grain Company, Decatur, Alabama, and the Retail Wholesale and Department Store Union, Local No. 451, AFL-CIO, stipulates that "the rest period schedules shall be one paid ten (10) minute rest period during the first four hours of the employee's shift and one paid ten (10) minute rest period during the second four hours of the employee's shift."

We acknowledge that adults need periodic breaks from work. We even acknowledge that apes in Hollywood need time and space to play. Requiring children to stay "on task" for a full day isn't just cruel and unjust; it is also nuts. No looking for ladybugs. No jumping rope, playing jacks, running races, hanging on the monkey bars, finding pictures in the clouds, looking for four-leaf clovers, making snow angels. And there's more: for kids who do poorly on the all-important tests, there is no time for singing songs, painting pictures, doing Black History projects, playing basketball. In many districts, poor test takers also miss out on art, music, P.E., and special project time in the library. While other children engage in these activities, poor test takers sit with the omnipresent skill workbooks. This is worse than monkey business; this is abusive.

What's more, there are schools in New York City and Los Angeles where teachers are forbidden to "waste time" by reading aloud to students. The Texas Assessment of Academic Skills (TAAS) *is* the curriculum. Science and social studies aren't tested in the elementary grades, so, more often than not, they are either dropped from the curriculum or treated in a cursory fashion. A veteran teacher, who recently moved to a large urban district in Texas from Oregon, notes, "We had our own standardized test woes there, but it was kid's stuff compared to Texas. Nothing in my wildest dreams could have prepared me for the lunacy of the TAAS and TEKS (Texas Essential Knowledge and Skills). Teacher orientation was filled with talk of teaching to the tests, and we are now bombarded with demands to document that we are teaching to the test. One administrator told us that we 'really shouldn't be teaching anything that isn't in the TEKS.'" This teacher adds, "This district lost 20 percent of its teachers last year. They're going to lose this one too." Nationwide, for every minute of every day, teachers are on call to prove they are doing only those things that will guarantee higher scores on high-stakes tests, the tests ordered by state politicians, tests that determine whether children advance from grade to grade, tests that determine whether high schoolers receive a high school diploma.

For every classroom activity, there must be a standard written on the board—so every word coming out of the teacher's mouth—and the children's—can be justified as enhancing a child's ability to pass the tests. One can only wonder what kinds of citizens children who have been denied art, music, P.E., and good stories will grow up to be. Treating young children like robots—or Wall Street brokers-in-training—cannot come to a good end. When the message is hammered to children from the moment they enter kindergarten, "You are never good enough," the results are tragic.

## THE BOY WHO ATE PENCILS

I taught third grade in a school that rigorously grouped children by their reading scores on standardized tests. My students, classified as the worst readers in third grade, made no bones about how they felt about reading. Throughout the day they told me how much they hated reading. Except Dennis. Dennis always had a library book in his hands. On the first day of school I learned that this eight-year-old had a deep and sophisticated interest in mythology and could rattle off the names of the gods and explain their functions. So what was he doing in the low reading group? I checked Dennis's permanent record. From kindergarten on, his standardized achievement test score rated him as functioning far below grade level in reading, language, and math.

I soon got first-hand evidence for the reason for the disconnect between Dennis's test scores and what I saw in the classroom. Believing that letter-writing is a surefire way to lure reluctant readers into books, I gave every student a little 3" x 5" spiral-bound notebook, and every day I wrote everybody a note, expecting an answer just as often. My reluctant readers were thrilled to read those notes, and they played by the rules: To get a new note, you had to write a note. Everybody but Dennis. As his classmates wrote their replies, Dennis looked at the ceiling, pulled on his hair, twisted in his chair. And then, just in case I hadn't noticed his hostility, he pushed a pile of books onto the floor.

"Did you read my note yet?" I asked him. Dennis nodded. "Going to answer it?"

"I don't have a pencil," he replied. Now, most children start off the school year with a kit of new supplies, eager to show their good intentions for the year. But I wasn't about to begin my own new year with a complaint. I handed Dennis a pencil.

A few minutes later, I prodded him again about answering my note. "I don't have a pencil," he answered.

"But I just gave you one," I said, looking on the floor around his desk.

"He probably ate it," Karen volunteered. "That's what he does every year. Crayons too." Karen added that she had lent her favorite Snoopy pencil to Dennis in first grade, that he had eaten it, and that she would never lend him another one.

Soon I discovered that Dennis destroyed pencils so he wouldn't have to face the trauma of using them to make marks on paper. When pressured, Dennis might take ten minutes to get his name down on paper—and then the *s*'s didn't always go in the right direction. On a diagnostic spelling test, he scored so poorly that the manual recommended a formal spelling test "not be attempted at this time."

These days, Standardistas, the corporate chiefs and politicians and media mavens who insist they know so much more than experienced teachers, would hold up Dennis as a failure of social promotion. After all, his abominable test scores proved how deficient he was in every skill area. Their solution would be something called direct instruction, a regimented approach with every move the teacher makes coming from a script devised by a publishing committee. One flaw in this approach was that, in contrast to test scores, classroom evidence showed that Dennis was an excellent reader. Every day he came into class, wanting to talk about what he'd read the night before.

I continued to write notes to the children, keeping a careful eye on Dennis, who very much wanted a new note from me each day. During note-writing time he tried to engage me in conversation about what he'd been reading. But I stuck firm to my rule: in this class, to get a note you had to write a note. And during note-writing time, we didn't talk about reading anything but notes. Before long, Dennis's longing for a note won out over his aversion to writing, and by October we had an ongoing exchange. Here's a sample:

Dear Dennis,
Wasn't it awfully COLD and DARK at 6?
My cat begs for food when I cook dinner. He
is greedy and he will eat EVERYTHING. Last
night he ate pea soup and grapes. I made a HUGE pot.
We will be eating it for a long time, even with the
cat's help.
Your friend,
Mrs. O.

[yes it was awful at 6:00. My dog begs for food too. He eats every thing I do. Last night he ate a whole turkey and a chicken. Your friend, Dennis]

I am the first to acknowledge that the spelling, the lack of spacing between words, the penmanship are all terrible, far below what we expect from third graders. These days, Dennis's note wouldn't pass official kindergarten standards. But because I'm a teacher, and not an automaton judging children only by skills checklists passed out by some state- department-of-education functionary, I also notice something else. Dennis is very aware of his audience and of the subtleties of telling a tall tale with which to entertain that audience. In my note I tell him a tall tale about my cat. In his reply he tells a taller tale about his dog. Dennis may not spell well, but he writes with voice and with wit and style, very much aware of the model his teacher has established. And anyone unduly alarmed by Dennis's penmanship should try reading Henry David Thoreau's.

Dennis is writing in a long-established genre, one that I have been reading aloud to children in the form of Sid Fleischman's *McBroom Tales*. For Dennis, art is informing writing. His classmates will eventually catch on to this approach, but at the beginning of the year Dennis is far ahead of the pack. Other third graders with perfect penmanship are not nearly so sophisticated in their appreciation of literary genre. So I work at capitalizing on Dennis's strengths rather than beating him up about his deficiencies.

Of course I was concerned, and I talked with Dennis's mother. She was cooperative, but she felt the school tended to exaggerate his difficulties, noting that Thomas Edison and Albert Einstein also had problems in school. She told me, "When he's a corporate president or a U.S. senator, he'll have a secretary to correct his spelling." Nonetheless, she gave me permission to consult the Learning Disabilities teacher in our school. This teacher observed Dennis in my classroom and then invited him to her class for more evaluation. She thought his writing dysfunction was serious—physical as well as behavioral, and she pinpointed specific ways Dennis manipulated teachers and materials to get his own way, to avoid work he didn't like.

With Dennis's mother's help, we launched a program to train him to use a pencil. It was a long, difficult struggle. Despite our hard work, there wasn't a totally victorious happy ending to Dennis's time in third grade. Dennis's spelling remained lousy, his penmanship barely readable—but with spaces between words. On the positive side: Dennis learned to use a pencil and even to keep one intact for an entire day; he learned to get his name on papers, to provide the minimal paper-and-pencil answers required in his math class, to be responsible for his homework. Dennis's story is one that can be told by millions of teachers across the country: When the Standardistas leave them alone, parents, teachers and students make decisions based on what they think is important for individual children in their care. They do what they can do.

In the spring, I made a bargain with Dennis. I promised him all sorts of extra reading time if he would just do the reading comprehension part of the standardized test administered every year. Not a high-stakes test, but one teachers used to inform their instructional practice. I told Dennis that he wouldn't have to fill in the bubbles for any other part of the test, but that I wanted him to prove what he could do on the reading part. "Show the world," I told Dennis. "This grade will be in your permanent record folder forever. Show everybody what you can do." He showed them all right. Dennis didn't miss a single question, achieving the highest score of anybody in third grade.

In most schools today Dennis would be floundering, and his teacher would not be allowed to use her own resources, experience, and imagination to rescue him. Based on his standardized test scores, Dennis would be forced to fill out multitudes of workbook pages on discrete skills, and would never have the opportunity to reveal and live out his talents. He would instead be defined by his deficiencies. And I suspect he'd avoid all that skill drill by continuing to eat pencils.

## AND THE NATIONAL GUARD SHALL LEAD THEM

A few years ago, a mother in northern California showed up at a school board meeting to protest that her four-and-a-half-year-old had failed the prekindergarten screening. The child was labeled "immature," with her thumb-sucking habit cited as evidence. "Of course she's immature," said Mom. "What is a four-and-a-half-year-old supposed to be?"

Good question. A Standardista push to make kindergarten and even prekindergarten academic turns age-appropriate behavior into an illness or a deficiency, and we see five-year-olds put on Ritalin because they can't sit still long enough to circle all the vowels on stacks of worksheets. In a move to circumvent charges that its new kindergarten standards are developmentally inappropriate, California has upped the eligible age for kindergarten entrance from four and one-half to five, and some districts are recommending that if children have a tough time with the new curriculum rigor, then these children should spend two years in kindergarten. Nationwide, kindergarten admission age has increased by four months.

*New York Times* education columnist Richard Rothstein calls this an "Alice-in-Wonderland effect," noting that "You push the first-grade curriculum down into kindergarten with one hand while driving the kindergarten entrance age up with the other." In a move reflecting more political strategy than concern for children's well-being, officials justify this deformation by saying that getting workers ready for what jobs in the twenty-first century demand, means tougher standards for kindergartners. Most teachers will tell you that when children can't perform well with certain material, something is wrong with the material, not with the children. In some affluent circles, parents have launched a countermove. Rothstein notes that the older eligibility doesn't fully offset the increased academics, so more and more parents, determined to protect their children from too much academic rigidity too early, are delaying their children's kindergarten entry till age six, hoping that by then they will be better prepared to meet the challenges.

But Standardistas feel kindergarten is too late. These days we have national curriculum expectations even for toddlers. In 1999, the state of Connecticut drafted six pages of "goals and benchmarks'" for math expectations for preschoolers, part of a 33-page guide to curriculum guidelines. The High/Scope Educational Research Foundation in Ypsilanti, Michigan, publishes a 539-page preschool curriculum. With all good intentions, the current Bush administration is advocating a rigorous skill model for Head Start preschool programs across the country. Three- and four-year-olds are drilled about letters, dividing words into syllables, and spelling. The plan is that this will prepare poor children to learn to read when they go to kindergarten. The Department of Health and Human Services, which oversees Head Start, is developing a curriculum that every Head Start teacher will be expected to follow. This notion of bypassing teacher savvy and handing out curriculum scripts has already infected elementary schools across the country (see Chapter 3). But the Head Start plan is particularly ominous. Plenty of developmental psychologists and teachers point out that teaching isolated components of language without the prior experiences of lots of reading aloud and lots of talk can do much more harm than good. It all comes back to money. One reason officials feel Head Start teachers need scripts is that they are high school graduates earning, on average, $20,000 a year.

So today's kids enter kindergarten identified as deficient in skills that weren't even introduced to kids a decade ago. It's called preparing future workers for the global economy. Keep the pressure on; keep people worried that they're never good enough. And it starts in kindergarten. Long regarded as the place where young children develop social, emotional, and verbal underpinnings on which their later academic achievement is based, kindergarten has become a targeted-skill zone. After all, if you are under a lot of pressure to get high test scores out of second graders, then first grade is already too late to start teaching them to read. So the Standardista mentality now pollutes the place that originated as a "children's garden," flooding it with such notions as "raising the bar" and "high stakes" and "zeroing in on skills." This may be language appropriate to those who train racehorses or the military. It is not appropriate to the care and nurture of children. Even *Time* magazine, hardly a voice for schoolhouse slouchers, lamented that with the speeded-up curriculum, kindergarten should be renamed "kinder grind."

Evidence of just how high the stakes are can be seen in the fact that throughout California children start preparing for the state-mandated

Stanford 9 test (SAT-9) when they are five years old. Children don't take the exam until second grade, but Standardistas insist that "too soon" is not a concept that applies to test savvy. In San Diego County, for example, kindergartners practice how to take timed tests. The teacher sets a timer and they draw a picture. They learn to fill in the bubbles on the answer form. The San Diego *Union Tribune* quotes a principal, "Unless a student becomes familiar with the [exam] format, they cannot zero in on the academic skills. Try passing a bar exam without preparation." Maybe someone should ask that principal what taking the bar exam has to do with being a kindergartner.

In North Carolina, the state-mandated social studies curriculum requires kindergartners to be able to "identify facts" in nonfiction material. In California, they must distinguish fact from fantasy as well as learn about probability and statistics. Increasingly, testocrats look at today's five-year-olds as tomorrow's computer programmers and engineers. Butchers, bakers, candlestick makers, and artists need not apply. Seventh graders hear the mantra "Algebra or bust!" For kindergartners, the pressure is just as great. In an Illinois school, the teacher sets a timer and the child reads the prescribed list of sight words aloud. If the child doesn't complete the list in the prescribed number of seconds, she is sent to the corner—just like the dunce chair of old. Blocks, finger paints, dolls, sand tables, and other materials to encourage free exploration are gone from this kindergarten. The focus is on preparing kindergartners for future tests. At least in New York City's Public School 9, kindergartners still get recess. In a seven-hour day, they get 25 minutes free from academics.

Things are even bleaker for kindergartners and their teachers in Chicago. Writing in the *New York Times*, Jacques Steinberg described the 53d day of the school year in a kindergarten classroom at Joyce Kilmer Elementary. The teacher knows it's the 53d day because "Day: 053" is printed at the top of the recommended lesson plan open on her desk, a thick, white binder crammed with goals for each day and step-by-step questions given to her and the city's 26,000 other teachers by the school system's administrators at the start of the school year. The page also identifies the section of the Iowa Test of Basic Skills to which that day's entry corresponds—even though the kindergartners will not take the test, which determines who will repeat the grade, until the end of first grade.

On my refrigerator I have a bumper sticker: *It's 10 p.m. Do you know where your cat is?* I used to think it was funny. Somehow, in light of Chicago timetables, I'm not laughing any more. The Chicago version could hang in the superintendent's office: *It's 10 a.m. I know what every kindergartner in the city is doing.*

Every teacher in Chicago gets this day-by-day outline of what should be taught in language arts, mathematics, science, and social studies. The *New York Times* reporter notes that some see this as the logical outcome of the standards movement, providing "an almost ironclad guarantee that all students will be exposed to the same material and that all teachers, regardless of qualification, will know exactly how to present it." Paul Vallas, Chicago-school-chief-turned-gubernatorial-candidate whose idea this is, says he got the idea from National Guard training manuals.

Stop and think about it. What's wrong with this picture? National Guard training manuals and five-year-olds. Nobody seems to have told Vallas that maybe children don't learn the same way as adults, that maybe all children don't learn the same way or on the same timetable. Teachers at Parlin Junior High in Massachusetts still write their own lesson plans, but the requirements are specific: Each day's lesson must be typed up on a page that details the objective, the content, and the related learning standard from the curriculum frameworks. A semester's worth of lessons fills a binder the size of a New York City phone directory.

## FIGHTING BACK

By state decree, every child in California starts taking the SAT-9, a test that purports to determine what children know, in second grade. Fresno, California, teacher Silvio Manno refused to give the SAT-9 to his second graders. The test is given in English, and Manno's students spoke Spanish, and Manno, who believes in offering appropriate academic challenges to the seven-year-olds in his care, judged that it would be cruel and nonsensical to make them take a test they could not decipher. For exercising his teacher judgment, Manno was suspended without pay. An administrator acknowledged that the test may not be fair, but "the bottom line is the state picked that, and our kids are going to have to do as well as they can on it."

The State rules.

Others are not so sanguine. Eugene Garcia, dean of the Graduate School of Education at the University of California, Berkeley, blasts the state's use of the SAT-9, calling it "reform by shame." Garcia is on record urging parents to request waivers, opting their children out of taking the tests. Under the letter of the law waivers are allowed, but many teachers are under the impression that they are not allowed to inform parents of their right to refuse testing of their children. Not so Silvio Manno. These days he doesn't give the SAT-9 because nobody shows up to take it. Parents submit waivers to opt their children out. This is not a widespread phenomenon. For 79,000 students tested in the Fresno Unified School District, only 342 received waivers. About one-third of the waivers came from Manno's school, which is classified with a student population of 55 percent "learning English."

The Allentown School District seems to have found itself caught up in similar testing craziness. The state of Pennsylvania sued the Allentown School District for refusing to give the state-mandated standardized test to 106 non-English-speaking students. In April 2001, the state agreed to drop the lawsuit only if they receive all test booklets from the district to ensure every student required by law to take the test did so. Although state regulations allow someone to read math questions to students in their native language, Allentown officials worried about finding translators for all of the 22 languages spoken by their students. State officials don't want excuses; they insist the district is violating federal law. Allentown officials still think they are right, but worry about the expense of fighting a lawsuit. Maybe the answer is to require members of Congress and state legislatures to take a few tests in Mandarin Chinese, Swahili, or Punjabi.

The New York City Board of Education reports that immigrants learning English in city schools are dropping out at nearly double the rate they were two years ago. Of 9942 students in the class of 2000 in bilingual programs, 31 percent quit school, a sharp increase from the 17 percent dropout rate in 1998. It's not hard to figure out why. New rules require all students to pass the English Regents exam. Based on a college prep curriculum, the exam made *New York Times* headlines for requiring students to write a response to a passage written by the sixteenth century essayist Roger Ascham (see Chapter 3). Seeing that they are not going to pass such a test, students are dropping out as early as ninth or tenth grade, and they are doing it in high numbers. Maybe we should build prisons next to the schools.

Critics blame bilingual programs, citing "the good old days" when immigrant children went to school, learned English, and did fine. But people are confusing economic success with educational success. USC Professor and noted literacy expert Stephen Krashen observes that in those good old days, when jobs in manufacturing and agriculture were plentiful, economic success preceded school success. "This is much less likely to occur today; economic success is much more dependent on school success." In *Condemned Without a Trial: Bogus Arguments Against Bilingual Education*, Krashen presents startling evidence of dropout rates among students with home languages other than English in those good old days: dropout rates exceeded 90 percent.

In *The Way We Were? The Myths and Realities of America's Student Achievement*, *New York Times* education columnist Richard Rothstein also presents a convincing argument that the good old school days were not so good—particularly for immigrant and minority children. Rothstein shows that the immigrant and minority students who dropped out of school in the first half of the century made dramatic gains in academic achievement in the 1980s and 1990s. It seems worse than perverse now to throw away these gains in the name of high-stakes tests.

## THE END OF CHILDHOOD

Knowing that third grade would be a challenge, the mother of an eight-year-old skipped the usual clown, pizza party, or trip to the beach for his

August party. The celebrant and nine guests attended a hitting-the-books party at the SCORE! Learning chain, where they spent the first half of the party in front of computers answering math and spelling problems. At these parties, participants earn points on their skill performance, points that can be turned in later for prizes. Cake and ice cream comes after skill drill. In a front-page article on this phenomenon, the *Wall Street Journal* quoted the mother of an eight-year-old who celebrated her birthday at a SCORE! center in Wellesley, Massachusetts. With all the focus on high-stakes tests, Mom says, "You can't expose them to enough, I feel." These parties are so popular that Great Neck, New York, parents book months in advance. SCORE! Learning, Inc., is owned by Kaplan Educational Centers, the Washington Post Company unit best known for its test-cramming schools for the SAT and the GRE (Graduate Record Examinations). Going after the elementary market is a relatively new venture for Kaplan. SCORE! also publishes parent guides for various state tests, defining this practice as "a public service to families." So far, SCORE!'s curriculum team has developed exam fact sheets and parent guides to state tests in California, Connecticut, Illinois, Maryland, Massachusetts, New Jersey, New York, Texas, and Virginia.

Maureen McMahon, Kaplan publisher, says, "Anyone could see there was a need for a guide that would take some of the anxiety away from this process." But even Massachusetts's test-happy education commissioner, David Driscoll, acknowledged that the test prep books may increase anxiety among children and their parents. "There's a danger in overemphasizing the test and the test results." Driscoll later changed his tune. In October 2001, Massachusetts contracted with Princeton Review for a $200,000 on-line test prep program for high schoolers who failed the state's high-stakes tests. Critics point out that the students most likely to need help are the ones most likely not to have home access to the Internet. Other critics ask what happened to the governor's plan to have 20,000 tutors in place by the summer of 2001, a plan that fizzled.

Princeton Review, the outfit that preps kids for the SAT, is making aggressive moves in the high school and elementary test-anxiety markets. The program Princeton Review sold to Massachusetts was piloted in Texas. In addition to contracts with states, Princeton Review operates Homeroom.com, a test prep service for individual schools. For the parent market it offers *The Princeton Review High School Edge* and *The Princeton Review Middle School Edge*. The latter is billed as "everything your sixth, seventh, eighth grader needs to get an edge in school . . . the ultimate Middle School Solution!" Seven CDs for $39.99 run more than *The Princeton Review: Inside the SAT and ACT 2002 Deluxe*. Parents might think twice about putting their children through an ultimate solution.

The curriculum at the Woodlands Elementary School in Amarillo is totally test-prep driven, and the kids don't even pick up their #2 pencils. Neither do their teachers. The kids take practice tests at Homeroom.com. The tests are graded on-line, and a chart is provided for the teacher, showing what skills students need to practice some more for Texas's high-stakes test. "I know exactly what kinds of questions they missed," a teacher told the *New York Times*. "I automatically know what that kid needs to work on, so I can focus my instruction on what they're weak in."

John Katzman, chief executive officer of the Princeton Review, claims that his test prep company is "diagnostic" and that it "offloads from the teacher one of the most difficult burdens she has." It would be interesting to know how many teachers would sign on to that statement. And maybe someone should ask the kids how they feel about life becoming one test after another.

The *New York Times* article covering this electronic phenomenon pointed out that one of the problems is "students need access to computers, and teachers must know how to use them." The article brushed aside deeper concerns of whether this kind of streamlined piffle should dominate classrooms. Workbook drill is workbook drill, and replacing a #2 pencil with the punch of a computer key doesn't make it any more legitimate. What parents should question is why such test prep is crowding out more important curriculum, and why the teacher has ceded away her professional judgment. Funny how the media rarely look at it this way. They just report on what the machinery can do, ignoring the professional, ethical, and moral questions inherent in doing it. The teacher interviewed talked about a student scoring 20 points higher on a practice TAAS test in February than in September, proof, she said, of the efficacy of the computer skill drill. Certainly if one drills students on the skills that are on the test, after five months they should do better on those skills. That's not the question. The question is, How should children be spending their time in school? The question is, What rich curriculum opportunities did the child miss as a result of daily drill on a narrow range of skills?

Another test prep outfit, Kaplan Learning Service, takes its services to the schools. El Camino Real High in Woodland Hills, California, hired Kaplan to come in and do teacher in-service, training teachers on how to prepare their students for the exam. Traditionally, teacher in-service sessions have focused on helping teachers deepen their pedagogy. Using this time and money for test prep strikes many as a professional affront and outrage.

In some states, test prep books are a growth industry. In Texas, teachers have quit the profession to open up shop selling test prep materials. At least 10 companies now market test guides in Ohio. The ubiquitous nature of these guides is made apparent in what happens to eighth graders who have failed the state test in North Carolina. They go into Prep School. Here are the books they use in this school:

1. *Buckle Down on N.C. Reading/Math*, 1996, Profiles Corporation
2. *Ketchup on Reading/Math*, 1996, Profiles Corporation
3. *Mastering Reading Through Reasoning*, 1995, Innovative Sciences, Inc.
4. *Preparing for the N.C. Competency Test in Reading/Math*, 1999, Amsco School Publications, Inc.
5. *Scoring High in Reading*, 1985, Random House, Inc.
6. *The Competitive Edge* (Reading/Math), 1997, Contemporary Publishing of Raleigh, Inc.
7. *The N.C. Literature-Based Coach for End-of-Grade Reading Tests*, 1997

And there's more. If parents think there isn't enough test prep and test taking already at school, then they can go on-line and test kids at home. Former U.S. education secretary William Bennett has announced his on-line venture to capitalize on parent anxieties over whether their kids are good enough. Parents can obtain diagnostic tests in every major subject in every grade. These tests are scored on-line for $50 to $100 a test. Chester Finn, a conservative spokesman who frequently rails against the quality of public schools and a member of the board of Bennett's proposed on-line venture, said the tests give parents a check on whether children are learning as much as they should be. Other on-line companies are already offering tests of everything from a preschooler's motor skills to a fourth grader's vocabulary. Plenty of education experts advise caution about these tests, which reduce a child's performance to a percentile number, but standardized test mania has made parents as anxious as their children.

Before they spend a lot of time and money training their children to pass the tests, maybe parents should consider this: In March 2001, the Virginia Board of Education voted to change some of the state's Standards of Learning (SOL) for history and social studies, revisions intended to give more students a chance to pass the state tests. Material judged too sophisticated for third graders was moved into the seventh-grade curriculum.

Read that last sentence again. Parents and teachers complained that the SOLs were too tough for third graders, so the board of education bowed to pressure and bumped the material up four grades. Something is wacko here, and it isn't children. "I think the process worked," Kirk T. Schroder, president of the board of education, told the *Washington Post*. Something worked? Sounds more as if something was terribly wrong for thousands of third graders for a number of years. Mickey Vanderwerker, leader of PAVURSOL (Parents Across Virginia United to Reform SOLs), says her third grader studied this standard: "Students will explain the term civilization and describe the ancient civilizations of Greece and Rome in terms of geographic features, government, agriculture, architecture, music, art, religion, sports and the roles of men, women and children."

When the unit was finished, Mickey asked her son if they could visit the people in Greece he was studying about. "Oh, no, mommy. We would need a real bus, not a school bus." Mickey called for a Virginia "Take the Test Day," asking 10,000 successful adults to take the Standards of Learning tests. "If more than 70 percent can pass them, maybe the tests and the standards really aren't so bad. But if they can't, then review and revise the standards and the testing program. Let's let the legislators go first." Mickey reports there have been no takers.

In New Jersey, parents and teachers complained about the way the tests were scored ever since the state put its standards in place. The fact that in the 1999–2000 school year, only six students out of 90,000 received the high mark of six (on a scale of one to six) indicates that maybe the complainers had a point. Six kids in New Jersey know how to write, and the rest are dodos? Even the Business Roundtable, the Fordham Foundation, the Heritage Foundation, and the U.S. Congress might find those statistics hard to believe. A panel of experts looked at the tests in August and decided that the grading standards had been too tough: fourth graders were being judged by eighth-grade standards. The New Jersey School Board Association had another bone to pick with the test: taking five days to administer, it's longer than the SAT and the state bar exam for new lawyers.

In California, children take the top-secret Stanford Achievement Test, Ninth Edition (SAT-9). Every teacher who administers the test must pledge in writing never to reproduce, store, or reveal the exam's contents or format in any way. According to Harcourt Educational Measurement, teachers shouldn't worry about signing away their rights to criticize the test because "All items are grade-level appropriate so that they are within the experience of students taking the test." A California teacher, whose name can't be revealed because he/she could be fired for talking about the test, points out the pressure to which children are subjected: a six-year-old child taking the SAT-9 has less time per test question than a college graduate applying to law school.

Another important question: Harcourt says all items are grade-level appropriate. Are we just supposed to sit back and take their word for it?

As any parent, pediatrician, or teacher can point out, there have always been plenty of children who don't toe the line: kids who don't listen, follow instructions, or turn in homework. These kids, more often boys than girls, are squirrelly, obstreperous, and now at risk for being labeled as having a neurological disorder or some sort of brain damage. Increasingly, schools tell the parents to get the kid on Ritalin or Prozac. Or else. And most family physicians acquiesce. But a number of dissident child psychologists warn that most pediatricians and family physicians are not qualified to distinguish between an abnormal child and a child who is exhibiting quite normal behavior in not wanting to sit through a seven-hour school day cramming for standardized tests—without recess, art, music, gym. At congressional hearings on Ritalin held in March 2000, Dr. Lawrence Diller, a behavioral pediatrician, suggested that these days doctors wouldn't hesitate to put Tom Sawyer or Pippi Longstocking on Ritalin. He could add Barney. As academic pressures increase in preschool, the Ritalin rage extends downward to younger and younger children. Diller has observed, ironically, that with about 5 million children currently taking Ritalin as they go to school with average class sizes of 30, "Why not increase the number of children taking Ritalin to 7.5 million so we could increase classroom size to 45 and save a lot of money?"

## LICE ABATEMENT AND THE BUSINESS EXECUTIVE DREAM OF ASSEMBLY-LINE EDUCATION

News coming out of schools today sounds more like stockyard quotes from grain futures. Or pork bellies. In the name of what they call educational standards, millionaire CEOs, politicians, and assorted pundits are rating our children as though they were so many slabs of beef. Like beef, schools are rated U.S. Government Approved, but parents and teachers aren't let in on what goes into the rating system. For the past decade, Standardistas have been waging a preemptive strike on public education, and it's past time for parents to realize that things are getting serious, that, in the name of standards, your child might be denied a high school diploma, no matter how he does on daily classroom work.

Even if your child is good at filling in bubbles on "Choose a), b), c), d)" tests, his education is in dire trouble.

Standardista rhetoric is revamped psychobabble: "I'm OK, you're OK, but those fellows in the schools stink." While downsizing and outsizing middle-class America, this hoary chorus is lamenting our so-called lackluster schools and teachers in the vain hope that their clamor will distract the public from noticing that buying power for middle America continues to drop. And so far, the Standardista rhetoric seems to be working. According to Gallup surveys, parents like the school their own children attend, but are convinced all other schools are lousy.

Which brings me to a recent incident at a drugstore in California. All I was trying to do was find something to read while waiting for the pharmacist to fill a prescription for my father. My eyes lit on a newspaper clipping taped to the counter. It reported that a new, virulent form of head lice is rampant throughout the land, and that plain old petroleum jelly is as good a treatment as more expensive products.

"That's interesting," I commented.

"Yes," nodded the clerk. "But if schools would only do their jobs, then there wouldn't be such a problem."

Thwack! There it was. Let's just add "lack of lice control" to the growing list of teacher inadequacies.

I wonder whether mastery of lice control should come before or after such newly inaugurated state standards from California to Virginia that require students to:

1. Analyze the role of the arts in civilizations past and present.
2. Master the fundamental concepts, principles, and interconnections of the life, physical, and earth/space sciences.
3. Understand the development of economic systems.
4. Read and understand literature representative of various societies, eras, and ideas.
5. Use geometric methods to analyze, categorize, and draw conclusions about points, lines, planes, and space.

I'm out of breath already.

And where does lice abatement fit? Maybe we can just slip it in between "just say no" to drugs and "just say yes" to condoms.

The clerk may never realize it, but everyone from President Bush to New York Commissioner of Education Richard Mills to California Governor Grey Davis to IBM CEO Lou Gerstner is responsible for the fact that I pounced on her instead of smiling politely.

"And what measures do you recommend that teachers take to stop those lice dead in their tracks at the schoolhouse door?" I asked in measured tones.

My question was definitely a conversation stopper, but unfortunately Louis V. Gerstner, Jr., was unavailable to hear my defense of the schools. Gerstner, chairman and CEO of IBM, a many-millions-a-year guy, may not have any suggestions about lice control, but he sure isn't shy about issuing plenty of other education edicts. He has plenty of ideas about how teachers should do their jobs. He leads the Standardista charge setting up roadblocks to your child's high school diploma. Gerstner leads a chorus line of public-schools bashers who insist that the "business" of schools is "the distribution of information." He advises teachers to pull up their socks and to follow his model: "Know what your job is; know what your outcomes should be; know how you will measure output."

Output. He's talking about children.

In that same California town, I spoke to the mother of an eight-year-old who is worried that she is only number four in her class. "How does she know she's number four?" I asked. The mother told me that the children are tested on skills every day, and every week the results are posted. Newspaper accounts describe similar skill displays in states across the country. Children are ever under the gun to measure up; increasingly, children are made to feel they can never be good enough.

Suzanne Tacheny, director of California Business for Education Excellence, insists that testing helps kids and parents. "California has a testing program around some basic content areas—English language arts, mathematics, science, and history/social science. Those subjects, especially reading and math, are the foundations of the education the public expects public schools to deliver." See Chapter 5 for further elucidation on the business advocacy of the conveyor-belt notion of schooling. See Chapter 7 for a look at what parents do and don't want from schools.

A fourth-grade teacher in Vancouver, Washington, who wishes to remain anonymous because he's hoping to transfer to a grade level where their state test isn't administered, says the Washington Assessment of Student Learning (WASL) doesn't test what students know or what they are capable of learning; it tests what the state wants them to know. "If you can jump three feet, they can raise the bar to three feet one inch."

Washington State University professor Donald Orlich reviewed a sample fourth-grade test given in Washington, analyzing the developmental difficulty of every question. He concluded that "between 60 to 70 percent of the math questions" were beyond the children's developmental level. "They simply don't have the ability yet to use the higher-level thinking skills that test required." In an article in the highly respected scholarly journal *Phi Delta Kappan*, "Education Reform and Limits to Student Achievement," Orlich observes "for nine- and ten-year-olds, there is a cognitive limit."

When 63 percent of fourth graders fail the state math test in Washington, what are parents supposed to conclude:

1. Their children are inadequate?
2. Their children's teachers are inadequate?
3. The test is loony?

Orlich did an item-by-item analysis of the test, and concluded that a significant number of the problems on the Washington test are as difficult as problems on a prestigious national test that only one percent of eight-year-olds answer correctly. So when Washington parents are told their children don't know math, they need to ask just what this means. Parents across the country need to ask the same question. They need to ask it loudly, and they need to ask it often.

And one way to ask this question is to study the questions released to the public. On the third-grade Minnesota Comprehensive Assessment

1998, there is a reading passage about Sylvester Graham, for whom the Graham cracker is named. Students read how Graham got the idea for a new food. "He watched people gulp down their food. Greasy piles of fried potatoes. Slabs of red meat. Pounds of pastries."

Three paragraphs later, they read, "With this graham flour, his followers, called Grahamites, baked bread and crackers. Instead of hot morning gruel, the popular breakfast at the time, Grahamites ate the first cold cereal, 'Granula,' made of crumbled rebaked graham crackers."

Here's a comprehension question from the test:

The story says the Grahamites did not eat hot morning gruel.
What was gruel most like?
a) Doughnuts
b) Oatmeal
c) Potatoes
d) Crackers

At first glance, this might seem to be a straightforward question that relies on what teachers call "reading in context," figuring out new words from the context of surrounding material in the reading passage. The trouble is the passage contains clues that would justify a choice for a, b, and c. And for good measure, the test writers stick in "'Granula,' made of crumbled rebaked graham crackers" as a further distracter item.

If a child does not come to the story knowing what gruel is, the context in the paragraph does not help him choose the right answer. And anyway, for many of today's children, "oatmeal" is just about as arcane as "gruel." This reading passage is typical in presenting material about life in a long-ago period, life that is alien to today's children who aren't fortunate enough to be hearing *Little House on the Prairie* read aloud each night. Likewise, there are many cultural assumptions embedded in a phrase such as "slabs of red meat," assumptions that many third graders whose parents aren't vegetarians will not pick up on during a reading test.

What parents need as a guide to the fairness of reading tests is to see a careful, expert examination of the content. They need to hear explanations of why children choose the answers they do. As famed and thoughtful educator Deborah Meier has pointed out, children's wrong answers are very convincing. There's the rub. Test makers claim "trade secrets," refusing to let the public see their tests. City and state education departments insist that it is illegal for teachers to talk about their tests and for scholars to publish critiques of specific test items. Test makers and the officials who buy their tests circle the wagons, keeping marauding questioners out. Think about this: The Chicago Board of Education sues a teacher for $1.4 million for publishing its test questions after students have taken the tests. Police from the Gwinnett County Georgia school system show up on my doorstep in Vermont making threats about a CTB McGraw-Hill test that had been mailed to Georgia media. Florida declares it against the law for a teacher to glance over a child's shoulder and take a peek at any part of the test. Their fear is real. Let professionals read the test, and sooner or later someone is going to squeal about the inappropriate and unfair content. The public now gets the tests interpreted through the lens of big business and education bureaucrats. Parents need to see tests interpreted through the lens of educators.

Instead of treating teachers like horse thieves, our legislators might consider treating them like professionals. Funny thing: While our teachers are being beaten up by politicians and the press as incompetent and worse, according to a November 2000 Gallup poll, school teachers rate highly with the public. Rated "high" or "very high" by 62 percent, teachers score considerably better than either governors or reporters, rated 30 percent and 16 percent respectively. At 23 percent, business executives didn't do any better. Instead of railing against teachers, maybe Standardistas should put their own houses in order.

## JUST THE FACTS, MA'AM

After five years of impeccable personal habits, my cat stopped using the litter box. Before facing the ultimate decision of choosing between husband and pet, I lugged the (four-legged) beast off to the vet's. The vet looked into the cat's ears, stroked his own chin, and said, "Well, it's hard to tell about these things. It could be behavioral or it could be medical. Let's wait and see." For that, the vet charged me 32 bucks and advised me to have a good day. It's called professional services.

At first, I was outraged. What kind of chutzpah was this? I wanted a diagnosis; I wanted a cure. But then I realized that teachers need the right to do the same: We need the confidence to admit there are certain things we cannot know, not right this minute anyway. We need the courage to say that we and the children need some wait-and-see time before passing judgment. If the vet hadn't been confident in what he did know, he could have gone to the data warehouse and given me a stack of computer printouts showing my cat's age, heart rate, reflexes, and so on. He could have given my cat an MRI and other high-tech evaluation. If he really wanted to snow me, he'd have given me a graph showing how the length of my cat's tail compared with those of other felines around the country and in Singapore. And I might have been so impressed by all those numbers that I'd have forgotten that the cat was still not using the litter box.

Americans love irrelevant information, but it's one thing to play silly games in your own living room and quite another to allow children's academic lives to be held hostage by the national mania for tedious statistification. In resigning ourselves to keeping track of each child's so-called skills pretty much the way handicappers figure the horses, we must be wary that we don't lose faith in our own observations, our own intuition. We must ask ourselves just what it is we know when we know a child tests out as a 3.2, and if we know something different when that number is 2.8 or 3.6. We must remind ourselves that teachers come to know quite a lot about the students in their charge—and parents know even more—long before the test results come in. And the numbers must not be allowed to obliterate what we know.

Value, for a McDonald's customer, is a predictable, standardized product. Parents need to be careful about trying to ask schools to deliver a streamlined product, one that is capable of being mass-produced and mass-judged—even though Standardistas like Colorado's former governor Roy Romer are "committed to entertaining many new forms of delivering a K-12 product." Delivering a product—as though kids were just another sack of dog food. A nation addicted to fast food should think again about producing fast kids.

Parents must not expect the classroom to be a neat and tidy place—like the kitchen in Anne Tyler's *Accidental Tourist*, where Rose "had a kitchen so completely alphabetized, you'd find the allspice next to the ant poison." When Rose's brother Macon goes grocery shopping, he takes three tagged books. One holds data from *Consumer Reports*, so that under B, there's the top-rated brand of bread. In a second book he writes down prices. The third book holds coupons. If Anne Tyler ever decides to write a sequel, Rose and Macon should be working for the state education department.

Bureaucrats with a Standardista mindset insist that standardized tests will tell you everything you need to know about your children. They claim an anecdotal system of evaluation, a use of student portfolios, making a judicious use of standardized tests as just part of the overall evaluation, is not practical. Parents need to realize that the important question in evaluation is not whether it's practical; the question is not whether it's efficient and easily stored in data banks. The question parents and teachers must ask is whether it's true. Secretary of Education Rod Paige insists, "Tests provide irrefutable data about which kids are learning what, and in which classrooms." Megan Farnsworth, Bradley Fellow at the Heritage Foundation, declares, "You can't manage what you can't measure." She quotes a charter school principal as saying, "The more you test, the better the students do," which seems just about as logical as saying the more you take your temperature, the better you feel. Ever looking for the quantitative knockout punch, public-school bashers don't admit to ambiguity. No anecdotes, please. Just the facts, ma'am. In 1943, William Faulkner wrote an unsolicited letter to fellow Southern writer Eudora Welty after reading her short story "The Robber Bridegroom." Faulkner wrote, "You're doing all right." We'd do well to give our children the same message.

And my cat? I fed him pills, and I tickled him under the chin and pleaded with him to be a good fellow and mend his wicked ways. Finally, I got him a new litter box, brown instead of blue. And my cat started using it. So the vet was right: it was either behavioral or medical. Mostly, it was a mystery.

*Chapter 2*

# Maybe College Shouldn't Begin in Kindergarten

In *As Good As I Could Be*, Susan Cheever describes her daughter's reaction to a question posed during an infamous nursery-school entrance test in New York City. Shown cardboard pieces of vegetables and fruits, the child was asked, "Which of these would a guinea pig be most likely to eat?" Cheever's daughter pondered the question and then asked, "Do guinea pigs eat puzzle pieces?"

In South Carolina, Zenobia Washington says her seven-year-old daughter Alexis loves school, but Zenobia worries about teachers "being boxed into a school system that does not allow them to teach to their full potential." Alexis's kindergarten teacher was very concerned that she did not know her colors. Zenobia couldn't fathom this. "I know my child knows her colors. What the teachers saw as the color green Alexis may have called sea foam because that's what I said. She called circles 'disks' and squares 'blocks' because I work with fabrics and beads, and that's what I call them."

The real insult, though, came in first grade, when Zenobia asked how her daughter was doing. "The first thing out of the teacher's mouth was that they had not started any testing, so she couldn't tell me how Alexis was doing. I thought, 'Well, you can tell me if she is getting along with other children, if she is paying attention, if she is participating. Is she listening?'" Zenobia continues, "Of course she could have told me these things, but teachers are under a lot of pressure to think only the test counts." Zenobia believes schools should be challenging and fun, and her wish list for Alexis echoes that of most parents. "I want my child to be computer literate, to read well and be good in math and science, because I know these things will help her live a fuller life. I want her to learn another language so that she can have friends who don't speak English." The list isn't unusual, and Zenobia's concluding remarks echo those of parents around the country who see that the emphasis on standardized tests is deforming their children's education. "I don't want Alexis to learn these things so she can be a whiz at taking standardized tests. I want her to know that she has learned a skill because she can apply it to her daily life, not because she gets a smiley face sticker and a free coupon for McDonald's french fries."

There is plenty of pressure pulling parents in another direction. "Last chance for a Learning Adventure!" trumpets an envelope sent to parents. Inside matter offers California parents in selected zip codes the summer 2001 schedule for College Admission Prep Camp. An outfit that has changed its name from TestTakers, Test Scholars promises camp participants that for $845, "we don't just teach tricks to get around the test—we teach a combination of skills and strategies that allow students to *master* the test!"

## BOMBING IN KINDERGARTEN

A *USA Today* report extolling the importance of summer school reported that "Summer scholars run the gamut from Baltimore and Houston tykes who've bombed in kindergarten to gifted high-schoolers in Atlanta taking 'enrichment' science from college professors." Wait a minute. How does a kid bomb in kindergarten? According to the report, these tykes have failed to meet tough new academic benchmarks and can't be "socially promoted." Kindergartners thus get early indoctrination in the competitive rat race that characterizes corporate America. And *USA Today* reports it as the accepted way of the world.

Fred Rogers of Mister Rogers told the audience at the Middlebury College commencement in 2001 that hanging in his office is a framed piece of calligraphy with a sentence from Antoine de Saint-Exupéry's book *The Little Prince*. It reads: "L'essentiel est invisible pour les yeux." (What is essential is invisible to the eye.) Rogers told graduating seniors, "I feel the closer we get to knowing and living the truth of that sentence, the closer we get to wisdom." Rogers is definitely paddling upstream against received wisdom from corporate America's insistence that kindergartners should be competing for a place in first grade as their first step up to the global economy, and let's all give him three cheers for his efforts.

What is essential is invisible to the eye. That's where the Standardista squads searching for evidence of skills buildup in schools miss the boat. In their efforts to make kindergartners ready for the Ivy League, they fail to see what is really going on in a developmentally appropriate kindergarten: children are busy taking care of plants and animals, building with blocks, experimenting with sand and water, engaging in dramatic invention in the playhouse, painting, singing, dancing. They are talking with each other. Because the skills kindergartners are learning are complex and difficult to notarize and post on charts for real estate agents to make hay over, in more and more schools kindergartners are losing out on finger-painting time, and poring over workbooks instead. Megan Farnsworth, Bradley Fellow at the Heritage Foundation, sums up the Standardista position: "Holding students to high academic standards without regular testing is like expecting high returns from a business without being able to check its quarterly earning report."

What an image: kindergartner as quarterly earning report.

Employing Skinnerian methods, skills fanatics can teach kindergartners to read. Probably they can teach the kids some version of quantum mechanics too. So what? Skinner taught pigeons to play Ping-Pong, but you have to ask yourself: Just what have you got when you've got a pigeon who plays Ping-Pong? I once witnessed a showcase performance of a second grader trained in a popular direct instruction method of reading. Handed a newspaper, the child read, "Brezhnev Employs New Strategy. . ." The audience applauded. She was a cute little girl, but you have to ask: Just what have you got when you've got a seven-year-old who can sound out "Brezhnev Employs New Strategy"? Looks like a trained pigeon, walks like a trained pigeon, reads like a trained pigeon. Some people might think you have a trained pigeon.

Even more disquieting is the way Standardistas ignore the classic study conducted in the 1930s by Carleton Washburn in Winnetka, Illinois. He compared children who were given formal reading instruction in first grade to those whose instruction was delayed until second grade. Although, as would be expected, the first graders showed an initial advantage on reading tests, this advantage disappeared by grade four. What is troubling—and of concern to today's parents—is that Washburn followed these children into junior high school. The young adolescents who were introduced to reading later had greater enthusiasm for reading than the other group. State-mandated kindergarten reading standards spew forth lists of detailed "musts"—use phonetic skills to decode simple words, identify consonant sound/symbol relationships, and on and on and on—without ever mentioning that the child should find a joy in words, should know that a book can provoke laughter, tears, and a desire to read another book. State-mandated kindergarten reading standards end up being one more example of child abuse.

## SLOGANS TO LOSE SLEEP OVER

Item: "College Begins in Kindergarten" screams the banner headline on the Education Trust home page.

Item: "I believe passing the Washington Assessment of Student Learning (WASL) as a 10th grader starts with the kindergarten teacher," asserts the principal of Shelton High School in Washington State.

Item: "Success at each level—high school, college, and beyond—depends on earlier preparation. . . . A cracked foundation threatens the whole." William Bennett quoting from his own book, *The Educated Child*, on the Web page describing the new kindergarten curriculum he is peddling on K12.com.

Item: "The notion that kindergarten is a place where kids come and play is an anachronism. The expectation by the professionals is that whatever children do, it's going to be time that leads to some kind of ultimate achievement," Karen Lang, deputy superintendent of schools in Greenwich, Connecticut, tells a *New York Times* reporter.

Ultimate achievement. Sounds like a perfume. Or an all-terrain vehicle, or maybe the $120 tasting menu at a boutique restaurant in Manhattan or Laguna Niguel. When applied to children, it's a recipe for ulcers. And worse. We'd better change that slogan: Give us your tired, your poor, your ultimate achievement kindergartners.

Art imitates reality and calls it a joke. In a *New Yorker* cartoon in May 2001, Robert Weber draws parents asking a young child, "Summer's coming. How does pre-med camp sound?" If college begins in kindergarten, then med school surely must begin before fifth grade.

But state ed functionaries have a way of upstaging even *New Yorker* cartoonists, TV satirists, and dot.com venture capitalists. In California, when 92 percent of the students in the schools not located in upscale zip code areas failed the state's exit exam in mathematics when it was first administered in Spring 2001, state superintendent of schools Delaine Eastin said that to bring students up to speed, the state will need to "focus like a laser" on the weakest schools. There's laser dentistry, but laser skill delivery? Or maybe Superintendent Eastin has in mind focusing laser beams on the poor-performing schools and vaporizing them. Or maybe teachers will be issued laser ray guns, ever-ready to zap students who don't buckle down. Algebra spectrometer analysis for the underachieving? What next? Killer tomatoes? Han Solo, where are you when we need you?

California teachers will soon get a version of Star Wars, custom-designed just for them. On May 22, 2001, 1:34 p.m. Eastern Time, McGraw-Hill launched its "online and onsite training program integrated with state standards and adopted textbooks." Educators' Professional Development/McGraw-Hill (EPD/McGraw-Hill) promises to deliver the goods. Billing itself as "a global information services provider," offering such brands as Standard & Poor's, Business Week, Open Court, CTB/McGraw-Hill testing, McGraw-Hill says it is "breaking new ground by developing teacher training programs that are aligned with state and national content standards . . . As the standards movement accelerates with calls for more accountability and testing, teachers are often frustrated by the pressure to quickly increase their students' test scores on standardized tests. EPD/McGraw-Hill will provide teachers with the training and resources necessary to meet these new challenges."

Funny thing: I was awarded the "banned in California" title a few years back. More than one hundred of us staff development "providers" filled out the California Board of Education's 27-page-long application form to become California literacy providers. No one would admit just why we all received an identical rejection letter, even though the law stipulated rejectees should be told how they could fix up the documentation they submitted. But we heard stories about state board of education member and passionate phonics advocate Marion Joseph going over the applications in her garage. The upshot is that an individual school may not use state money to invite me to provide staff development. God forbid: I'd be out of control. I might talk about the importance of students reading riddle books and exchanging notes with the teacher, about getting adolescents to read novels instead of ugly little paragraphs with their tagalong multiple choice questions.

The issue is considerably broader than whether or not I can set foot in California schools. The same crew that established the list of banned literacy providers are now systematically attacking the state college education departments, screaming that professors of education are lazy, inept, and stupid. Who will be left when the California Board of Education gets rid of everybody they don't like? Ahem, McGraw-Hill, publishers of direct instruction, is poised to deliver anywhere from $3\frac{1}{2}$ to 120 hours of staff training to every teacher in California. Coming next: Florida and Texas.

The Education Trust home page proclaims, "Our basic tenet is this—All children will learn at high levels when they are taught to high levels." Teachers who believe that the educational materials and strategies they offer children should be suited to the child's age, development, and interests aren't proclaiming that children should be taught to low levels. But that's what the Education Trust, the Business Roundtable, state education functionaries, and their brethren choose to claim. Maybe what this country needs is a rebirth of the Un-American Activities Committee. Change its name to the Un-Excellent Activities Committee. This time, U.S. Congresspersons can call teachers to testify: "Do you now teach, or have you ever wanted to teach to low levels?" Presumably, like Joe McCarthy, each Congressperson will have in his briefcase the list of "known low-level teachers."

In spring 2000, Karen Terrell, 1996 MIT graduate with a degree in architecture, accepted a signing bonus to become a high school math teacher at an inner-city high school in Boston. Karen tells her students, "Let your imagination soar!" knowing full well that most inner-city children don't hear this injunction after kindergarten or first grade. If Standardistas have their way, children will never hear it. These words are not in the direct instruction scripts teachers are supposed to follow.

Karen told *Newsweek* magazine that she switched careers to become a high school math teacher because she "liked the idea of being able to affect my own community." Karen insists, "Teaching is not just about academics, but also about ministering to kids. This means that we serve them, often help change them and propel them into their destinies."

Watch those verbs: This woman wants to minister to and serve kids, not skill target them. As influential jurist Learned Hand pointed out, "Words are chameleons, which reflect the color of their environment." Corporate leaders want to target students, bureaucrats want to laser beam them, teachers want to minister to them. John Dewey said, "Every teacher should realize the dignity of his calling: that he is a social servant set apart for the maintenance of proper social order and the securing of the right social growth." No wonder ed-whiz-biz wise guys hold Dewey in such low regard these days. What if, instead of blathering on about kindergartners in Hawaii being able to identify the spine of the book and fifth graders in Louisiana being able to explain "the political, cultural, and economic developments and trends of major world regions that resulted in the transformation of societies in the fifteenth through the mid-eighteenth centuries," we followed Thomas Jefferson's advice on education and taught people what it means to live in a democracy? Democracy is dangerous to the power elite. Keep everybody scurrying to line up behind impossible standards, and nobody will have the energy to demand democracy.

## A LIZARD CAREER PATH

In *The Boilerplate Rhino*, premier science writer David Quammen tells an amusing and illustrative tale of two men working with 32 lizards in a motel room in Mexico. One man, a Ph.D. candidate in biology, is timing lizard speeds. The other, a journalist, is watching. The research question is: How fast will a lizard run down a rubber track when chased by a human hand, figured to two decimal places of precision? Will a side-blotched lizard from La Ventana run as fast as a side-blotched lizard from the mainland? If not, what could that mean?

One has to wonder if this is why parents send their kids to college—so they can grow up to design rubber racetracks for lizards. After describing 15 minutes of belly-crawling and fervent profanity as the two men tried to catch a runaway lizard, Quammen concludes, "What the biologist is doing is called science. What the journalist is doing has no dignified name."

We learn that some lizards improve their time on repeated trials; others get worse. One lizard has to be pushed over the finish line. "She's getting tired," says the journalist. "Or else she's getting wise to the game and isn't interested anymore," replies the biologist.

Hmmm. Are the people who insist that children must be tested and retested and then tested some more listening? Plenty of kids are exhausted. Others, wise to the game, simply aren't interested any more. Sad to say, they've lost interest not just in tests but in school. At least none of the lizards vomited.

A Florida teacher who chooses to remain anonymous works in a school where children must take schoolwide multiple choice reading tests every eight weeks, and both their and their teachers' evaluations are based on the results. Children's scores determine whether or not they "move up" to the next level in the program. A teacher's evaluation is based on the percentage of her students who "move up." Like the lizards, a group of fifth graders got wise to the game, figuring out that since they were moving on to middle school—and a different reading program—their final test didn't count. Their teacher pleaded that scores always count, that future teachers would look at their transcripts. The students weren't buying it, and as a group they scored only 69 percent. This brought the teacher's unit test average for the entire year down to a 79.3, meaning she didn't get the necessary 80 percent to be considered a successful reading teacher. Her official evaluation for the year reads "Needs Improvement." Small consolation, perhaps, but this teacher should know that the lizards' performance is followed to two decimal points.

The following story may well be apocryphal, but here's how one teacher got her students to march in step when the occasion required. Visiting the classroom for a scheduled official observation, the principal noticed the teacher applying bright red lipstick with a heavy hand as he walked through the door. The students' behavior was exemplary. All were alert and eager to respond to the teacher's questions. Afterwards, the principal commented that he knew it was a difficult class and wondered how she'd achieved such exemplary behavior. "Oh, that was easy. Just before you came, I told them I was going to give the first one who misbehaved a big, fat kiss."

## HOMEWORK TOXIC BUILDUP

Parents don't need a University of Michigan study to tell them that very young children are getting three times as much homework as kids received 20 years ago. In the summer of 2001, the *Chicago Sun-Times* ran an article about a second-grader who spends 45 minutes a night on homework, while her little sister also toils on her worksheets brought home from preschool. Their brother in seventh grade works two hours a night on his homework. The children's mother points out that it only takes the second grader 45 minutes because "she knew how to do it." Chicago mom Donna Mosley says that after working all year on homework from 5 p.m. to 9 p.m., her sixth-grade son still had to go to summer school. "That's how I know it's not working," she says. "The schools are pushing homework, but at the end, when they give the tests, kids can't pass them."

In a Chicago suburb, ten-year-old Marie wants to take dancing lessons, but since homework takes her two or three hours a night, there's no time for such extras. "She doesn't watch any TV. She gets to play on the weekends if she gets her homework done," says her mom, who sees the homework crunch affecting her own life. Mom feels she can't participate in the church gospel choir because she has to keep tabs on her daughter's homework.

Back when he was U.S. Secretary of Education, William Bennett announced that "Homework is the single most reliable indicator of success in school. We spent $100,000 to prove that, to prove what people knew from common sense." When this elicited a chuckle from the audience, Bennett continued, "That's okay. They spent a lot more than that in the sixties and seventies trying to *disprove* common sense."

I was sitting in that audience, and because as a teacher I struggled for years with the frustrating realities of homework assignment, collection, and evaluation, I was startled by the secretary's bald assertion. I phoned his office the next day and asked if I could have a citation of the study he'd mentioned—or, better yet, a copy of the study itself. Bennett's staff members were courteous and prompt; they got back to me within the hour to explain that the secretary had been speaking without notes and did not have a citation for the study. They thought he must have been referring to page 42 in the Education Department's report, *What Works*.

That royal "we" can be a tricky rhetorical device, and Bennett uses it frequently in his speeches and his writings—sometimes referring to official departments, to books he's written, to committees he sits on, to the community of right-thinking, loyal Americans who are striving to defend the nation from ignorance. Sometimes, it seems, the "we" refers to Bennett himself and his alter ego. When he said, "We spent $100,000 on a study," I thought it reasonable to assume that the "we" referred to his own department, the U.S. Department of Education of which he was chief. But people at this department were in the dark. And there is nothing on page 42—or anywhere else in *What Works*—that comes even close to supporting Bennett's vehement public assertion about homework.

The lizard-timing biologist admits that some days he thinks this racing lizards thing is so much malarkey. "They behave so differently on the track from how they do in the field." Hmmm. Funny thing: what's true for lizards is also true for students. But the Education Testing Service (ETS) isn't likely to admit to malarkey any time soon. SATs have almost no predictive value as to how students will do in college after the first year, and books like Thomas Stanley's *The Millionaire Mind* become bestsellers by debunking any connection between doing a lot of homework in third grade, or being a stellar student in tenth, and becoming a millionaire. The author presses home the point that obtaining high marks in school does not translate into becoming a millionaire "because analytical intelligence is not a strong correlate of leadership ability." What habit do millionaires have in common? According to *The Millionaire Mind*, 70 percent of them get their shoes resoled.

## CRITICAL KINDERGARTEN SKILLS

The jury is still out on the predictive value of a preschooler knowing whether a guinea pig would be more likely to eat a cardboard picture of a banana or a cardboard picture of an asparagus stalk, but plenty of schools insist that kindergartners be able to read a basic sight vocabulary. A kindergarten newsletter sent out in Newtown, Connecticut, is typical: Parents are informed that in school the word families of the week feature *ing, ig, ip* words as well as word families with the short *o* sound. Parents are reminded, "Please practice the K-show words at home. We continue to practice in class and in music." This works for plenty of kids, but David Elkind, professor at Tufts University and author of *The Hurried Child*, warns that international research shows that pushing children to read early causes later reading problems. *Pushing* is the key word here. Children who are ready and eager to read early should be encouraged; but pushing others too early can do a lot of harm.

Nonetheless, lists of skill requirements get longer. Here are some of the kindergarten information literacy requirements at an elementary school in Honolulu:

- Identify the parts of the book: front/back cover, spine, title, and author.
- Identify a "made up" story and differentiate it from "real" information.
- Access information efficiently and effectively.
- Use information accurately and creatively.

These are called *benchmarks* (see Chapter 4), and they were written not by kindergarten teachers but by librarians. Perhaps this explains the emphasis on knowing the spine of a book. Declaring that a kindergartner should use information accurately and creatively is nonsense. But no skills benchmarks these days are complete without their tagalong rubrics, and here are the rubrics for kindergartners—presumably provided so moms can distinguish between basic and exemplary book spine skills.

No question about it: rubrics have an exaggerated sense of their own importance. Writing a so-called skill down in three different boxes and labeling these boxes "occasionally," "frequently," and "consistently" is of minimal use to anybody. Most parents, and teachers, too, if truth were known, simply eyeball the categories and then interpret them as grades of A/B, C, D/F. One can imagine the late E.B. White taking a look at rubrics and repeating his famous *New Yorker* cartoon caption, "I say it's spinach and I say to hell with it." Today we read rubrics and think, "I say it's a C and I say to hell with it."

Information Literacy Standards: Benchmarks for Collaborative Teaching Kindergarten Performance Rubric[1]

| Information Literacy Skill | Basic | Proficient | Exemplary |
| --- | --- | --- | --- |
| *Standard 1: The student who is information literate accesses information efficiently and effectively.* | | | |
| Identifies the library as a source of information. | Identifies the library as a source of information occasionally. | Identifies the library as a source of information frequently. | Identifies the library as a source of information consistently. |
| Identifies the parts of the book: front/back cover, spine, title and author. | Identifies the parts of the book: front/back cover, spine, title and author with assistance. | Identifies the parts of the book: front/back cover, spine, title and author with little assistance. | Identifies the parts of the book: front/back cover, spine, title and author easily. |
| Listens for specific information. | Has difficulty listening for specific information, can do it only on a piece-by-piece basis. | Listens for specific information with some cueing. | Listens for specific information with little or no cueing. |
| Understands that the library is arranged in order. | Needs reminding that the resources in the library are arranged in order. | Frequently shows an understanding that resources in the library are arranged in order. | Consistently shows an understanding that resources in the library are arranged in order. |
| *Standard 2: The student who is information literate evaluates information critically and creatively.* | | | |
| Identifies a "made-up" story and differentiates it from "real" information. | Can identify a made-up story with assistance. | Can differentiate a made-up story from real information only with assistance. | Can identify a made-up story with little assistance. |

(continued on next page)

Information Literacy Standards: Benchmarks for Collaborative Teaching Kindergarten Performance Rubric[1] (continued)

| Information Literacy Skill | Basic | Proficient | Exemplary |
| --- | --- | --- | --- |
| Chooses books for information needs. | Needs assistance in defining information needs and choosing book for needs. | Needs some assistance in defining information needs and choosing book for needs. | Knows information needs and chooses book easily. |
| Aware of terms: fiction and non-fiction. | May be aware of terms: fiction and non-fiction. Needs much assistance when cued. | Is aware of the terms: fiction and non-fiction. Needs some assistance when cued. | Is aware of the terms: fiction and non-fiction. Can recite it when cued. |
| Tells where information was found. | When asked can tell where information was found only with assistance. | When asked can tell where information was found frequently. | When asked can tell where information was found consistently. |

*Standard 3: The student who is information literate uses information accurately and creatively.*

| Information Literacy Skill | Basic | Proficient | Exemplary |
| --- | --- | --- | --- |
| Retells information gathered. | Can retell about information only with assistance. | Can retell about information with some assistance. | Can retell information gathered with little or no assistance. |
| Assesses the retelling. | Can assess the retelling only with assistance. | Can assess the retelling with some assistance. | Can assess the retelling with little or no assistance. |

[1]http://www.k12.hi.us/~cfoster/standards/rubk.html

The direction in which this particular list of kindergarten information literacy skills seems headed is of greater concern than how it's packaged. Here we can see the groundwork for requiring young children to write research papers. It is rather mind-boggling to witness apparently reasonable adults on the precipice of declaring writing a research paper a kindergarten skill. One can only stand in the yawning divide below their precarious perch and yell, "Don't do it! Don't do it!"

Likewise, adults who think that listening for specific information is an appropriate kindergarten skill should consider their own abilities of taking in information orally when they have to stop the car and ask someone for directions. Some people can do it; some need other cues.

Around the country, people seem anxious to declare kindergarten a skill-intensive zone. Here are a few of the "Fundamental Computer Skills" for kindergartners in the Olathe, Kansas, School District:

- Use and understand basic computer-related terms such as Login and Cursor.
- Demonstrate appropriate care and use of special keyboard keys (ESC, Shift, arrow keys, spacebar, backspace, Delete, Enter, Alt, Ctrl, etc.).
- Use basic computer management skills.
- Show understanding of appropriate legal/ethical conduct by:
    - Demonstrating appropriate use of computers.
    - Demonstrating appropriate computer etiquette.
    - Following the District Policy regarding technology resources.
    - Respecting the privacy of all users through use of security rules outlined in District Policy.
    - Obeying copyright laws.

Imagine the shame of being the parent of a kindergartner who flunks copyright laws.

The state of California has identified about 40 goals kindergartners should achieve. These include knowing how to read high-frequency words; count syllables in words; locate a book's title and table of contents; distinguish fact from fantasy; describe and classify plane and solid geometric shapes such as sphere, cube, rectangular prism; identify traffic symbols and map symbols; and construct maps incorporating such structures as police and fire stations, airports, hospitals, harbors, places of worship, and transportation lines.

And schools with money to burn find ways to ratchet up the high stakes even more. For California students, the SAT-9 test is not required by the state until second grade, but in Saddleback Valley Unified in Mission Viejo, Orange County, kindergartners take a beginner's version. Kindergartners. For those with faith in the training bra of academia, it's never too early to give a child a standardized test. School officials say they use results from this test to identify students who need extra help as early as possible—and to compare children's performance with others nationwide. Surely it's just a coincidence that when one does an Internet search for the Saddleback School District, the first page that pops up is sponsored by a real estate agent. Maybe parents should consider that the increase in property values might be coming out of their kindergartners' hearts and souls.

When you're in a rat race, the only ones who can win are the rats.

Mission Viejo is an affluent community proud of its selection as "safest among cities with a population between 75,000 to 100,000." What's more, it was named a "Tree City USA" by the National Arbor Day Foundation and is recipient of the 1999 Fitness City Award. Isn't this enough? Do the five-year-olds have to compete for national acclaim too? Certainly it's worth considering what criteria would go into the award Kid City USA. How would a city recognize that its kindergartners are tops? Surely not many people would hold out for knowledge of copyright law or ability to count syllables in words.

Robert Fiersen, assistant superintendent in Manhasset, New York, where the schools now include beginning conversational Spanish in kindergarten, worries that, "In this business, as in any other, everybody looks down. The high schools look to the middle schools, the middle schools look to the elementary schools, and the elementary schools look to kindergarten. Ultimately, you're going to end up with prenatal reading." In Manhasset, where average pupil expenditure in 1996 to 1997 was $18,063, they just might pull it off. It's not that encouraging the children in our language-phobic nation to learn another language isn't a good thing. One just worries about the kids when a school district that already sends over 98 percent of its graduates to college is still insistent on upping the ante.

Robert Rayborn, director of California's testing program for Harcourt Educational Measurement, which produces the SAT-9 tests, acknowledges that the test is controversial: "There are those educators who believe that kindergartners are too young to operate in a testing situation." He adds, "There are others who believe it's important to know what kindergartners are doing in relation to the rest of the country." And it doesn't seem likely that Harcourt Educational Measurement would try to talk Saddleback Valley Unified out of spending an extra $45,000 on testing kindergartners and first graders. District officials believe the early testing might give schools a leg up when children are required to take the test in second grade. Some parents and teachers wonder about how many books $45,000 would add to the school library. But in an affluent community, probably this isn't a serious consideration. They can have both.

Remember *All I Really Need to Know I Learned in Kindergarten?* Excerpts from Robert Fulghum's celebration of kindergarten were published in "Dear Abby" and in the *Reader's Digest*. Paul Harvey and Larry King read it on the air. It was read into the *Congressional Record*. Maybe our testocrats need to read it again: Nowhere in his paean to kindergarten does Fulghum mention reading and math skills. No mention of rectangular prism competency or computer literacy. His vital kindergarten skills include: Share. Play fair. Clean up your own mess. Say you're sorry when you hurt somebody. Flush.

Funny thing. He didn't mention PowerPoint, the new craze in the primary grades. Kindergartners do it, but plenty of people doubt that it's a good idea for them or for fifth graders either. Immediate computer graphics and formatting encourage presentation pizzazz to become a substitute for thinking things through. And the pizzazz is of a cookie-cutter mentality, provided by the AutoContent Wizard's template.

## PRIMARY UPGRADES

Consider a history course of 108 lessons, which includes these topics:

1.  Basic Geographic Awareness
2.  Ancient Rome
3.  From Caesar to Augustus
    Includes the significance of the Roman Republic (government by consuls, chosen by the citizens, and by the Senate) and the rise, rule, fall, and legacy of Julius Caesar.
4.  From the Roman Empire to Constantine
    Includes Rome under the rule of Augustus Caesar and subsequent emperors, the historical beginnings of the religion of Christianity, and the relocation of the Empire's capital to the eastern city of Byzantium.
5.  Rome Falls and Byzantium Rises
    Includes the significance of Attila the Hun, how Rome fell to invading warrior tribes, Rome's lasting contributions to society, and exploration of the new heart of the Roman Empire, Constantinople.
6.  The Early Middle Ages in Western Europe
    Includes the early settling of England and France, the legendary saga of King Arthur and his court at Camelot, and the love of learning and preservation of knowledge within the monasteries.
7.  The Rise of Islam
    Includes the historical origins of the religion of Islam, and the major figures, events, and cultural achievements of the Islamic Empire.
8.  A World in Turmoil
    Includes the significance of Charlemagne's struggle to unify the fractious European tribes; the lives, beliefs, and heroes of the Vikings as they raid, conquer, and settle lands on both sides of the Atlantic.

9. The Feudal World

   Includes the concept of feudalism, the knight's code of chivalry, and real and legendary acts of honor, courage, and courtliness.

10. Crusades Abroad and Changes in Europe

    Includes real-life and legendary heroes from the time of the Crusades and the Hundred Years' War and the significance of the terrible plague that swept Europe.

11. Medieval African Empires

    Includes the rich, varied lands and people of medieval Africa, including Ghana, the Kingdom of Gold in the west; the scholarly city of Timbuktu; Sundiata, the "Lion King" of Mali; the monumental carved churches in eastern Ethiopia; and the travels of Ibn Battuta through Asia, Africa, and the Mediterranean.

12. Medieval China

    Includes life during the Sui, Tang, Sung, and Yuan dynasties, the major figures and architectural feats in Chinese history, the discoveries of the compass and porcelain, and the development of Chinese trade to Europe.

13. Feudal Japan

    Includes the history and governance of feudal Japan, and the code of the samurai, and the Shinto religion, haiku, and a popular Japanese folk tale.

This could be the Advanced Placement World History course issued by the College Board. Many of the topics, such as attention to medieval China and feudal Japan, are similar. It could also be a course based on the California seventh grade history standards. Or Virginia. Or countless other states whose history standards prove they haven't been in the presence of many seventh graders. But it's neither of these. This outline is part of what William Bennett terms "the frontier of high-quality, high-performance education reform." It is the outline for the K12.com history course for second graders. No, not history for second-year college, but history for seven-year-olds.

For $225, William Bennett, the mouthpiece of this venture, will send parents a history course they can teach their seven-year-olds at home. He calls it "world-class"; I call it insane. He was U.S. Secretary of Education. I was a classroom teacher for 20 years.

If parents want to go for the whole curriculum, for $895, K12.com offers a bargain: The complete academic program online includes history, math, language arts, science, art, and music. K12.com is owned by Knowledge Universe Learning Group, cofounded by former junk-bond king Michael Milken and his brother Lowell. Media mogul and sultan of sensationalism Rupert Murdoch sits on the board, as does Chester E. Finn, Jr., president of Thomas B. Fordham Foundation and John M. Olin Fellow at the Manhattan Institute, both institutions noted for their vicious, statistics-skewed attacks on public education. Bennett says there's nothing in President Bush's education plans that will benefit K12, but he and his cronies are out stumping for increased funding for charter schools and educational savings accounts that parents could bring to private ventures of their choice. Bennett also notes that once huge numbers of parents associate national testing with the need for academic rigor, here K12.com is positioned, offering plenty of rigor. Or rigor mortis.

Funny thing: just a couple of years ago *The Educated Child*, by William Bennett in large letters and Chester E. Finn, Jr., and John T. E. Cribb, Jr., in small, gave a Kindergarten Readiness List that seems almost ludicrous in its lack of oomph. Kindergartners should be able to name familiar objects such as chair, spoon, soap; identify such common animals as dogs and cows; know own full name, age, and gender; count aloud to ten. But a few pages later, when the tutoring trio start talking about curriculum, they get down to brass tacks: they want kindergartners, who have given evidence they know what a spoon is, to study the seven continents, including landmarks and animals on each; discuss how an illustration of Iwo Jima inspires people; learn about Teddy Roosevelt. Kindergarten. In first grade kids move on to the Code of Hammurabi. And the history of world religions, early exploration of America, the American Revolution, and the exploration of the American West. Parents whose children are in public schools are warned to study the social studies curriculum of their children's school carefully and make sure it isn't "an odd jumble." What else would one call putting the Code of Hammurabi next to Cortés, Martha Washington, and Daniel Boone?

This is not to say the book does not offer specific strategies for producing an educated child in its 664 pages. Here's one to inculcate writing skills. "Ask your child to pretend he is a mountain. . . ."

When he was U.S. Secretary of Education, William Bennett gave a speech in Allentown, Pennsylvania. In answer to a school board member's question of how his plan for reforming education would work, Bennett replied, "I deal with wholesale; you're going to have to work out the retail for yourself." It appears that Bennett has finally worked out the retail. Whether he can convince parents of first graders that their kids need to know the Code of Hammurabi is another matter.

## KINDERGARTEN: THE GREAT DEBATE

In the May 17, 2001, *Sacramento Bee*, editorialists declare, "It isn't just sandbox etiquette, story time and learning how to sit still anymore." The editorial outlines California's new academic content standards for kindergartners:

- Read simple one-syllable and high-frequency words.
- Ask and answer questions about essential elements of a text.
- Write uppercase and lowercase letters of the alphabet independently.
- Attend to the form and proper spacing of letters.
- Count, recognize, represent, name and order a number of objects (up to 30).
- Recognize when an estimate is reasonable.

In advocating that kindergarten be made mandatory, the editorial acknowledges the new academic crunch: "higher standards have converted kindergarten to what used to be first grade." Although the editorialist takes this academic pressure cooker as a given, parents might well ask, "Who decided that kids don't get kindergarten as a children's garden any more? Who decided it has to be a pressurized skill zone?" And they might also ask, "Who made play a four-letter word?"

Lucy Haab, longtime kindergarten teacher in San Jose, California, points out that not one preschool, kindergarten, or primary teacher sat on the committee that produced the standards in the California publication *Every Child a Reader*. The result, says Lucy, is that "I am told to teach skills that my professional experience, knowledge, and judgment tell me are better learned at a later time." Lucy continues, "I am tired of being asked to ignore what I know about children's growth and development and told that every child must learn the same thing at the same time. I am tired of the attitude that seems to serve politicians that if children have a difficult time learning something at age five, let's fix it (and them) and ask them to learn it at age three. This is not just unrealistic; it is abusive. I am tired of being asked to push children to learn things that could be better and more quickly learned later." Lucy points out that a good example of this is the standard of "telling time" in kindergarten. In the name of rigor and raising standards, a 35-year veteran teacher is forced to ignore what she knows about young children and teach a skill few will grasp, wasting time and frustrating children about a skill they could learn in about 20 minutes in third grade.

In his commencement address at Middlebury College in May 2001, Fred Rogers, the beloved Mr. Rogers of television fame, suggested a different approach to life.

> I wonder if you've heard what happened at the Seattle Special Olympics a few years ago? For the 100-yard dash, there were nine contestants, all of them so-called physically or mentally disabled. All nine of them assembled at the starting line; and, at the sound of the gun they took off—but one little boy stumbled and fell and hurt his knee and began to cry. The other eight children heard the boy crying. They slowed down, turned around, saw the boy and ran back to him—every one of them ran back to him. One little girl with Down's Syndrome bent down and kissed the

boy and said, "This will make it better." The little boy got up, and he and the rest of the runners linked their arms together and joyfully walked to the finish line. They all finished the race at the same time. And when they did, everyone in the stadium stood up and clapped and whistled and cheered for a long, long time. People who were there are still telling the story with obvious delight. And you know why? Because deep down we know that what matters in this life is much more than winning for ourselves. What really matters is helping others win, too, even if it means slowing down and changing our course now and then.

This is the opposite mindset to the administrators in a Washington school who decided to line graduates up at high school commencement according to their Grade Point Average. Universities don't even rank and sort to this degree, but, increasingly, high schools seem compelled to make a public display of who's at the bottom. Most people don't quarrel with acknowledging the accomplishments of a high school valedictorian, but plenty of child psychologists argue that the ranking and sorting of young children does as much harm to those at the top as to those at the bottom.

Mr. Rogers suggests an opposite mindset to the school officials in Birmingham, Alabama, who pushed 522 students with academic difficulties out of high school. Reason given: "bad attitude." By instituting this push-out right before the administration of the high-stakes state test, the district raised its scores and averted takeover by the state. Adult-education instructor Steve Orel, who is working to reclaim these students, observes that "The maximum fine for low-achieving high school students who may lower test score averages if they are allowed to remain in school is death on the city streets." Birmingham is playing catch-up to a long-established plan in Chicago. The front-page headline in the Chicago-based education newspaper *Substance* says it succinctly: "10,000 Students Pushed Out." Editor George Schmidt's thorough analysis reveals that between September 1995 and September 1999, the first four years that Mayor Daley had complete control over the city's public schools, more than 10,000 students were pushed out of

Chicago's public high schools. Most of these students, African-American and Hispanic, were from Chicago's poorest neighborhoods.

Mr. Rogers's approach is opposite to the mindset of government policymakers who are determined to turn kindergarten into a skills upgrade factory and high school into a revolving door of fodder for minimum-wage misery. The litany of child abuse grows longer and longer. We need to remember that there are two types of people in the world: There are those who stop for tears and those who don't. We'd better be sure we have people making education policy who do stop. And those people who are convinced that education is a race should reread Aesop's fable "The Tortoise and the Hare." Someone should read it into the *Congressional Record*, and send a copy to the Secretary of Education and to the President, who hijacked the slogan of the Children's Defense Fund, "Leave No Child Behind." If he means to stand behind this slogan, then he needs to know that the race goes not always to the swiftest.

**TEST Booklet**

**WARNING:**

Experts on child development have determined:

* This test may cause your child to vomit, have palpitations, nightmares, and school phobia.
* This test will make your child feel insecure, ignorant, and helpless.
* This test will distort your child's understanding of why people read.
* This test has no academic value. Nobody but $8-an-hour test correctors get to see your child's answers.
* By definition, 50% of the children who take this test must score below average.
* Because of this test, your child will no longer have recess.
* Because of this test, you will become the warden of homework mania.
* Because of this test your child becomes the property of the State.

*Chapter 5*

# Child Abuse: Test Absurdities and Outrages

In California, children as young as seven sit for five straight days of testing on the SAT-9 achievement test, also known as the STAR. When thousands of public school students across Arizona started taking the four-day national assessment test in April 2001, first graders were included in the testing pool for the first time. "That's too young," said Adriana Rincón. She kept two of her children home, first grader Jose Luis, 7, and Gabriela, 8, a second grader. In Washington, D.C., Caleb Rossiter led a parent boycott of the test, keeping his first grader home on testing days. He finds all the test prep disheartening as well as a waste of time. He worries about the ways the test is debasing the curriculum.

Rossiter has reason to worry. Professor Walt Haney of Boston College's Center for the Study of Testing points out that tests of young children are much less reliable than those of other children. Research shows that the very mechanics of test taking—such things as following the directions, filling in the bubbles on the answer sheet (and keeping them in the right order)—are often harder for young children than is the test itself. This means that the results show more about second graders' abilities to fill in bubbles than their ability to understand what they read.

Worse than this, the tests scare young children. There are good reasons for the National Association for the Education of Young Children's stance against standardized testing of young children. One can only wonder why the nation's politicians, corporate CEOs, and other testocrats ignore these arguments.

In Montgomery County, Maryland, kids take standardized tests for 50 hours. This is not counting PSATs (Preliminary SATs), SATs (Stanford Achievement Tests), and AP (Advanced Placement) tests. The MSPAP (Maryland School Performance Assessment Program) plus three other state testing programs aren't enough for Montgomery County. They also have a county-imposed CRT (Criterion Reference Test). Maybe it's past time for parents to step in and protect their children from ETS: Excessive Testing Syndrome. Psychiatrists and child-development experts have urged President Bush and Congress to rethink their push for annual testing of children beginning in third grade. In 1999, Boston College researchers asked students to draw pictures about taking the Massachusetts high-stakes test. About 20 percent of the students expressed positive feelings, but 40 percent exhibited negative feelings, ranging from anxiety to despair. Boston College professor Walt Haney told a *Dallas Morning News* reporter that the hype surrounding the tests panics students. "Kids are stressed not just by the test but by all the public discussion of the consequences of the test," he said. "Their fear and anxiety has been exacerbated by all the mania."

While the adults in the community are screaming about whether the schools are world-class or in-the-toilet, the kids are slogging through exams that aren't going to prove anything to anybody, least of all to the students. Anyone who thinks he knows anything about the quality of schools should answer this question before being allowed to orate: "When was the last time you or your kids were in a school for two days in a row?" Kids are good sources of information.

Mickey VanDerwerker, mother of five, is cofounder of Parents Across Virginia United to Reform SOLs. (SOL stands for Standards of Learning, and is Virginia's entry in the "test 'em till they drop" marathon.) Mickey is adamant that her job as mom is to keep her children safe. "So my third grader, who is very afraid of the tests, is staying home during this week's SOL testing at his school. He won't get a fail; he'll get a DNA (did not assess). He won't fail because his mom makes sure he gets excused absences. One day he has his 10-year-old birthday checkup (a bit early). The next day he has the tests that go with the checkup (a blood stick, maybe his ears. Maybe an x-ray for the suspected scoliosis caused by book bags that cause kids to keel over). The pediatrician simply can't do it all in one day. She is *sooo* busy. Doctor stuff is all approved absences. I am keeping him healthy with regular health care. And I am keeping him safe from terrible anxiety and panic. That's my job. I'm his mom."

At their annual meeting in July 2001, delegates to the National Education Association voted to support any legislation that permits parents to let their children skip the tests. The legislation passed by the 2.5-million-strong directs union lobbyists to fight mandatory testing requirements at the federal level. and offers union support to state delegations in lobbying for laws allowing parents to opt their children out of testing. "If you want to know how your child is doing, you don't wait seven months to get the results of a standardized test," said Judi Hirsch, an Oakland, California, algebra teacher who introduced the measure. "You ask your kid's teacher."

Politicians, media pundits, and their Fortune 500 CEO cronies commend high-stakes testing rituals as proof of state educrats' devotion to "high standards," but increasingly, parents and educators at all levels are calling it child abuse. Acclaimed Denver principal Lynn Spampinato resigned in protest over the governor's report-card rating of schools, saying, "As a true believer in public education, I cannot be a participant in its demise."

Birmingham, Alabama, adult-education instructor Steve Orel knows firsthand about the destruction of public education. Steve was fired for questioning why, right before the SAT-9 tests were administered, 522 high school students were pushed out of city schools that were under threat of state takeover because of low test scores. When these students began showing up at Steve's adult-education courses, he asked the obvious question: Why are students whose official withdrawal papers read "lack of interest" in school voluntarily enrolling in a school? Asking that question cost Steve his job and shut down his program, but he found a way to reopen, establishing the World of Opportunity for pushed-out students to work on literacy and job skills. On the program's first anniversary, September 5, 2001, 504 students abandoned by the Standardistas had enrolled. Five had earned their GED (General Educational Development) certificates.

Steve reflects that when the push-outs first occurred, "Each household thought it was their own deficiency. First, parents blamed their children, and each child felt abused and misunderstood. Then, realizing the systemic cruelty that had injured their children, parents cried. We are a city familiar with police dogs and fire hoses, but we were blindsided by the insidiousness of this attack." Steve says that at first they thought it was happening only to them. Gradually they've learned that Birmingham is just "the tip of the iceberg."

Alabama Governor Don Siegelman speaks with pride, "Recently Alabama was ranked among the top five states in America for strong accountability standards." He doesn't say who's doing the ranking, but the Thomas Fordham Foundation published *The State of State Standards 2000*, in which Alabama gets generally high marks. One must wonder what the Alabama Department of Education functionaries were thinking of when they titled their guide to Alabama's high school graduation exam "Great Expectations." To use this title in the sense of "high goals," in the face of the Birmingham 522 *and* in the face of the deep, multilayered irony of Dickens' title, is almost beyond belief. But one learns, when dealing with Standardistas, to be ready to believe anything. Let's take them at their word and assume they are admitting that their accountability system is dishonest and destructive; by using the title "Great Expectations," maybe they are announcing to the world that many educated adults could not pass their exam, loaded as it is with esoteric and/or trivial facts. After all, as University of California Professor Murray Baumgarten observes, we ask students to read *Great Expectations* not so they will set high goals but so that they will "consider questions of money and social position, gender and power, caste and class to account for their own experience." Certainly these are questions that need to be considered in the Birmingham school district.

Funny thing: Standardistas in Massachusetts also need to brush up on their Dickens. *Great Expectations*, a four-page booklet printed in the *Boston Globe* "as a public service" in Spring 1999, was prepared by the Boston Plan for Excellence in collaboration with the Boston Public Schools and the Boston Annenburg Challenge, and sponsored by Bank-Boston, Bell Atlantic, and Fidelity Investments. Another big push by big business to degrade public education.

## BRIBES FOR TEST SCORES

In Marysville, California, Debbie Johnson was upset to learn that her sixth grader was one of 40 students in the junior high school excluded from a party teachers threw for kids who scored well on the high-stakes SAT-9 test. Invitations to the party, which was held during the last two periods on a Friday afternoon, were handed out in class. Two hundred students were feted; forty were excluded. According to the district superintendent, other schools in Marysville give medallions to high-scoring students, throw parties, or take them on field trips. Marysville Joint Unified School District Superintendent Marc Liebman told a *Sacramento Bee* reporter, "Most of our schools are significantly above average in terms of the improvement they made this year. This congratulates students for the way they performed last year and can be a motivator for what they can do this year." Maybe the reporter should have asked Debbie Johnson's son how motivated he felt. In New York City, a low-scoring school offered bicycles and karaoke machines as prizes. In Hernando County,

Florida, two middle schools handed out cash prizes to students who did well on the FCAT (Florida Comprehensive Assessment Test). The money comes from Coca-Cola sales and local business partners. As one school board member said, "If it works, it works." A great moral message for students, reminding one of convicted arbitrageur Irving Boesky announcing "Greed is good" at the commencement address of the School of Business Administration, UC Berkeley.

Not everyone in Florida agrees. Nearly 250 teachers in Pascoe County, Florida, tore up the state-proffered "incentive" checks, saying that accepting Governor Bush's cash incentives would make them complicit in what they see as a flawed school-ranking system. Six more teachers and a principal at Gulf Gate Elementary School in Sarasota, which was identified as an "A" school in the FCAT rankings, also refused the bonus money. George Sheridan, a second-grade teacher in Cool, California, calls such bonuses "blood money." George says, "This is a bribe to keep us quiet. My seven-year-olds had to sit still for eleven tests—eight hours. They were physically and emotionally wiped out." George donated his bonus to the California Coalition for Authentic Reform in Education, a group organized for test resistance.

The tests surround kids with threat and fear. A kindergartner in Manatee County asked his mom, "When am I going to have to take the FCAT?" A fourth grader in California worries she's only number four in her class. How does she know she's number four? They take test-prep skills tests every week, and their scores are posted on the classroom wall, from high to low. In Florida, a Sunday-school teacher asks her students if anything is worrying them a lot, anything they want to pray about. So, joining hands, they form a prayer circle and pray to pass the FCAT. In New York City a nine-year-old interviewed by a *New York Post* reporter confessed that she was afraid she might fail the upcoming test and thereby shame her school, her family, her neighborhood, and her country.

In Duval County, Florida, Brandon was interviewed by a *Times Union* reporter about being required by state law to attend summer school. Brandon was in an all-or-nothing situation: Pass the test at the end of summer school and go on to fifth grade; fail it and repeat fourth.

Brandon told the reporter, "I'm really nervous for my parents. If I pass they'll be glad and I'll be happy too. I don't want to let them down. I'm trying hard, but I don't think I'm ready. I think I may let down my parents."

How many parents want this kind of pressure put on their 10-year-olds?

A third-grade teacher in Brooksville, Florida, asks a question every adult responsible for the nurture of children should ponder: "How are children going to do well on a test if they are crying over it?"

Consider the little girl in Arizona, so worried about the test that she started crying in school and couldn't stop. Not even when her daddy arrived to hug her and reassure her. She couldn't stop crying when she got home. This child spent her 10th birthday in a psychiatric hospital, diagnosed as a victim of anxiety disorder.

If there is any question about whether or not we have, as a nation, overemphasized standardized testing, and if there is any question that this overemphasis has taken a whole lot of the excitement out of teaching and learning for huge numbers of people, a recent article in the *Baton Rouge Advocate* puts those questions to rest. Louisiana is in the process of implementing high-stakes tests called LEAP (Louisiana Educational Assessment Program). This article addresses how schools and students near Baton Rouge are dealing with the preparation and stress. The test, which lasts five days, will determine, among other things, whether students will be promoted and whether schools will face sanctions for poor performance.

A teacher summarized her own reaction and that of her students, "I'm thinking about letting us have a scream day sometime in March, when we just go outside and scream." The principal in this school told teachers during a faculty meeting that he expects some students to throw up during the test. He assured them that he'd arranged to have all of the school's janitors on duty to clean up the messes.

What's wrong with this picture?

Is this where parents want their children to spend their days? Where it's considered a normal state of affairs that school makes them vomit? It is no wonder that students are anxious. To make sure children's and teachers' hysteria gets ratcheted up to fever pitch, for eight weeks before the test, the school's billboard is updated daily with the number of school days left until the test. Maybe it's time for parents to replace those "My child is an honor student" bumper stickers. New ones can read, "My kid puked on your high-stakes test." Maybe it's time for parents to have their own scream day.

Parents and teachers must join hands, vowing not to make children cry or vomit over any test, never mind one that is put to high-stakes uses even the test-makers call illegitimate. Officials at Harcourt Brace Educational Measurement, for one, state clearly in the guide *Stanford Achievement Test Series, Ninth Edition* that using standardized achievement test scores in making promotion and retention decisions for individual students is "misuse."

The manual states:

> "Achievement test scores may certainly enter into a promotion or retention decision. However, they should be just one of the many factors considered and probably should receive less weight than factors such as teacher observation, day-to-day classroom performance, maturity level, and attitude."

School must be a place where children know they are safe, where they are nurtured and protected. School must not be a place that harms children, makes them vomit, or makes them think they need to pray for survival. School must not be a place that makes fourth graders feel that the fate of the nation rests on their shoulders. No matter what the Business Roundtable claims.


## SHHH! IT'S A SECRET!

When a Massachusetts fourth grader came home from taking the writing portion of the MCAS (Massachusetts Comprehensive Assessment System), her parents were thrilled when she told them that she had written about her grandmother in response to this writing prompt:

GRADE 4

Think about people you know or have met. Choose one person who has made a big difference in your life. Write about that person and describe his or her positive effect on your life.

The fact that, of all the people she knew, this little girl had chosen to write about her grandmother was especially poignant for this family, because the grandmother had died just months before. Mom called the school, asking for a copy of her daughter's essay for the family to savor. Mom was informed this is not possible: All test answers are the property of the state. Not even parents can see them.

Sure, the Massachusetts parents can ask their daughter what she wrote on the test. They can even ask her to write a similar essay at home. But obviously a rerun at home is not the same thing as the essay written at school—in the heat of the testing moment. These Massachusetts parents feel such an academic exercise misses the point. For other parents across the country, labeled conservative in some quarters, there's another issue: they don't want schools to collect, and label as top secret, information their children reveal about private family matters.

Beyond the labels of liberal and conservative, the real concern is for children. Somehow it snuck up on all of us when we weren't looking that the test a child takes in third or fourth grade (though if the corporate honchos and their political lackeys have their way, the testing mania will extend down to prekindergarten) has become the definition of who that child is. Parents and teachers can try to offer an opinion, but the State is trying hard not to listen.

In Mendota Heights, Minnesota, Sydney Swaden's dad wasn't even offering an opinion; he was just asking a simple question: What math questions did she miss on the state test? After being told that Sydney, a ninth grader, had failed the high-stakes math test (it's called high-stakes because no student will receive a high school diploma without passing it), Marty Swaden asked to see the test. For a year, Sydney had been receiving extra tutoring in math, and Marty Swaden wanted to see where she had messed up, where they needed to concentrate their efforts.

The education department stonewalled him. Like most states, Minnesota has strict security rules; they want to keep test questions secret so they can be recycled year after year. Some New Jersey teachers report that security is so tight there that even teachers are forbidden to look at the tests while they are proctoring the exams. The idea that teachers and parents cannot see the material by which their children are being rated seems worse than crazy.

Marty Swaden, a lawyer, persisted, and after three months of repeated phone calls to state education department functionaries, he finally got an appointment to look at Sydney's test. As he told a *Chicago Tribune* reporter, "We were going through the questions one by one. . . . then we hit a block of five questions where her answer appeared to be the correct answer, and their key appeared to be wrong. To his credit, the [staffer] was increasingly upset—not with me, but with the situation."

National Computer Systems, paid $2.9 million annually to grade the tests, had rearranged the last page of test questions but neglected to change its answer key. The company apologized to Minnesota seniors who missed their graduations as a result, and offered college-bound seniors $1,000 scholarships.

This doesn't help Jimmy Dressen, who had planned to become a pipe fitter after graduating from high school, a job requiring a high school diploma. When told that he had failed the state's math test in both February and April, Jimmy dropped out of school. He wasn't going to get a diploma, so why bother? As it happens, Jimmy had actually passed the math test in both February and April. But by the time he got this news he was a high school dropout who'd found a job collecting shopping carts at a Kmart.

Jimmy is among 226 seniors incorrectly labeled as math failures who missed out on their high school graduations. Since he wasn't college-bound, National Computer Systems didn't offer Jimmy the $1,000 apology.

The Business Roundtable, the members of Congress who passed President Clinton's Goals 2000: Educate America Act in March 1994, the Minnesota legislature—they all owe Jimmy Dressen an apology. Our country needs pipe fitters. We need beauticians, bricklayers, carpenters, forestry workers, auto mechanics, butchers, bakers, and candlestick makers. We don't need to downgrade students by saying their missed high school graduation was worth less because they weren't headed to college.

About 8000 Minnesota students were told they'd failed the test when they'd actually passed. When 8700 New York City kids were sent to summer school, and 3500 held back a grade, because of a test-grading error the first time the Terra Nova exam was used to make these determinations, CTB/McGraw-Hill offered profuse apologies. But Mayor Giuliani had a different take. He said parents should say "Thank you"—because their children got those extra months of education [in sweltering buildings]. Giuliani had no words of advice for the district superintendents who were removed on the basis of this erroneous reporting. This same error affected the rankings of one million students who took the tests in Indiana, Nevada, South Carolina, and Wisconsin. Tennessee results were also affected, but testing officials there caught the error. Actually, people involved in assessment in New York City also caught the error, but, assured twice by CTB/McGraw-Hill that nothing was wrong with the data, and under pressure to release the scores, the city went ahead and released them. Funny thing: Standardistas won't accept the evaluation of teachers, but never doubt the testocracy.

But some administrators are speaking up. Benjamin Brown, Tennessee's testing director, told *Education Week*, "When you begin to hear all the problems this is causing, and you begin to hear the words 'promotion' and 'retention,' you have to remind people that these tests contain substantial standard errors. I think teachers having a student all year would certainly have something more substantial to say than a state achievement test."

In Columbus, Ohio, Mitch Chester, assistant superintendent for the Ohio Department of Education's Office of Curriculum and Assessment, says a study commissioned by the state shows that scores on the reading portion of the Ohio fourth-grade proficiency test can't predict whether students will succeed in fifth grade. "That's why the scores should not be the sole determinant in whether a student should be held back." This man holds a high office at the Ohio Department of Education. If he worked in Chicago, the city's whole system of curriculum and assessment would fall apart. But Ohio has just passed a law that reading scores can only be used as one factor among several in deciding whether to retain students.

Of 765 students in the study who failed the reading test, 577 were judged "academically successful" in fifth grade. The others were judged "not academically successful." Amazingly enough, in a move bucking the national trend of demeaning and discounting teacher judgment, Ohio teachers were the judges of fifth grade success.

## ALL THE NEWS THAT REPORTERS WANT TO PRINT

Asking teachers for their opinions is no fun. More entertaining for media pundits is to proceed full steam ahead on the theory that school standards started on a steep nosedive the day after they, the pundits, graduated from high school. These reporters seem to take a special delight in putting a nasty spin on their coverage of test scores. In April 2001, in a *Washington Post* column titled "F for School Reform," reprinted around the country and on the Web, Michael Kelly sneered that National Assessment of Educational Progress (NAEP) results foretell "the joyous prospects of bike-messengering, table-busing, weed-pulling, hamburger-flipping, and broom-pushing—episodically relieved by unemployment and descents into deep poverty" for America's youth, that 47 percent of urban students scored below basic, that 60 percent of poor and minority children are "shoveled through the schools and out the other end, largely illiterate and innumerate."

It sells papers.

But as David Berliner and Bruce Biddle showed so powerfully in *The Manufactured Crisis: Myths, Fraud, and the Attack on America's Public Schools*, and as Gerald Bracey explains persuasively every month in the leading journal of education professionals, *Phi Delta Kappan*, as familiar as the statistics parroted in the press have become, they have been distorted by spin and outright fraud. In *What Really Matters for Struggle Readers*, nationally recognized reading expert and scholar Richard Allington notes that in 1992, American fourth graders ranked second in the world; American ninth graders were right in the middle. In addition, the most economically disadvantaged U.S. students performed around the middle in both grades. "So," says Allington, "if American elementary schools are failing, virtually all schools across the globe must be failing also." Allington presents plenty of data and sums it up with the conclusion that "at all grade levels children today outperform children from earlier eras of American schooling."

One can only wonder what it would take to get this displayed in banner headlines in newspapers across the country. Imagine any of the networks leading with a startling announcement: "At all grade levels children today outperform children from earlier eras of American schooling." Imagine the President calling a press conference to congratulate teachers because "at all grade levels children today outperform children from earlier eras of American schooling."

Don't hold your breath. For the U.S. press corps, bad news leads, and good news is an oxymoron.

Gerald Bracey, a testing expert, observes that the way the NAEP is graded—with levels set at advanced, proficient, basic, and below basic—makes little sense. Adults decided which questions kids should be able to answer. They didn't look at how kids performed on the tests; they didn't talk to kids about why they answered the questions as they did. They sat at their desks—or maybe they lay in their hammocks—and thought about which questions kids should be able to answer. Bracey's observation is crucial for anyone who hopes to understand not just the NAEP but other state and national tests. Any time educators examine tests, they point out serious disconnects between "right" answers as perceived by adults and the way children actually think and reason. Educators aren't able to publish comments about the tests—because test publishers invoke copyright restrictions. One must have top secret clearance to see the tests, and even then, one is prohibited from publishing critiques that discuss specific items.

Why do test-makers want to fool children into choosing wrong answers? Because norm-referenced tests require winners and losers. One-
half the test-takers on a norm-referenced test score above average, and
one-half score below average. That's how the tests are designed. When
a test is being normed, if most low scorers answer a question correctly,
that question is thrown out. If most high scorers miss it, it is also
thrown out. On a nationally normed test, when an affluent community
like Scarsdale, New York, or Palo Alto, California, has most of its children scoring way above average, there has to be another community,
like the Bronx, New York, or East St. Louis, Illinois, or Los Angeles,
where most of the children are scoring way below average. Nationally,
everybody can't be above average, a fact that seems to elude our politicians. Or maybe it just suits their purpose to obfuscate this fact.

On June 22, 2001, front-page headlines in *The Post-Crescent* in Wisconsin's Fox River Valley screamed "School test scores plunge." Here's
the lead paragraph:

> Statewide test results for fourth-, eighth-, and tenth-grade stu-
> dents in Wisconsin show lower proficiency in many categories,
> even after the testing company reviewed the tests to make sure
> they weren't flawed, officials announced today.

Letting CTB/McGraw-Hill—or any testing company—decide if
their own tests are flawed seems rather like letting Firestone decide if
their tires on the Ford Explorer are OK.

But this issue extends far beyond one state's results on the tests of one
test-maker. Reliability and validity are continual questions about tests
across the country. Here's how the Florida Department of Education
answers the question on their Web site:

> The FCAT is extensively monitored for statistical reliability and
> the results are reported in the technical reports.

The passive construction is telling. Parents and teachers need to
know "Who's minding the store?" And they need the answers to be

written in English, not in unreadable technical reports. It's long past time for letting the fox into the hen house to rank and sort the ill-fated chickens.

## WHEN READING ABILITY IS NOT GOOD ENOUGH

When children sit down to a reading test, they face much more than just understanding what they read. Children must pick their way through the torturous maze of distractor items among the multiple-choice questions traveling along with the reading passages. These distractors aren't simply wrong answers. These distractors are written by adults trained in making the miscue bait so tempting that kids will bite. In fact, a distractor item does not make it onto a high-stakes reading exam unless it has proven to be able to lure a certain percentage of hapless students into falling for it. The purpose of standardized achievement tests has never been to measure what people know, but to differentiate among people, to determine who gets into gifted and talented programs, who might need special ed services, and so on. These tests are wholly unsuited to measure the progress or achievement of students, schools, districts, states, or nations.

Parents need to remember that all of the children can be above average in Lake Wobegon because kids there don't take high-stakes tests. By definition, 50 percent of the kids who take a high-stakes test have to score "below average."

Distractors are what makes the differentiation happen. If you want to rate children from best to worst, then you must have a system that makes those separations. As Clifford Hill and Eric Larsen observe in *Children and Reading Tests*, "Test-makers must construct distractors that are genuinely attractive, and the most attractive distractor is one that results from an inference that the passage invites readers to make."

Hill and Larsen offer a detailed analysis of both the reading passages and the accompanying multiple-choice questions from a famous pilot reading test they were allowed to write about. After children took the test, they talked with Hill and Larsen about their answers. Children's reasons for wrong answers are sometimes poignant, sometimes amusing, and very often persuasive. Hill observes, "If ever there's a place you should not use multiple-choice tests, it's in fourth-grade reading." Yet now schools are using these tests with first graders too. Years ago, famed educator Deborah Meier also interviewed children about their answers on reading tests and reported the same phenomenon. Not only do children have very good justifications for their "wrong" answers, usually they can't be talked out of these answers. The answers have little to do with reading comprehension and everything to do with child psychology and the way children see their world.

The proposition that children see the world differently from the way adults do seems to have eluded the test constructors, and since the tests are secret, there's nobody blowing the whistle. We can pose a general question, however: Can distractors ever be legitimate? If a child can read a passage and make sense of that passage, does the fact that he can be tricked into choosing a clever distractor mean he no longer understands the passage? Should a child's reading ability—and promotion to the next grade—depend on his ability not to "fall for" devious tricks?

Walk down a hallway a few weeks before test time, and you'll hear the chant: "Three in a row? No, no, no!" Such chants, of course, are unrelated to reading. They are concerned with spotting tricks. Worse, such tricks badly distort children's notions of reading. Do we really want to train seven- and eight-year-olds to believe that reading is a trick? In ever-increasing numbers, school districts across the country think we do. They are drilling students on test prep materials, and directing parents to such commercial products as Kaplan's *No-Stress Guide to the 8th Grade MCAS, No-Stress Guide to the 8th Grade FCAT, No-Stress Guide to the New York State 8th Grade Tests, Parent's Guide to the MCAS for Grade 4*, and so on. My favorite is a Kaplan suggestion for a game parents can play with their kids:

> Try to sneak in simple questions at the end of ordinary sentences, so that "Please pass the potatoes" becomes "Please pass the potatoes if you know how many multiple-choice questions there are in the math exam."

Please don't try this at your house. The insurrection during dinner, with mashed potatoes dripping from the ceiling, wouldn't be pretty. Clearly, whoever wrote this suggestion either has no children or avoids mealtime contact with them.

Walmart.com offers the *McGraw-Hill Test Prep Grade 1: Standardized Test-Taking Skills for Reading, Math, and Learning*, and McGraw-Hill has its own on-line site for test-prep materials, a different book for each grade. Riverside Publishers offers "fundamental test-taking skills" in *Test for Success* and *Test Alert*, noting the importance of familiarizing children with the standardized test format starting in kindergarten. Funeducation.com offers to prepare a child for the SAT-9—$19.95 for an annual subscription to the computer-based version, or a book *How to Prepare for the SAT-9* for the same price. Funeducation, indeed. Alfie Kohn, the author of *The Case Against Standardized Testing: Raising the Scores, Ruining the Schools*, observes, "They're like circling vultures. They find a place where there's a new test, and then they offer their services."

Now Massachusetts is offering to bring test-prep companies into the schools. Acting Governor Jane M. Swift says that starting in the fall of 2002, the state will pay for test-prep tutors for students who repeatedly fail the MCAS exam and don't get the extra help they need at school. On the 2000 exam, 45 percent of 10th graders failed math and 34 percent failed English. No one asks if something might be wrong with the tests. Instead, the state will pay test-prep tutors to come in and apply a drill-fix for the students.

Schools do parents and children a terrible disservice when they promote this sort of offal. Test-prep exercises are the Fen-Phen of education. Not just a gimmick, they do real harm, distorting the vision of what it means to be a competent reader. Diet drugs don't teach you to eat properly. Test-prep exercises don't teach kids how to read. Even when it says "Higher Score Guaranteed," a workbook crammed with 210 pages of practice exams will serve only to make children hate reading. The guides give advice on strategic guessing, formulaic essay writing, pacing one's time. Any child would be better off reading Beatrix Potter, Rosemary Wells, Steven Kellogg, the *Just-So Stories*, *The Time Warp Trio* series, the *Junie B. Jones* series, the *Sammy Keyes* series, the *Professor Poopy*

*Pants* series, *The Rats of NIMH*, Robert Louis Stevenson, Douglas Florian, Nikki Giovanni, Kristine O'Connell George, E.B. White, Katherine Paterson, Karen Hesse, Jean Fritz, Gary Paulsen, Avi . . . the list is wonderfully long and wonderfully irresistible.

If you have a "reluctant reader" in your house, hand him a riddle book. In my third grade classroom, *Dinosaur Riddles* convinced Chris that he wanted to become a reader. I took our daily challenge from the book, writing on the board, *What kind of dinosaur do you find in a rodeo?* Through the day, children wrote suggestions under the question. We played this tomfoolery every day, and often the children's suggestions were better than the printed riddle answer. After I read the answer at the end of the day—*A Bronco-saurus*—Chris insisted he had to have that book, not a common request from a boy with a Boston hospital-diagnosed learning disability. Chris studied the book's pages during our silent reading period every day—for a month. He frowned, he sounded out, he asked me for help. And on the 28th day he volunteered to read three dinosaur riddles aloud to the class.

Having read one book, Chris was ready to look for another one. And that's the miracle every teacher looks for. One of my definitions of a reader is *Someone who expects to find something worthwhile in a book's pages*. Test-prep trickery can never do this for children. This is why it is our duty to show children a better way. But test-prep is swamping curriculum offerings across the country.

A survey of North Carolina teachers indicated that 80 percent of them devote at least 20 percent of instructional time to test preparation. In a searing chapter titled "Collateral Damage," in her must-read book *Contradictions of School Reform*, Rice University Professor Linda McNeil documents what happens when test prep is, in effect, mandated by the state. McNeil points out that the legislated reforms in Texas have had "the effects of de-skilling teachers' work, trivializing and reducing the quality of the content of the curriculum, and distancing children from the substance of schooling." McNeil concludes that "the clear picture that emerges is that the standardized reforms drastically hurt the best teachers, forcing them to teach watered-down content required because it was computer-gradable." One specific result is that children read fewer novels and full-length nonfiction books. Instead, they read short, disconnected passages, and answer multiple-choice questions about these passages—just like on the tests.

In North Carolina, eighth-grade teacher Teresa Glenn requested a subscription to a metropolitan newspaper such as the *New York Times* or the *Washington Post* for her classroom. She was interrogated, "Why do you need this? Newspaper articles aren't on the test." As her own daughter gets ready to start school, Teresa worries about letting her "set foot in a school in North Carolina, knowing what I do about the focus on test prep." Teresa continues, "I can already tell you with certainty that she'll get close to no history or science. For poetry she'll get a bunch of literary terms, but there won't be time to communicate the passion, the beauty, the fun of words. In math, she's not going to use manipulatives or do simulations; she's going to practice finding one right answer from among four." North Carolina earns high praise from President Bush for its rigorous testing program.

## CHOOSING THE BEST PANCAKE TOPPING

According to the Florida Department of Education FCAT Briefing Book, the FCAT measures what the people in charge want it to measure. These people offer no explanation of why they want third graders to be able to figure perimeter and fourth graders to know about obtuse angles in triangles. Age-appropriate material is a critical issue in testing. Sometimes children can understand every word in a reading passage but still "fail" the questions because the psychology of the questions is out of whack. For example, on the 1999 CTB/McGraw-Hill test in New York, nine-year-olds across the state were shown pictures of labels from different brands of pancake syrup and asked to choose "the real Mc-Coy," defined in the reading passage as "anything of true worth or value." The labels show maple-"style" syrup, 2 percent maple syrup, syrup with artificial maple flavor, and 100 percent pure maple syrup.

Such as question is more a can of worms than a fair assessment of a fourth grader's reading comprehension. Deconstructing food labels is *not* a regular part of a fourth grader's curriculum, not to mention any child's psyche. One might also wonder about the income level required to put 100 percent maple syrup on the family pancakes. In the real world, where plenty of nine-year-olds accompany their parents to the grocery store, 24-ounce containers of Aunt Jemima Lite and Vermont Maid, with maple syrup contents of 2 percent and zero respectively, cost $3.59 each. An 8-ounce container of Butternut Farm Grade A Medium Amber pure maple syrup costs $12.95. How many consumers opt for the $1.62-an-ounce product over the one that costs just $0.15 an ounce? Even in my grocery store—in Vermont, no less—you have to go to the pricey specialty section to find 100 percent pure maple syrup.

And what's a fourth grader to think? That his momma doesn't put "true value" on the family breakfast table? If we don't trust the chowderheads who wrote this question to buy our groceries, how can we trust them to rank and sort our children? How can we let them decide who moves on to fifth grade and who doesn't?

## A PICTURE IS WORTH A THOUSAND WORDS

A seldom-reported distractor item on tests is the huge disturbance caused by wildly inappropriate artwork. What was a high schooler hoping to pass the Spring 2001 California High School Exit Exam to make of the illustration stuck below "The Courage That My Mother Had," a poem by Edna St. Vincent Millay, showing a stocky, middle-aged African woman? Edna St. Vincent Millay, the first woman to win the Pulitzer Prize in poetry, a woman who was arrested marching for Sacco and Vanzetti, a woman whom Thomas Hardy declared one of the two great things in the U.S. (the other being the skyscraper), was described by a student in the audience when she gave a reading at Yale:

Her bright hair shining, she stood before us like a daffodil.

Nancy Milford, author of an acclaimed biography of Edna, describes that hair as "fire" and her skin as "pale as milk." Far from stocky, Edna was small in stature, often described as ethereal. Ralph McGill, recalling that "she wore the first shimmering gold-metal cloth dress I'd ever seen," called Edna "one of the most fey and beautiful persons I'd ever met." The illustration accompanying the Millay poem is the opposite of fey. It is the portrait of a dark, prim, stolid, middle-aged woman who, frowning in her suit, might be a church deacon, an undertaker, a high school principal facing an inquisition from the board.

As every English major knows, poetry is universal and the speaker in a poem is not necessarily the poet herself. But the California testocrats forestall this interpretation, by inserting this bald statement in the directions for reading Millay's poem: "The following poem is about the poet's inheritance." What's the reader to think? That Edna was adopted? Come to think of it, the African-American woman in the illustration looks like she could be the head of an orphanage.

Some will say I quibble. After all, probably not one high schooler in ten will know that Millay was a daffodil, not an oak tree. But consider what happened to *More Stories Julian Tells* when the testocrats got hold of it. Most third graders in the land know that the acclaimed Julian series features an African-American family. So what were seven- and eight-year-olds to make of the Illinois reading test, with its excerpt from *More Stories Julian Tells* showing Julian as an Anglo kid?

Author Ann Cameron, described by *Parents* magazine as "a virtuoso storyteller with a gift for revealing the heart and soul of childhood in her stories," worries about the unconscious racism embedded in the assumption of the test producers that the smart, successful, loving family in the stories must be white. Ann worries about what children seeing the test item will think. She asked the Illinois state board of education to issue an apology—to be read to third graders across the state, who might feel tricked by the mistake. Cameron's publisher, Random House, asked the board to stop distributing the test and to destroy remaining copies. MetriTech, based in Champaign, Illinois, who produced the test for the board of education, said the artist had not read the story.

A spokesperson for the board of education said the state reviews tests to ensure diversity in the drawings. So does California. So does every other state in the union. Testocrats will do what they damn well please and then cry "Diversity!" Some bean counter noticed that the California test needed another black and the Illinois test another white. Years ago a story circulated about the efforts exerted to create racial balance in a basal reading series. An executive told the art director to make sure the art in a story "showed diversity." The art director pointed out that it was a story about dinosaurs.

Readers bring who they are and what they know to any text they are reading. But when the tests distort literature, readers are put in a no-win situation. What's a kid to think? Either the test-maker is trying to trick the reader by pretending that Julian is Anglo, or the test-maker is just plain ignorant and doesn't know Julian is African-American. Either way, an eight-year-old knows he can't trust the people who wrote the test.

And the real assault goes much deeper. The real assault is that writers and publishers allow literary passages from stories and poems children love to be put on tests, tests that determine whether a kid goes to summer school, whether a kid passes from third to fourth grade. Is there any author of any repute who bows each morning to the Vocabulary Test muse? To distractor items? If not, then it seems legitimate to ask authors why they are allowing their work to be distorted and defiled.

This is a difficult issue. One can make a good argument that the best writing from acclaimed children's authors should be used on tests so as to engage and interest young readers. The trouble is that the tests distort the way people read. Test prep promotes bad reading habits. And when young readers encounter, say, Katherine Paterson's *Bridge to Teribitha* on a test, they think she wrote it to test them. Nothing could be further from the truth. The cost of using beloved authors' work on tests is too high. Arnold Lobel's stories and fables should not be used to test children. That's a fact. Shel Silverstein's poems should not be used to test children. That's a fact. The publisher who allows this to happen is immoral. That's a fact.

In Chicago, authorities want to make certain teachers and students are on the same page. Teachers are provided with the Structured Curriculum Lesson Plan for each day, showing them how to use such favorites as *Miss Nelson is Missing* to prepare children for the ITBS/TAP (Iowa Tests of Basic Skills/Tests of Achievement Proficiency) and ISAT

(Illinois Standards Achievement Test) tests. Testocrats direct teachers to take this book, which celebrates young children's instinct for anarchism, and "discuss the fact that the students are being rude, making faces, and they are out of their seats. Ask: *Can the class learn when they are behaving like this?*" (Emphasis in original.) Oh, my. Testocrats demonstrate how bad things can happen to good literature. Testocrats in Chicago may find this hard to believe, but *Miss Nelson is Missing* is not a story about teaching children good manners. And third graders know this. Third graders will acknowledge that the teacher still gets the upper hand (for the time being), but in this story they are on the side of anarchy, not Emily Post. Or Chicago's updated version of Dickens's Gradgrind.

Perhaps it's time for authors to step up and declare that they didn't write children's stories to be weighed and measured. They should do this for the sake of the stories as well as for the children.

A Maryland test (MSAP, Maryland Student Assessment Program) given to eighth graders in 1996 offered a way around the difficulty. Three different pieces of literature are described: an African folktale, a science fiction story, and a humorous story. Students choose which story they want to read, and then are given 85 minutes to read it and then answer eight questions. Here are three:

1. You and your friend have probably chosen different stories to read. Write a note to your friend summarizing the story. Include the major problem and how it was solved.
2. Write the title of the story you read. Using details from the story, explain why this is or is not a good choice for the title.
3. Think about a character in the story you read. Write a paragraph for your teacher comparing the story character to yourself or someone else. Include details from the story.

This method of questioning children about things they read has its flaws. For one, it judges their ability to read by how well they write. Nonetheless, anything that offers students choices and acknowledges the importance of their own insights seems to be an alternative worth trying.

Some years back, *Library Journal* published an article about a little girl who had never spoken and who had withdrawn from the world around her. She spoke her first sentence after a teacher read Maurice Sendak's *Where the Wild Things Are*. She said, "Can I have that book?"

Those are the magic words that literature elicits from children. We must stop debasing that literature with multiple-choice questions, and instead inspire children to ask for more books.

Children's authors are in the perfect position to help us do this.

## STEALING CHILDHOOD

Writing in *The Washington Post*, Marc Fisher described a fifth-grade girl standing in the foyer of Bethesda Elementary School "capsized in tears." When a concerned parent asked what was wrong, the child kept crying. Finally she gulped that she missed the bus and because she's a few minutes late she can't go to the special Maryland School Performance Assessment Program (MSPAP) playground. The school set up this special playground—with extra games and triple playtime—for those children who come to school on time every day. Principal Michael Castagnola explains, "It's a motivator. The kids get penalized if they miss a day of the test. They know that if you work hard, you're going to have fun." Fisher describes other "supposedly ethical ways in which schools twist and tweak kids to get them to take the tests seriously." Parties, test coaching worksheets, practice tests. On Fridays, to improve their self-esteem, kids make posters about the Standards of Learning (SOLs).

That's a good one for parents to try at the office. On Fridays, instead of casual dress day, institute Make-a-Poster day. Poster teams can make posters about Workman's Compensation, Social Security, or maybe OSHA regulations.

At least the school still has recess. The *New York Times* ran a front-page story showing the picture of a kindergartner in Atlanta, telling the reporter she'd like to go outside and look for ladybugs. But in the name of improving children's skills, Atlanta no longer has recess. Some

Virginia districts axed the 15-minute recess to cram in more test prep time. When the Virginia Board of Education ordered elementary schools to reinstate a daily recess, some schools figured out how to get around this by having adults lead kids on a three- or four-minute walk after lunch and calling it recess. In Florida, *News-Journal* columnist Mark Lane visited his daughter's old elementary school playground, which now occupies barely a quarter of the space of the one there when she was a student. After reminiscing a bit about his own and his now-teenage daughter's blister-inducing monkey-bar triumphs, Lane concludes, "There is no section of the FCAT devoted to measuring monkey-bar skills, so playgrounds don't have much of a place in the test-prep oriented schools of today."

In a survey of 64,785 elementary schools in 15,000 districts, the American Association for the Child's Right to Play (IPA/USA) found that about 40 percent of America's public schools have cut one or more recesses from the children's school day. The association issued a statement on the importance of recess, declaring recess as "vital to the child's overall healthy development." Among many points, IPA/USA points out that:

- Recess responds to the child's social and emotional needs.
- Recess is a contributing factor for cultural exchange, children playing with children of different cultures.
- Recess contributes to the child's cognitive and intellectual needs.
- Unstructured play gives the children opportunity to exercise a sense of wonder, which leads to exploration, which leads to creativity.

The on-line document points out that in Japan, long classroom sessions alternate with intense periods of play outside (http://www.ipausa.org/recess.htm).

Numerous home pages feature the *Certificate of the Right to Play*, intended for adults as well as children.

## Certificate of the Right to Play

By this Certificate, know ye that:
_____ is a lifetime member
and in good standing in the Society of Childlike Persons and forever entitled to: Walk in the rain, jump in mud puddles, collect
rainbows, smell flowers, blow bubbles, stop along the way, build
sandcastles, watch the sun and the moon and the stars come out,
say hello to everyone, go barefoot, go on adventures, sing in the
shower, have a merry heart, read children's books, act silly, take
bubble baths, get new sneakers, hold hands and hug and kiss,
dance, fly kites, laugh and cry for the health of it.

Wander around, feel scared, feel sad, feel mad, feel happy, give
up worry and guilt and shame. Say yes, say no, say the magic
words, ask lots of questions, ride bicycles, draw and paint, see
things differently, fall down and get up again, talk with animals,
look up at the sky.

Trust the universe, stay up late, climb trees, take naps, do
nothing, daydream, play with toys, have pillow fights, learn new
stuff, get excited about everything, be a clown, enjoy having a
body, listen to music, find out how things work, make up new
rules, tell stories.

Save the world, make friends with other kids on the block and
do anything else that brings more happiness, celebration, relax-
ation, communication, health, joy, love, creativity, pleasure, abun-
dance, great self-esteem, courage, balance, spontaneity, passion,
beauty, peace and life energy to the above-named member, and to
the other human beings on this planet.

Further, the above-named member is hereby officially author-
ized to frequent amusement parks, beaches, meadows, mountain
tops, swimming pools, forests, playgrounds, picnic areas, summer
camps, birthday parties, circuses, cookie shops, ice cream parlors,
theaters, aquariums, museums, planetariums, toy stores, festivals,
and other places where children of all ages come to play.

_____

Maybe no child should start on the homework grind each evening until he's checked off that he's achieved at least half a dozen items on the Right to Play list that day. A happy childhood is a much better legacy than completing worksheets as preparation for becoming a future worker, global economy or no.

When a third-grade teacher who has taught in a Fairfax County school for 30 years thinks about the things she has had to eliminate from her classroom since the SOL tests took over the curriculum, she worries about what legacy her students are forfeiting. Her third graders used to write autobiographies and biographies; they wrote poetry in each of six forms, binding this collection in a book. "Something for them to keep forever." Now students read some poems and pick out the rhyming words so they can pass their SOLs.

Kathy Vannini, an elementary school nurse in Longmeadow, Massachusetts, says she dreads the springtime weeks when children must take the MCAS, the lengthy test required of Massachusetts children starting in third grade. "My office is filled with children with headaches and stomachaches every day. One third grader was beside himself on the morning of the test—he could not stop sobbing."

Sometimes the abuses are more subtle. A Virginia mother reflects that pressure for the test provoked her eight-year-old daughter to cheat. "She just spent three days learning about electricity for the SOL tests. Today she was tested on such things as static electricity, electric charge, electric current, electric circuit, closed circuit, open circuit, lightning, conductor, insulator, filament, switch, Benjamin Franklin, Thomas Edison, Lewis Latimer, and so on. She was so worried about doing well on this test that she cheated." Mom has kept a list of the factoids that her child has been required to memorize, a list she labels "abusive." This mother wonders, "What leads a child who has never been in trouble at school, a child who consistently receives citizen awards, to cheat on a test?" Then she answers her own question. "The stakes are high. Test scores determine grades in science and social studies. The curriculum and test preparation in Virginia are out of control."

In Missouri, Mary Lowe says that because of the MAP (Missouri Assessment Program), "the bus routes to our schools are paved with the souls of our children." Mary was assigned as reader and scribe to a student we'll call Dave. Dave has a reading disability, and was taking a three-days-long social studies exam for the MAP. "I can't believe how hard the social studies test was. Each question had multiple steps, and I can't believe there are many fourth graders who have the sophisticated reasoning and organization skills to work through each step. Afterwards, I cried all the way home." One can get a glimpse of Dave's torture by looking at the Grade 4 Social Studies "Sampler" on-line at the Missouri Department of Education Web site. One question asks the child to look at a map of the Oregon Trail and then answer this essay question: "How have territorial boundaries in the western part of the country changed since the days of the Oregon Trail?"

This is what teachers are talking about when they talk of the cultural bias of tests. Children who have taken family trips in the West are much more likely to have an idea of Oregon's location these days, never mind 1850. Here's another essay question: "Your family just arrived at Fort Bridger on the Oregon Trail. Why will food be much more expensive in Fort Bridger than it was in Independence, Missouri, where your family began your journey?" Supply and demand and other capitalist theory is a big item among Standardistas. It is anyone's guess what nine-year-olds are to make of it.

One of the questions Mary read to Dave asked why freedom of speech is important. Dave replied that it is important because if he were president he would get up in front of the whole country and tell everyone how dumb the stupid tests are and how unhappy the tests are making everybody—miserable and sick. Dave added, "I understand freedom of speech now. When you believe something really a lot and feel scared to say it, you say it anyway."

Julie Woestehoff, Executive Director of PURE (Parents United for Responsible Education) in Chicago, says, "I don't think any place has Chicago beat for student humiliation and terrorizing." Chicago's habit is to notify an eighth grader right before school picnics, class trips, and graduation rites are to take place that he can't participate. Julie comments, "Suddenly you become a nonperson in your school. This would happen even for honor students, students with good grades throughout the year." Publishers of the Iowa test decry this use of their test. But they don't stop selling tests to the Chicago school system. People who think it's only right and proper for kids who don't measure up to be held back should know that overwhelming research indicates that students who are held back are five times more likely to drop out of school than students with the same skills who were not held back. Hold a student back twice, and the likelihood of his dropping out is 100 percent.

Insisting that testing is an "essential ingredient in ensuring that no child is left behind," Texas commissioner of education and chair of the Education Leaders Council, a group representing eight state education chiefs, Jim Nelson concedes that testing is stressful, but he insists that "learning to manage stress is a part of learning to live." He says that testing is "an essential ingredient in ensuring that no child is left behind" and that "it is unfair not to test kids."

No one wants to see kids reach high school without adequate reading and math skills, but schools must be encouraged to develop alternative curriculum to meet the needs of students. Members of the Business Roundtable and their political allies and bureaucratic toadies should be made to prove they have spent serious time in the presence of students before they are allowed to orate on "essential ingredients" of school curricula. Lock them up for a few days with 28 third graders and then ask them what students need.

## WRITING FOR A TEST

Here's a variation on the old algebra nightmare—where you dream you've overslept on the morning of your final exam in algebra. Imagine you're in a classroom and the examiner tells you that you have 45 minutes to write an essay explaining your favorite thing to do after work and why you enjoy doing it. Or maybe you'd rather write about your favorite day of the week? In 2000, Florida fourth and eighth graders were told to write an essay explaining why a day of the week is their favorite. This is termed an "open-ended" question. What's the problem? A kid has a choice among seven days. But once he picks it, he'd better write carefully crafted paragraphs. New educational jargon is born. In Florida, teachers now teach "demand writing." Fourth graders take the *Florida Writes* test, part of the FCAT, so practice for demand writing begins in third grade. This is not an option. Students are expected to memorize the steps of demand writing:

Step I    10 minutes: Think Plan, which includes webbing ideas, big ideas, supporting ideas, details, and examples.

Step II   25 minutes: Organize and write, with a beginning, middle, and end.

Step III  10 minutes: Replace tired words, write strong sentences, correct punctuation, grammar, and spelling.

Forty-five minutes from start to finish. That's why it's called demand writing.

Teachers receive directives on how to get the kids ready, and they drill these techniques each day, starting in third grade. "Explain that demand writing is the type of writing done in real-life situations when time is limited." No adult required to produce writing on the job does it this way. Even the required college essay assignment allows the student time to think about it, to consult with peers, to make false starts. The 10-minute Think Plan of the FCAT is a parody of real world writing—except perhaps at the rewrite desk of a large city newspaper.

Here's a modest proposal: Ask your local school board members, the op-ed page editor of your newspaper, local TV pundits, and everybody on your block to write an essay on the topic of their favorite day of the week, how to clean the parakeet cage, or whatever. Extra credit: Suggest the same topic to your state legislators, the governor, and the fellows you send to Washington. Make them stick to the time limit and remind them that there's no talking allowed. Be sure to tell them the whole world will be reading the results.

Or how about hummingbirds? On the high school exit exam given in March 2001 to California high schoolers, students were asked to read an essay about hummingbirds and then perform this writing task: "Write an essay in which you discuss the author's purpose for writing about hummingbirds." Probably the simple fact of the matter is that the author was paid to write about hummingbirds. In any case, how many people agree that the ability to understand an author's motivation for writing about hummingbirds should decide whether one is worthy to receive a high school diploma? Or that a kid's willingness to go along with this ritual should determine whether his teacher and school are labeled adequate? Florida high schoolers taking the FCAT in 2001 were asked to write about the pros and cons of a year-round school, examining the issue from different perspectives—including that of the organization Phi Beta Kappa. Yes, Phi Beta Kappa, a college honor society whose members are invited based on high academic achievement.

Maybe Public Agenda should take a poll and find out how many people give a hoot about Phi Beta Kappa's opinion one way or another. Or how many know who or what Phi Beta Kappa is.

New York students trying to pass the New York State English Regents exam were told to write a "unified essay about the power of nature" as revealed in a passage written by the sixteenth-century English essayist Roger Ascham and another passage written by Jack London. They were instructed to use evidence from each passage to develop their controlling idea about the power of nature. Jeanne Heifetz, a summa cum laude graduate of Harvard with a specialty in Renaissance literature, an M.A. in English from New York University, and experience teaching at high school and college levels, says she was hard-pressed to decipher the Ascham without the Oxford English Dictionary. (One of the key words in the passage was defined in the OED, listed as "obscure"—the example the dictionary cited was: Roger Ascham!) And the clock wasn't ticking nor a high school diploma hanging in the balance for Jeanne.

Five English Language Learners at Sleepy Hollow High School flubbed the writing exam. They passed all their courses and all the other Regents tests. Some had the biology Regents on the same day as the ELA (English Language Arts), so this meant nine hours of testing. Four of the five had been accepted to college. The five took the exam several times, so they had the experience of writing about Roger Ascham's prose as well as Anne Lamott's. Here's the writing prompt for the latter:

The Situation: As a member of a class on fiction writing, you have been asked by your teacher to prepare an instructional manual for your classmates on the reasons and techniques for using dialogue to improve their writing. In preparation for writing the manual, listen to a speech by published writer Anne LaMott [sic]. Then use relevant information from the speech to write your instructional manual.

Your Task: Write an instructional manual for your classmates in which you give some reasons and techniques for using dialogue to improve their writing. . . . Use specific, accurate, and relevant information from the speech to support your discussion. . . .

Several questions come to mind. First, is it too much to expect the people grilling students on the work of an author to spell that author's name right? Someone working at the New York State Department of Education must have a fondness for Anne Lamott. She also showed up on the 2000 Regents writing prompt. There, as if writing an essay comparing Roger Ascham's view of nature with Jack London's weren't freakish enough, students were told that their task was to discuss these works "from the particular perspective provided in the Critical Lens." Here's the Critical Lens: "When writers write from a place of insight and real caring about the truth, they have the ability to throw the lights on for the reader. Anne Lamott (adapted)"

At least they got her name right that time.

Let's get this right: Students must write an instructional manual on using dialogue to improve one's writing—based on information they get from listening to a reading taken from the work of Anne Lamott. Wait a minute: How does writing dialogue prepare students for life in the global economy? How many people need to know how to write dialogue in the scene Lamott suggests: The boy in the leather overcoat meets the beautiful girl with the harelip and the Gucci bag . . .? Was this, maybe, meant to balance the Ascham of the previous year's exam? If the Business Roundtable can provide me with the names of five CEOs who have found occasion to write a line of dialogue in their professional lives, I'll eat their annual reports.

What chance did the five English Language Learners at Sleepy Hollow High have when faced with the sly, edgy humor, Bay Area alternative Christian lifestyle persona, and staccato delivery that make Anne Lamott a popular on-line diarist for Salon.com? What were they to make of her lessons on dialogue writing, for God's sake? Anne Lamott's *Bird by Bird* has gone from cult status to popular respectability. It is on the recommended reading list for English 401 at the University of New Hampshire, where they give lessons on dialogue writing.

The New York State Regents High School examination in global history and geography, administered January 23, 2001, shows students that they can be in worse jams than trying to write a manual on dialogue writing. Just a few questions make it obvious that high-stakes testing is a form of corporate terrorism against the young.

"If a son has struck his father, they shall cut off his hand. If a nobleman has destroyed the eye of a member of the aristocracy, they shall destroy his eye. . . ."
    The idea expressed in this quotation is found in the:
    1. Ten Commandments
    2. Twelve Tables
    3. Justinian Code
    4. Code of Hammurabi

One way in which the Eightfold Path and the Five Pillars of Faith are similar is that that these rules:
    1. Represent codes of behavior
    2. Restrict social mobility
    3. Stress the spiritual being in all natural objects
    4. Suggest a deep respect for nature and reincarnation

One conclusion that can be reached from the evidence about Mansa Musa's rule of Mali is that:
    1. Christianity was a dominant religion in Africa in ancient times
    2. Complex civilizations existed in West Africa before the arrival of Europeans

3. Trade was not necessary for a civilization to survive
4. The slave trade originated in West Africa

The purpose of the encomienda system in Latin America was to:
1. Control overpopulation in urban centers
2. Convert native peoples to Protestantism
3. Obtain labor and taxes from the native peoples in the Spanish colonies
4. Introduce political ideas into the colonies gradually

Maybe New York kids should consider themselves lucky. The Code of Hammurabi is in the sixth-grade standards in South Dakota, and listed as essential for second graders in William Bennett's K12.com curriculum.

Anyone critical of the New York Regents for lowering the passing grade to 55 should find six people to take the full test, and ask the hometown newspaper to publish the results. Maybe everyone on your block could take it—and figure out who is and who isn't worthy of living on your block. How about everybody in your place of work? Replace Dress-Down Fridays with Take-a-State-Test Fridays. Find out if your place of business is ready for the global economy that Lou Gerstner and his CEO cronies are so crazy about.

## SOILED TESTS

Virginia parent activist Mickey VanDerwerker remarked, "Thou shalt not make the test so difficult my son throws up on it." Executives at testing giant Harcourt Educational Measurement, a San Antonio-based firm that publishes the Stanford 9, also known as the SAT-9, acknowledge that tests can make kids throw up, and advise that when this happens the correct and legal thing to do in such a circumstance is send them the vomit. In an interview with the *Sacramento Bee*, Bob Rayborn explained that every school must account for every test it receives. If tests are missing, Harcourt investigates why. If a test is missing from a classroom, the teacher must write a letter explaining what happened. Rayborn explained about vomit, "I've seen where kids have thrown up on the test. Kids do get sick at school. In those instances, teachers might have thrown the test away. The appropriate way to deal with that would be to put [the test] in a plastic bag." And send it back to Harcourt. It has the makings of a good slogan: "Send them your vomit!"

There are plenty of parents for whom this isn't a joke. A Pompano Beach, Florida, mother could find no way to prevent her son from being forced to repeat fourth grade—even though he had B's and C's in most of his course and A's in mathematics. When he came up three points short on the FCAT, his parents were informed that he wouldn't be promoted to fifth grade. Mom couldn't find anyone willing to answer the question of why her son's satisfactory work all year counted for nothing.

Young children are used to their teachers answering questions. But if children don't understand the directions on a standardized test and ask for help, they have been warned that it is against the law for their teachers to give that help—even to clarify unclear directions. Fourth graders taking a math test in New Jersey faced a very problematic question. Not only could teachers not clarify things, they were forbidden even to look at the tests. Authorities figure that if teachers don't look at the tests before or during their administration, they can't be accused of cheating.

Later, when teachers at the Bret Harte School did get a look at some of the questions, they said it was obvious that whoever wrote the question had never met a fourth grader. Teachers also protested the fact that nine- and ten-year-olds are tested for five days in a row. When they don't understand the directions and their teacher can't explain, the only alternative is to quit. And maybe cry. Or vomit. Or all of the above. Juanita Doyon, parent activist mom in Spanaway, Washington, known as the Button Queen of FairTest's listserv, ARN (Assessment Reform Network), has designed a T-shirt: "My kid puked on [name of school]'s high stakes test!" Another T-shirt turns Bush's slogan on its ear: "Leave No Child Untested." Juanita reports a national demand for her buttons,

## HIGH STAKES TESTING
## KNOW THE REAL SCORE!

Juanita insists, "I would have failed the fourth grade WASL and the seventh grade WASL. I might fail them if I took them today. I would probably overthink the writing and underthink the listening. And I'd write obscenities across the math." Juanita wants to know why, in 10th grade, her son just barely passed the WASL, but then, as a senior, scored in the top 25 percent on his SATs. "We have to watch out for our own kids," she cautions, "and for everybody else's too."

Peter Peretzman, a spokesman for the New Jersey State Department of Education, said, in effect, that parents and teachers should knock off the whining. "Our students and our parents will have to get used to taking much tougher tests," he told a *New York Times* reporter, launching into a canned spiel about the need for higher standards and tests to prepare New Jersey students for college and the job market. Then New Jersey spent tens of thousands of dollars to mail a letter trying to justify the tests to parents.

Dr. Caleb S. Rossiter, a Washington-based consultant on national security policy and adjunct professor of statistics at American University, urges parents in Washington, D.C., elementary schools to boycott the tests, saying "Teaching to the test is all cost, no benefit." Dr. Rossiter points out that many first and second graders, particularly boys, "who will become superior students later in life have not at this point developed the reading level and attention span needed for the SAT-9."

Here's a sample of what Dr. Rossiter is so concerned about. Try these questions on your favorite second grader:

1) If you want to find out where the Indian Ocean is, you should look in:
   a) A dictionary
   b) A thesaurus
   c) An atlas storybook

Or maybe you don't have atlas storybooks in your house. On the other hand, the Geographical Names section in the back of my dictionary tells me where the Indian Ocean is. Here's an item to test your second grader's writing savvy.

A very important person came to our class yesterday. He was a firefighter. He told us how to be safe at school and at home. We liked listening to him because he was very friendly.

1) Which of these would go best after the last sentence?
   a) After he talked to us, we asked him many questions.
   b) He spoke to us after we had finished reading a story.
   c) This important person was someone from our town.

How about all "of the above"? Which option a writer chooses depends on how she plans to move the narrative along. This is one more example of test writers working in a void, uncontaminated by classroom reality. Teachers carefully prepare for special visitors. This is likely to include reading a story about firefighters. The second-grade writer might want to comment on whether the real-life firefighter's account was similar or dissimilar to the story. The questions asked and answered would, of course, make for compelling narrative. Including the observation "This important person is someone from our town," though a teacherly thing to do, is definitely not the only option, nor even the best one.

Is there a parent alive who thinks his child's promotion to third grade should depend on how his child answers such inquisitions?

Concern for her son has led Lisa Guisbond to become co-chair of Brookline Coalition for Authentic Reform in Education (CARE). Lisa says she's an unlikely candidate. "I was an excellent test-taker." Lisa says that if her son were born with a replica of her own brain's wiring, she might not be spending hours each week organizing parents and teachers to protest the MCAS. "Thanks to MCAS, I have a new avocation." In a statement posted on the WGBH Web site, Eye on Education, Lisa says that in second grade, her son Max "is still struggling to learn to read, has a tenuous grasp of the simplest math concepts, and is just beginning to have the fine motor control to be able to write, although he is a prolific artist." A neuropsychologist says Max's disorder is in the subcortical region of the brain; he expects Max to be able to reason at a fairly high level but to have ongoing problems with basic math functions.

Max has a rich vocabulary. In second grade he defined "extraordinary" by saying that it's similar to "sublime, which means beyond wonderful." Speaking with great pride of Max's talents, Lisa expresses great optimism for his future, "assuming he is encouraged to develop his natural abilities and does not become mired in frustration and hopelessness. I fear his talents and skills will be given short shrift, and school will become the place where he is constantly reminded that he does not measure up to his peers." Lisa says Max has made great strides in reading; she talks about how funny and creative he is.

Where's the test for humor and creativity? Should Max be denied a diploma because he doesn't pass an algebra test?

The national mood about the testing mania is shifting. Jackie Dee King, CARE coordinator in Boston, reflects, "Many people stand up in the audience where I give talks, in towns like Swampscott or New Bedford, and say, 'I'm not that kind of a person, but this thing has gone too far.'"

Funny thing: On the WGBH *Eye on Education* Web site, people speaking against the MCAS talk about individual children. A parent, a teacher, a principal, and an education policy analyst talk about Max and Allyson and Sylvie, about 10th graders at Madison Park Technical/Vocational High School, and about how the testing insanity hurts them. People who promote MCAS talk about a global marketplace and the needs of the business community. The president of Mass Insight, a Mass Insight education manager, and a school superintendent repeat the pat phrases circling the nation: "a highly competitive world," "anticipated high failure rates," "coin of the realm." Russell Dever, superintendent of the Barnstable Public Schools and cheerleader for MCAS, states with pride that "the long composition section of the MCAS is virtually identical to the essay component of the English placement exam that most incoming college freshmen must take." He calls passing such an exam "the basics." Parents need to ask when college admission became a basic for all students. Why should a child be denied a high school diploma if she doesn't write well enough to be admitted to college? Dr. Dever is proud that the MCAS is similar to "the renowned Regents exams."

Parents in New York don't refer to the Regents quite that way. In fact, parents in Scarsdale are so adamant about not letting the Regents ruin their high schoolers' education that they are opting to ignore the Regents and give their own diplomas. "We don't want our schools to be test prep centers," Debbie Miller, a Scarsdale mother of an eighth grader, told the Los Angeles *Daily News*. "The national movement of our president to standardize education throughout the country is something that we should all be fighting."

The three toughest tests in the country, called "world class" by Standardistas, are New York, Virginia, and Massachusetts. California is working hard to catch up. Governor Gray Davis laid out his plan in his 1999 State of the State Address: "While a number of other states require students to pass a statewide minimal-skills exam to graduate from high school, California does not. I believe we need to do even better. I am proposing a rigorous high school graduation exam, second to none in America." So now we have a competition among governors as to whose is bigger.

Sometimes state officials are forced to withdraw bad tests. After Massachusetts high schools scrapped rich humanities courses to march in line for the state's rigid world-history framework, in spring 2001, the state dumped their world history exam and announced they will work on developing one in U.S. history instead. Ever eager to put a positive spin on anything related to MCAS, Abigail Thernstrom, member of the

Massachusetts Board of Education, had no problem with scrapping the much-mocked world history test, insisting that the switch just lets students know that it's more important for students in the United States "to know who Thomas Jefferson was than to know about the Ming Dynasty."

Eileen McNamara, *Boston Globe* staff writer, put her finger on the truth of the matter. This embarrassing snafu reveals "all that is wrong with the nation's current infatuation with high-stakes educational testing. What, exactly are we testing for? Are we asking for a demonstration of analytical thinking or the rote regurgitation of memorized material? If it's the latter, and we have simply substituted a demand for knowledge about Reconstruction for knowledge about the Russian Revolution, how can we argue that what we expect our children to know is not arbitrary?"

The real tragedy of the testing is that teachers feel compelled to prepare students for the tests, and that means the day-to-day curriculum is arbitrary and wrongheaded. Speaking at Columbia University, reading-test researcher Clifford Hill observed that "In order to coach to the test, you're teaching a way of reading which I don't think is the way we really read, or the way we should read." This is an important consideration for parents: Every day a child spends in test prep reinforces a wrongheaded notion of what reading is all about. The tragedy is that poor readers are drilled and drilled on wrong reading, which means they have little chance to glimpse the power and pleasure good readers obtain from books. Schools used to have DEAR programs: Drop Everything and Read. Now the appropriate acronym is DEAD: Drop Everything and Drill.

Advocates of testing argue that being able to pass reading skills tests is better than not being able to read at all. But as many researchers have documented, training students for test taking may actually hamper their ability to learn to read for meaning. Trained on short passages simulating test material, young readers have difficulty concentrating on longer texts. Rice University Professor Linda McNeil notes that high schoolers report that "they frequently mark answers without reading the sample of text; they merely match key words in the answer choice with key words in the text." That's what years of drilling about "key words" will do for a kid.

## A TESTING POTLUCK

Testocrats and all their kissin' kin should be required to spend a day with the New York State Grade 5 Social Studies Test Sampler Draft, March 2000. Students are given a document-based question, a terrific idea—for an in-class project for older kids. But demanding that fifth graders juggle eight historical documents in high-stakes testing conditions is worse than excessive. Here's the task.

> Historical Background: In June 1985, the people living in the town of Rose, New York, were told that the United States Postal Service planned to close their town's post office. This meant that the people of Rose would have to get their mail from another town's post office, and would have other post office services (such as buying stamps and sending packages) for only three hours each day with no Saturday service.
>
> The attached [8] documents are from June 1985 through April 1994. They tell and show what the people of Rose, New York, did in their town after they heard the news.
>
> TASK: Write an essay about the people of Rose and their post office. In your essay, tell how the people of Rose felt about their post office and give examples of what the people did together as a community, or separately as citizens, to help save their post office.

Students must examine eight documents in a variety of formats: news item, announcement, invitation to a potluck dinner. How many fifth graders in Manhattan—or anywhere else in New York State—will know what a potluck dinner is? How many of their parents or grandparents know what a potluck dinner is? And think of 10-year-olds synthesizing the information in eight widely disparate documents. Based on your experience with education reporters, politicians, and state education functionaries, answer this question: How many documents can they balance on the head of a pin?

This news item is one of the eight documents students must examine.

Rose News by Eudora Fox
Have you noticed how neat and attractive the triangle in front of the Rose Post Office is? At one time there were shrubs, but they became so tall that they obliterated the dates on the monument. Since these have been cleared off, flowers have been planted and Arlene Case has taken it upon herself to take care of them. We thank her for this little beauty spot in the community.

Here are some questions for New York State Commissioner of Education Richard Mills and his minions.

1. How many New York fifth graders will realize that a "triangle" can be a geographical location as well as a figure in their math book? How many of their parents and grandparents would recognize this meaning?
2. To what does the pronoun "these" refer in the sentence beginning "Since these have been cleared off . . ."
3. Why is "take" repeated in this sentence, which is already lamentable in its construction? "Since these have been cleared off, flowers have been planted and Arlene Case has taken it upon herself to take care of them."

The hapless fifth grader still has seven documents to go. And then he must synthesize the information contained in each and write an essay characterizing how various townspeople felt about the post office. This is a difficult task for adults, never mind 10-year-olds.

## WASHING THE DOG

Texas fourth graders slog their way through the *Writing TAAS Booklet: Sentence Structure Objective 5*, which is 74 pages of choose-the-best-answer drivel. Bad as the very concept is, what makes it even worse is the fact that students received what looks like 382d-generation photocopy, so that the blurry selections are barely readable. And note: this is Objective 5. There are similarly ugly workbooks for all the other objectives. There is no indication who wrote or published this offal.

Choose the best sentence:
- Dedicated joggers think midday is just too hot for jogging, they are waiting until twilight to run.
- Even dedicated joggers in our neighborhood are waiting until twilight to run because midday is just too hot to jog safely.
- Since midday is too hot. Dedicated joggers in our neighborhood wait until twilight.
- No mistake.

Everybody knows that only mad dogs and Englishmen go out in the midday sun. Only testocrats think this is how children learn sentence structure.

A Texas mother who wishes not to be identified for fear of labeling her daughter as "trouble," tells of the agony of her fourth-grade daughter trying to prepare for the TAAS writing test. "For one solid month the assignment was to write an essay every single night." Here is a sample assignment—for just one night:

How to Wash a Dog
Opening: What you need to wash your dog . . . 5 sentences
    1st supporting paragraph: Washing the dog . . . 15 sentences
    2d supporting paragraph: Finishing washing the dog . . . 15 sentences
    3d supporting paragraph: Drying the dog . . . 15 sentences
    Concluding paragraph: 5 sentences

The mother reports, "My daughter was crying every night for an entire month."

What Texas needs is a law requiring every legislator and newspaper editorialist to do this homework assignment. Nightly news could feature how-to-wash-a-dog essays after the weather report.

It isn't just Texas. Take a look at the primary-grade writing exemplars from Delaware, available on-line, and you will know that they start drilling kindergartners on such stuff. Since authorities in Delaware identify good writing with amount of detail, kindergartners' drawings are rated on the basis of how many details they contain. The detail obsession increases with each grade. Not to pick on Texas and Delaware. Every state has its version of wash-the-dog formula writing. This is a parody of how to write. It is writing to pass a test, certainly not writing that anyone (except the writers of test prep manuals) ever does. You wonder how many fourth graders who get this kind of homework every night are going to stick it out for eight more years. Not to mention college.

In 1998, at the time of a lot of discussion about dyspeptic New York City Mayor Giuliani's determination to force the police to crack down on every manner of petty crime—from kids carrying spray paint cans to the opportunistic squeegee panhandlers to pick-up games in open fields without a permit to walking across the street against the light to tickets for double-parking ("I am the M-A-Y-O-R and I want them to write tickets")—Jules Feiffer published a cartoon on the *New York Times* op-ed page showing a man ranting about Mayor Giuliani's priorities. In the last panel a police officer arrests him for—*jaytalking*.

Jaytalking. It's a powerful image for what the Standardistas have done to our schools. From monkey bars to field trips to black history projects to writing outside the box, they've outlawed jaytalking ("I am the C-O-M-M-I-S-S-I-O-N-E-R and I want them to take high-stakes tests.") In the name of boosting standardized test scores, kids and teachers are locked into verbal strait jackets when what they need is more jaytalk, more opportunities, in the words of the *Magic School Bus* series' indomitable Ms. Frizzle, to "take chances, make mistakes, and get messy." Albert Einstein once observed that "It's a miracle that curiosity survives formal education."

Learning won't happen without jaytalking. Learning requires some measure of uncertainty, and uncertainty in turn implies jeopardy. For the illusion of learning without jeopardy, Standardistas created workbooks. After the airing of a segment on Texas barbecue, the host of

NPR's *Weekend Edition* read this letter: "Our priest's blessing at the annual Episcopal church pig-picking was, "Lord, we give you thanks for barbecue, which is so terrible for our arteries but so beneficial to our souls." Requiring students to slavishly follow a strict procedural blueprint, not only frustrates learning, it stifles the soul. Schools must insist on the right to curriculum pig-picking.

Used with permission, Mike Konopacki, Huck/Konopacki Labor Cartoons.

*Chapter 4*

# One Shoe in the Chicken Coop: Keeping an Eye on What Really Counts

Her six-year-old tried to tell her something about his shoe, but Nevada mom and English professor Michelle Trusty-Murphy, distracted by tasks more pressing than footwear, put him off with, "Yes, honey, that's okay. We'll get it later." The next morning, when Mom concentrated on finding the missing shoe, she discovered what her son had been trying to tell her hours earlier: he'd lost the shoe under the main perch in the chicken coop. By then, the shoe was full of poultry poop.

As the philosophers note, poop happens. For Michelle, mother of three and activist against high-stakes testing, the parallels with what's happening in the schools are striking. She sees the Nevada state test as the poultry poop fouling education. "We have to pay close attention to the testing mania. That small shoe gets filled with chicken doo before you know it. And the stench lingers forever. When the school curriculum narrows to the skills that can be measured, teachers and parents forget to look at the idiosyncratic and quite wonderful things children can do." The story of Michelle's battle with a school principal over her refusing to allow the state to test her 10-year-old son Connor, and the story of how Connor lost the battle but won the war, is recounted in Chapter 7.

*Texas Monthly* executive editor Mimi Swartz doesn't have anything good to say about her state test either. Writing in *Slate* in Spring 2001, she recounts that after living with the tests all year, she and her 10-year-old son Sam are all "TAASed out." She tells the story that has been circulating among parents—about a kid who wrote a narrative instead of the assigned "compare and contrast" essay. So she got a 0 on the infamous Writing TAAS.

That's zero for zero tolerance.

The same thing happened to Beth Levine's son Levi. Writing in *Rosie* magazine September 2001, Levine explains that her third-grade son bombed a practice writing test. When Levine looked at what Levi wrote, she saw a "wildly funny, whimsical piece written with lots of dialogue and sly jokes." So what's the problem?

"He didn't follow the writing prompt," the teacher explained. Levine learned that children were given explicit directions: what they were to describe, how to describe it, where to begin and where to end. Children who do not follow this rigid outline are considered underperformers. Levine concludes, "To get his writing scores up, he will have to suppress his natural storytelling ability and write like a robot."

In *The Luzhin Defence*, a movie based on Vladimir Nabokov's novel *The Defense*, Natalia Katkov asks chess genius Alexander Luzhin, "How long have you been playing chess?" He replies, matter-of-factly, "Nine thousand, two hundred and sixty-three days, four hours and five minutes." This is an answer schoolchildren across America can appreciate. Beth Levine documents that her son is getting skill-drilled for the state writing test for a full year before he has to take the test. In reality, this skill drill now starts in kindergarten (see Chapter 2). Welcome to the world of preparing five-year-olds to pass the tests that will prove they are ready to join the global economy. As Education Trust declares on its Web page, "College Begins in Kindergarten." Education Trust and its corporate brethren call this education excellence. Others call it academic abuse.

The classic nightmare of finding oneself rushing into a huge lecture hall half an hour late for an algebra exam has been updated for the global economy. These days it's the nightmare of finding out that your stubborn kid insisted on writing outside the lines on the state writing test.

What a message for parents to take to their children: Do it the testocrats' way or else. No points for coloring outside the lines; certainly no points for marching to one's own drummer. Before preaching this message at the dinner table, though, parents might want to consider the reflections of eminent zoologist Knut Schmidt-Nielsen, who opens his autobiography *The Camel's Nose* with a wry comment. "It has been said that the primary function of schools is to impart enough facts to make children stop asking questions. Some, with whom the schools do not succeed, become scientists." Schmidt-Nielsen attributes his own lack of success in school to an inquisitive doggedness, to the fact that he "never stopped asking questions." In his autobiographical writings, Albert Einstein makes a similar complaint. "One had to cram all this stuff into one's mind, whether one liked it or not. This coercion had such a deterring effect that, after I had passed the final examination, I found the consideration of any scientific problems distasteful to me for an entire year. . . . It is in fact nothing short of a miracle that the modern methods of instruction have not yet entirely strangled the holy curiosity of inquiry."

These days, instead of encouraging children to ask questions, we push them to provide trunkfuls of answers. The notion that subjecting an eight-year-old to a 17-hour test will prove that the state has standards is a colossal fraud as well as child abuse. In terms of educational excellence, it is, to put it boldly, a huge load of chickenshit.

Yes, chickenshit. Kids know it. Teachers know it. Parents know it. Next thing you know, newspaper editorialists and lawmakers might catch on.

The test itself would be bad enough, but what more and more parents are protesting is that high-stakes tests provoke schools into year-long test prep. Test prep has become the curriculum. Willing partners in this swindle include the test developers, consultant call girls ever-willing to pimp for the latest gimmick, corporate CEOs who form august committees calling for the need for each state to prove theirs is bigger and better, political minions who line up to provide whatever legislation is needed, and the media pundits who scream, "Yes! Yes! Yes!" What such testing mania does is improve the bank statements of a host of testing companies as well as the tagalongs: consultants, test prep centers, workbook publishers, not to mention doctors, lawyers, and psychiatrist chiefs whose services are required by frantic parents. Ironically, the test item *readers*, the people whose judgment determines whether a child's essay gets a thumbs up or not, are the only ones not getting rich off the testing enterprise. They make anywhere from $8 to $11 an hour.

Make no mistake about it. Teachers welcome some form of testing, either standardized testing, or portfolio, or a combination. But the current mania for number crunching has propelled the idea of "seeing how kids measure up" beyond sanity. Getting kids ready for the test has become a prized stock market item and a dreaded year-round enterprise in the schoolhouse. Texas is infamous for not offering subjects that aren't on the test. Plenty of other states are no better. Testing has become more useful to realtors with property to sell in affluent zip codes than to anyone else.

This account from Florida offers a searing view of what test prep does to children and to teachers. The names have been changed because teachers can be fired for expressing negative views about the test on which politicians have staked their political futures.

Penny is a math specialist whose job has been transformed from teacher of model lessons to tutor of children in danger of failing the test. One day when Penny went to pick up her fifth-grade charges, they weren't in their classroom. She tracked them down in the media center, doing research on famous black Americans. Jacqui, a beautiful, well-behaved girl, refused to leave the media center, repeatedly asking to be allowed to finish her work. "It's the only fun I've had in a long time."

The assistant principal intervened, admonishing the child that the FCAT (Florida Comprehensive Assessment Test) was looming, insisting that black history can be learned any time. She pointed to other students in the group, children retained in fifth grade. "Aren't you sorry you didn't knuckle down last year so you could have passed?"

The assistant principal continued, "Don't you learn about black history at home?"

The fifth grader hung her head and said, "No."

The assistant principal replied, "Well, you should."

Penny tried to teach the planned lesson on how to analyze number sequences, trying not to see the large tears rolling down Jacqui's face. When the children lined up to return to their classroom, Penny said, "Sometimes black history is more important than math."

Jacqui whispered, "Thank you."

The rest of the children were stunned. Penny knows they think she lives and breathes math and science. She wants them to know she lives and breathes children. Test prep makes this more and more difficult for children to see.

A second terrible incident followed immediately. Penny encountered a fifth grader attempting to jump from the second-floor railing, an act of desperation, not derring-do. A child who has always done well in school, Joseph currently was failing all the fifth-grade benchmarks. Probably a two-floor drop wouldn't have killed him, but the point was a fifth grader feeling this desperate.

Penny concludes:

I must stop bringing my heart and my head to work. Being one of 5000 Nationally Certified teachers in the country counts for nothing. What I must do is read the teacher's manual and follow state and district guidelines. I cannot think that black history is important. I cannot think that failing to meet your own expectations, never mind the expectations of others, is devastating to children.

I used to love teaching about the famous Italian, Fibonacci, but there is no more room for him than there is for our beloved Benjamin Bannecker in FCAT prep work. Both must take a back seat to the importance of a school grade. If we don't move from a "D" to a "C" my fast-running principal will be sent to another school, as was threatened two weeks ago. If we move from a "D" to an "F" we will be closed. Then both of these FCAT child casualties will face half-hour bus rides next year, while they repeat fifth grade.

I have never seen the FCAT. The governor made it a felony and automatic revocation of our teaching certificate for a teacher to look at the FCAT while proctoring students taking the test.

I can only do what the administrators tell me to do to improve test scores. I have four children and a mortgage. I can't afford to think about schema and metacognition and memory retention and brain-based learning and multiple intelligences and divergent thinking and creativity and holistic experience and curriculum differentiation and cooperative learning strategies and synergy and habits of mind and problem-based learning and thematic units and cognitive inferencing and guided discovery.

These children have a test to take, and their lives depend on it.

Penny signs herself: Child of God, Student, Philosopher, Researcher, Scientist, Parent, Poet, Teacher, Professor, Artist, Musician, Citizen, Fan of Frederick Douglass.

She adds, "Jacqui passed on to sixth grade, by the way. Her dark, flashing eyes caught mine at the end-of-the-year ceremony, and her noble head nodded. She didn't smile. We weren't celebrating; just acknowledging the end of our endurance test. She is a better person than I am, because she stands for what she believes in and yet she does what she must. I am lucky to have known her. She taught me well. I was her remedial student."

As it happens, taking a peek at the very test that defines a teacher's professional career as well as the futures of her students is *not* a felony in Florida. The fact that an experienced, savvy, National Board-certified teacher thinks it is, shows the level of intimidation, threat, and paranoia engulfing teachers. Teachers in half a dozen other states have told me the same thing: "It's a felony for me even to look at the test while the kids are taking it." Maybe this is the great school urban legend, but more likely, it's a deliberate attempt by school administrators to keep teachers in line, to enforce secrecy about the tests. And looking at the test is a misdemeanor in Florida, a crime with potential for jail time. And it is a fact that in Penny's school the assistant principal announced at a faculty meeting, "A fast trip out of here and into jail is available for anyone who reads over the shoulder of a child or looks at the test during breaks. You can pay the $1,000 fine out of your own pocket, since you won't be teaching anymore. And you will lose your teaching certification. Looking at the test is a felony and it will be enforced."

Penny adds, "The assistant principal told us she'd received these orders from the county administration because there was a teacher shortage and we couldn't afford to lose any teachers as an FCAT fatality."

There's a term to improve education: FCAT fatality.

Funny thing: Florida teachers are forbidden even to peek at the test. But, according to Maureen McMahon, the publisher of Kaplan/Simon & Schuster's *Parent's Guide to the FCAT: 4th Grade Reading, 5th Grade Math* and *No-Stress Guide to the 8th Grade FCAT: Expert Tips to Help Boost Your Score*, the state of Florida gave Kaplan sample questions. As the Massachusetts state education commissioner, David Driscoll, commented when asked about the *Parent's Guide to the MCAS for Grade 4* and the *No-Stress Guide to the 8th Grade MCAS*, "All's fair on the open market." And there you have it: corporate power squeezing democracy in its for-profit vise.

This is part and parcel of the policy in numerous school districts in California—when it comes to high-stakes tests and their tagalong prep materials: hear no evil, see no evil, and most definitely speak no evil. California teachers in many districts are expressly forbidden to utter anything negative about SAT-9 to parents. What parents don't know about, they won't protest. Or opt their children out of. California has the opt-out provisions: Test refusal is a parent right. All a parent has to do to protect a child from the test abuse is to write a note to the principal echoing Melville's *Bartleby the Scrivener*, "I would prefer not to." But if teachers don't tell them of this right, most parents won't know—a definite Catch-22. If parents opt out, then administrators start looking for who's been talking. North Carolina teacher Teresa Glenn was suspended for five days for commenting on two oddball test items on a listserv set up by the state as a place for teachers to discuss educational concerns.

## WHAT'S IN A NUMBER?

Counting things is always problematic. A whole lot depends both on the counted and the counters, not to mention officialdom's determination to fit the numbers into the available categories. The 1990 Census is a case in point. Some people who shared a household with a person of the same sex also reported being married. Since the Census Bureau categories did not recognize same-sex marriages, census accountants, for the sake of consistency, changed either the person's sex or the relationship to the other person. Just like that. The need to make the numbers fit the available categories supersedes all else. Wendy N. Espeland, a sociologist at Northwestern University who studies numbers, points out that the problem with such fiddling is that these numbers travel. The numbers "leave the people who produced them, the people who know exactly all the assumptions, all the uncertainty, the people who know where the bodies are buried." Strange as it may seem, the farther they travel, the more hard-and-fast the numbers become. And policy is made on the basis of those numbers.

Espeland is talking about the Census. She could be talking about schools in just about any state in the land. Look at the way the numbers connected with NAEP (National Assessment of Educational Progress), TIMMS (Third International Mathematics and Science

Study), and SATs travel onto every op-ed page in the country, never mind that the person writing about them usually doesn't have a clue what these numbers mean. It is enough to be able to write a school-bashing headline. They treat test numbers like some gross national product: "Numbers not up" or "Numbers not up enough." Ironically, those who are statistics-disabled make the numbers more real than do the people who actually understand them—because the press so enjoys a good school-bashing story. Case in point: Every month in *Phi Delta Kappan*, research psychologist Gerald Bracey offers detailed and cogent explanations about the test numbers that swarm around schools, frequently pointing out that much of the news is pretty good, even excellent. Readable as Bracey is, the reader must have an attention span larger than a geranium to take in what he says. In his book *Setting the Record Straight*, Bracey points out that the scores of our best students are the best in the world. Tops among 32 nations. And when you take all U.S. students and come up with a ranking of 13-year-olds ranking 13th of 15 nations on an international test, the U.S. score is only 3 points below the international average. Insignificant. But it's more fun for newspaper headlines to scream "U.S. Kids Near Bottom" than to discuss the real numbers.

As Bracey points out, what should concern us is the enormous gap between our high scorers and our low scorers. On international mathematics tests, U.S. students in affluent suburbs outscore everyone in the world. Again, we're tops. More than 70 percent of U.S. public school students score with the top three nations. But our bottom students are at the bottom internationally. These are the scores we need to worry about. Instead of focusing on students in trouble, providing them with the specialized help they need, politicos are forcing state boards of education to deliver the same curriculum to every student.

Here are some other insane numbers that take on a life of their own. They are the formula by which a Citrus County, Florida, middle school decides whether a sixth grader goes into advanced math in seventh grade.

| Criteria | Weight |
|---|---|
| Grade average | 100 |
| FCAT score | 500 |
| STAR math test | 100 |
| NRT percentile | 100 |
| Work ethic | 3 |
| Saxon test | 100 |
| Total possible points | 903 |

So an "A" (96 average) student who flubs the FCAT is transformed into a "D" student as soon as the FCAT numbers arrive in the mail—and told that "work ethic" counts for nothing. On the basis of these heavily weighted FCAT numbers, she is eliminated from advanced math, even though her teacher recommends that she take it. It matters not that this girl scored a 95 on the year-end final exam. Governor Bush has staked his career on the FCAT, and so these are the numbers that travel and become harder than cement. Giving the FCAT, a secret test the public is not allowed to scrutinize, a weight five times that of a full year of class work demonstrates the contempt the politicians have for teachers and for children.

Teachers are beginning to fight back. The following letter was written by a teacher in Hillsborough County, Florida, and passed out at Open House at the beginning of the school year in 2001.

To: Parents of students
From: teacher

I am happy to have your child in my class this year. I anticipate that we will enjoy the next nine months learning about math class. I would like to tell you how I plan to arrive at your child's grade for this class.

Although we will learn many topics during the course of these 37 weeks, your child's grade will be determined by a single test score given in February on material that will encompass only a very small portion of all that we learn during the year.

I did not write the test, nor am I allowed to look at it, although I have a pretty good idea of what will be on it. The test changes from year to year, so the test may not be reliable. Part of the test is multiple-choice, part gridded-response, and part free-response. I have not decided whether the free-response section will count toward the test score or not. I will probably wait until the day before the test to make that announcement.

I will not be grading the test. I plan to send it out of state to a company that handles huge volumes of such tests. I have no guarantee that the answer key they will use for the multiple-choice and gridded-response sections will be entirely correct.
I have no guarantee that all tests will be returned.

The free-response problems are certainly open to interpretation. The company plans to hire people who are not math teachers to grade this section for $10 an hour. Although they are not paid per test, they are expected to grade a certain number per hour. Students who provide valid solutions that do not match the scoring rubric might receive only partial credit or no credit at all for those questions; it is vital, however, that the students answer the questions inside the little boxes provided. That's important.

I have not determined what will constitute a passing score yet, but I understand that some business people who have never been in a classroom will help make this determination. The numerical grade your child earns will be based on a completely arbitrary scale that can be adjusted any way I like. This number has no relation to the scale used to score all of the other work students do during the year.

Some of my students have Individual Education Plans which take into account their diverse learning styles, but all students must take the same test under the same testing conditions. Regardless of how well your child does in my class throughout the year, passing the class will be contingent upon passing a test I had no part in creating or grading.

I wish all of my students good luck. They are going to need it!

Teacher-satirist Scott Hopkins adds a comment to parents, "This is why teachers are opposed to FCAT. We are not opposed to accountability. But this method of high-stakes testing cheats our students and unfairly criticizes our teachers and schools. What we seek is a voice in the accountability process. Currently we have none."

## LET ME COUNT THE WAYS

The corporate-politico-media cabal collect and contort numbers to paint an ugly picture of U.S. public schools, smearing all schoolchildren with the same broad brush of failure. Waving their trumped-up numbers showing universal failure, they rush to enact politically expedient but goofy measures to "reform U.S. education." This means every first grader being on the same page of the same book in Sacramento, to name just one district with a mandatory reading program.

School works pretty well for about 80 percent of the nation's children. We need to look carefully at those kids who truly are failing. At the same time we need to look at the fact that one in four children in this country lives in poverty. We need to examine what this means. For starters, Barbara Ehrenreich's searing *Nickel and Dimed* details what it's like to try to make ends meet on $7 an hour. We need to ask ourselves how parents working the jobs Ehrenreich worked—as a waitress in Key West, Florida, as a cleaning woman and a nursing home aide in Portland, Maine, and in a Wal-Mart in Minneapolis, Minnesota—could ever summon the energy and resources to help their children with their homework or find the extra cash to buy the long list of school supplies. Despite the advantages of her race, good health, education—and the knowledge that she could return to a comfortable middle-class life when her experiment was over—Ehrenreich could barely make ends meet only when she worked seven days a week at two jobs, one of which provided free meals. Ehrenreich observes, "My very ability to work tirelessly hour after hour is a product of decades of better-than-average medical care, a high-protein diet, and workouts in gyms that charge $400 or $500 a year. If I am now a productive fake member of the working class, it's because I haven't been working, in any hard physical sense, long enough to have ruined my body."

In 1999, CEOs in America made 458 times as much as production and nonsupervisory workers. If the minimum wage had risen as rapidly as CEO pay in the 1990s, it would have been $24.13 an hour in 1999 instead of $5.15. Lester Thurow, an economist at the Massachusetts Institute of Technology, warns, "It is a stupid society that runs an experiment to see where its breaking points are." It seems particularly stupid to run this experiment in schools.

The Standardistas want us to compare the test scores of fourth graders in Palo Alto and Grosse Pointe with fourth graders in the South Bronx. Okay. But while we're at it, maybe we should compare the test scores of fourth graders in Palo Alto and those in East Palo Alto. Let's talk about the disposable income of the families of the children. Let's talk about the families that lack adequate housing, health care, and food, not to mention the leisure time to go to libraries and cultural events, to play baseball with their kids and take family trips to the ocean, the mountains, to historic landmarks. Knowledge of the ocean and historic landmarks are embedded in the tests children take, so it's not surprising that children who have been on trips through eight states do better on the tests than children who've never been out of the Bronx.

Even with the cultural assumptions embedded in the tests, there are easy ways to raise the scores of the kids at the bottom. Richard Rothstein, research associate at the Economic Policy Institute and author of a column on education for the *New York Times*, says that if raising test scores is our goal, food might be the easy answer. There's evidence to suggest that giving every schoolchild a good breakfast will raise test scores more than ending social promotion, increasing accountability, or Congress passing a bill requiring more testing. It's a fact that iron deficiency anemia, twice as common in low-income children as in better-off children, affects cognitive ability. In experiments where pupils got inexpensive vitamin and mineral supplements, reports Rothstein, "test scores rose from that treatment alone." But so far no politicians are mounting campaigns for "Eat for Success."

School breakfast costs about a dollar a day. No one can even imagine the cost of testing every child in reading and math every year. In California, the *San Francisco Chronicle*, among others, bills the SAT-9 as the $44 million test, but it is difficult to find out just what that means. For starters, there's the additional $12 million paid out to National Computer Systems to process the tests. Then there's all the test prep material. *A Handbook of Performance Activities: Kindergarten*, published by Harcourt Brace Educational Measurement, comes in at $24.50. Although Harcourt's SAT-9 testing doesn't begin until Grade 2, it doesn't hurt to get a head start. Individual handbooks are available for grades K-12. Harcourt also offers *KeyLinks: The Connection Between Instruction & Assessment*. For $42, the teacher can get a manual and 24 student booklets with multiple-choice and open-ended questions in Language Arts. For another $42, she can get the same thing in mathematics. For another $42, she can get the same thing in science. After all, test prep comes in many subjects. Individual test prep packages are available for grades 1 through 12. At $34, the *Stanford Guide for Organizational Planning* helps administrators "use Stanford 9 test results to assist with program evaluation, to measure growth in achievement, to develop in-service programs for test interpretation, and to provide updated information to the public." Harcourt also sells the *Stanford 9 Test Booklet Place Marker*, to help kids "retain their place as they work in their test booklets." Seven dollars for a package of twenty-five.

What's next? Stanford 9 beanie babies?

And there's more. For about $1 per student, a teacher can send home *Preview for Parents*, Harcourt's test explanations and sample questions for each content area "to inform parents about the skills and abilities measured by the subtests."

Remember, that dollar would also buy a child breakfast.

SRA McGraw-Hill's *Scoring High* test prep series, available to students in grades K-8, promises to help students "understand test formats," "master time management," "optimize test-taking strategies."

The *Scoring High* series takes a different approach from many test prep materials produced by companies that also publish tests. Most promise to train students in generic test-taking strategies. *Scoring High* features test-specific versions of their materials, so one can get *Scoring High on CTBS/TerraNova*, *Scoring High on the Stanford Achievement Tests*, *Scoring High on the Iowa Tests of Basic Skills*, and so on. Or one can go the state-specific route, getting test prep for the *Florida Comprehensive Assessment Test*, the *Texas Assessment of Academic Skills*, the *New Jersey 8th Grade Early Warning Test*, and so on.

Early Warning Test? Sounds like those radio announcements, doesn't it? We interrupt this program to bring you this special emergency announcement about approaching tornados, hurricanes, and eighth-grader skill deficiency.

Test publishers constantly increase the pressure. Riverside Publishing, for one, offers a number of test prep materials, urging teachers to start in kindergarten getting kids ready for tests coming three years later. For $141.50, a teacher can get a classroom package for *Test for Success*. This program claims to deliver "Ethical test preparation for any standardized test," complete with overhead transparencies.

Ethical test preparation. An oxymoron for the New Millennium.

Here is a letter sent to every school principal in Illinois, where state testing starts in Grade 3.

Know How Your Primary Students
Score *Before* the Grade 3 ISAT

Announcing a new series of assessments
—The Multiple Assessment Series for the Primary Grades—
from Riverside, the publisher of The Iowa Tests.

How The Multiple Assessment Series Can Help You

Give these assessments to your grade 2 and grade 1 students at the same time you administer the grade 3 ISAT in February. Use test results to identify need areas for targeting instruction.

Test grade 3 students in the fall—prior to February. Use test results to focus grade 3 instruction early in the school year. These multiple-choice and open-ended assessments will help identify students who demonstrate lack of proficiency so you can focus instruction to help students meet or exceed ISAT standards.

Your Illinois assessment consultants will be at
    The Illinois principal's meeting Monday., October 18th.
    Please stop by Booth Number 224 for a sample of the new product, assessment assistance, and snacks.

**Don't wait until grade 3 to find out if your students will NOT meet state standards.**

RIVERSIDE PUBLISHING
A HOUGHTON MIFFLIN COMPANY

So for $31.56 per student, plus shipping and handling, Riverside provides the opportunity for schools to give youngsters the pre-ISAT three times before they have to take the real thing. For an additional fee, affluent schools won't even have to score it. "Central scoring is done by professionally trained scorers and provides a complete report package for each student. The Basic Score Report Package provides a set of reports that meet the communication needs of all those involved in student learning and achievement, including teachers, parents, and administrators."
    Sez who?
    When was the last time a parent felt her "communication needs" had been met by a printout of a test taken by her child? When has a teacher or principal? If everybody is so happy, what are all the noisy parents around the country complaining about?

## LEAVE NO CHILD . . . IN A
## CRUMBLING SCHOOL BUILDING

In *Savage Inequalities*, Jonathan Kozol quotes a 14-year-old girl. "We have a school in East St. Louis named for Dr. King," she says. "The school is full of sewer water and the doors are locked with chains. Every student in that school is black. It's like a terrible joke on history." Senator Paul Wellstone has documented the conditions of East St. Louis schools: backed-up sewers that flood school kitchens, faulty boilers and electrical systems, dangerous structural flaws, exposed asbestos, emergency exits chained shut, locked or nonexistent school libraries.

Children don't need just food and housing; they also need adequate facilities. With all the focus on the disparities in test scores, few people are calling for building standards, for equal educational facilities. Modest proposal: Why don't we stop the testing for a couple of years and use the money to fix the broken-down schools? The estimated cost nationally for repairing the infrastructure of crumbling schools is $127 billion or $300 billion, depending on whose figures you believe. The Department of Education cites the lower figure, the National Education Association the higher. In 1999, the New York City comptroller, Alan G. Hevesi, pointed out that one-half of New York City's public schools are more than 50 years old, and nearly 82,000 children are without appropriate classroom space. Hevesi reported that the Board "spends only one-tenth of what it should on building maintenance each year." So the buildings just get worse.

When the American Society of Civil Engineers released its 2001 Report Card for America's Infrastructure, school buildings received the lowest mark, a D–. ASCE president Robert W. Bein, a civil engineer, noted, "When you've got . . . kids in Kansas City attending class in a former boys' restroom, something is desperately wrong."

Nationwide, more than 60 percent of schools need major repair of roofs, exterior walls, windows, plumbing, and lighting. Our schools are in worse shape than our bridges, our transit systems, our hazardous waste disposal. Funny, isn't it, that the crumbling concrete we wouldn't stand for in a highway seems okay in a school? Not surprising, the largest number of schools reporting deficient conditions are in center cities serving 50 percent minority students or 70 percent poor students. Affluent suburban districts would not stand for the conditions that poor urban and rural populations have to put up with. Parents whose children go to Camarillo High School in the Oxnard Union High School District in California are up in arms. Their school has bathrooms without doors on some stalls, rusty lockers, and a leaky roof. In the same district, the new $60 million state-of-the-art Pacific High School has a $30,000 weight room and a gymnasium large enough to hold three full-court basketball games simultaneously.

California ranks 43d in the nation on spending on public education; it ranks first on spending for prisons. *San Francisco Chronicle* staff writers Nanette Asimov and Lance Williams wrote searing articles about how for 24 days in the summer of 2001, high-priced attorneys grilled 13 witnesses, whose ages ranged from 8 to 17, "trying to topple their testimony that California students don't have enough textbooks and that many classrooms are vermin-infested, overcrowded, and with temperature either sweltering or freezing." Up to September 2001, the case had cost California taxpayers $2.5 million and it hadn't even gone to trial. The class-action lawsuit, filed by children and parents across the state, asks the state to set minimum standards for "basic educational necessities," such as up-to-date textbooks and schools free of rats and mice. The state's attorneys tried to prove that the problems weren't so bad, asking 17-year-old Alondra Jones, "Did the mouse droppings you saw on the floor affect your ability to learn U.S. history at all?" The law firm's attorneys charge $325 an hour to ask these questions and to browbeat children into crying. State Senate President Pro Tem John Burton said, "It would be better to sit down and negotiate than depose a bunch of kids and scare the s--- out of them."

California resistors should sign this man up to witness the administration of high-stakes tests.

In 1998, of the $17 billion spent nationally on school construction, the federal government contributed just 2.5 percent. It allocated $218 billion to address the needs of crumbling highways and bridges. But why quibble on whether freeways are more important than schools? By the estimate of the American Society of Civil Engineers 2001 Report Card for America's Infrastructure, the total investment needed to repair America's infrastructure—the whole tamale—is $1.3 trillion. That would fix roads, bridges, transit, aviation, drinking water, wastewater, dams, solid waste, hazardous waste, navigable waterways, energy, and schools too.

Heads up! The tax-cut package approved by Congress in the spring of 2001 is $1.3 trillion. It is a staggering number. For the price of a tax boondoggle that rewarded the rich, gave a bare nod to the middle-class, and excluded the working class, we could have rebuilt America's infrastructure, improving the lives of every American. Decades ago, famed U.S. Supreme Court Justice Louis Brandeis warned, "We can have democracy in this country or great wealth concentrated in the hands of a few, but we can't have both."

In August 2001, the Minnesota Public Radio program "Marketplace" carried a segment that brings the undercutting of school finances home. Children's back-to-school lists are getting longer because schools can't come up with the money for supplies. At the same time that state boards of education offer questionable bonuses for improved test scores, schools don't have enough money to buy toilet paper. The parents of a Florida six-year-old in the Orlando area carried a back-to-school list of 24 mandatory items—plus an additional wish-list—into Wal-Mart. The supplies set them back $80—for things like paper and pencils—and antibacterial soap, paper towels, and toilet paper. Wal-Marts around Birmingham, Alabama, have posted school supply lists. Here's the kindergarten list for one of the poorest schools in the state:

1 box of crayons
1 pair of scissors
2 pocket folders
1 box of Kleenex
1 roll of Scotch tape
1 bottle of glue
10 pencils
1 clear or mesh book bag
1 tub of baby wipes
1 box of Ziploc bags
1 roll of paper towels
1 towel for naps
1 pack of paper plates
1 pack of paper bags

Parents are warned that this is the generic list, that individual teachers may add more specific requests when parents register.

In North Carolina, eighth-grade teacher Teresa Glenn has 74 students, including Maria and Teresa who don't speak much English and share the classroom's one Spanish-English dictionary. Teresa receives $150 for supplies—to last the year. With this she must buy replacement novels, construction paper, teaching aids, videos, and so on. She asks students to bring in extra paper, notebooks, and pencils when they can—to help out kids who can't afford supplies.

A mother in Kansas City reports shelling out over $600 in book and supply fees for her kids to attend public schools. A mother in Sandwich, Massachusetts, told the *Cape Cod Times* that she plans to use her federal tax-rebate check to finance her four children's school supply lists—and she is buying generic. Cape Cod reporters said that shopping at Staples for 16 items on the list for seventh graders at Mattacheese Middle School set them back $78. One reason this is happening is that school supply budgets were frozen in 1994. Never mind that the schools' populations have increased.

In the Puyallup district in Washington, supply lists for kindergartners include "2 boxes of snack crackers, 1 roll of scotch tape, and 10 glue sticks," along with the good news, "We will provide a Pee-Chee folder for all students. You do not need to purchase a Pee-Chee folder." First-grade moms will have to decide whether they are willing to follow directions: "Using a permanent marker, print names on all items AND initials on the end of *each* crayon!" Many lists ask each child to bring a ream of 20-lb. printer paper.

Lois Bridges, a parent in Palo Alto, reports that she has never been asked to send in basic supplies to her children's schools. "Don't all schools supply the necessities?" she asks. Only schools in wealthy and solidly middle-class areas, it seems. Parents working minimum-wage jobs have to send in soap and toilet paper to their children's schools. Lois also recalls that in the late 1970s, when she taught at Sells Elementary on the Tohono O'odham Reservation, 75 miles southwest of Tucson, all the necessities were provided as part of the school budget. "The school was so crowded that I taught first grade in a storage shed out in back, but we had the basics. I didn't have to ask the kids to bring soap and paper towels." Maybe those were kinder, gentler times. But the rules are different, depending on zip codes. Take Connecticut, with its highest per capita income in the nation. Senator Paul Wellstone has documented that school systems across the state spend an average of $147.68 per student per year on textbooks and instructional supplies; but Hartford can afford just $77, only 52 percent of the statewide average. Hartford school enrollment, incidentally, is more than 92 percent minority, whereas nearby towns are less than 5 percent minority. The city of Boston budgets about $4 million a year for instructional supplies. That comes out at $55 for each elementary school pupil, $62 for each middle school student, and $71 for each high school student. Out of that money, a school is supposed to pay for photocopy expenses, postage, classroom libraries, blackboards, easels, print cartridges, file cabinets and folders, reading tables, floor mats, pens, paper, textbook and workbook replacement, and other basics.

These days, children whose parents can't afford the supplies must rely on charity. Oakland County, Michigan, residents participate in the Stuff-a-Bus Campaign, which collects supplies for needy students. The superintendent of schools in a neighboring county says families there go to the Salvation Army for back-to-school supplies. In Virginia, a law firm donates backpacks filled with school supplies to every student at the Graham Road Elementary School nearby, from Head Start through sixth grade. Certainly such generosity is to be celebrated, but does anyone ask why schools don't receive enough revenues to make basic supplies a part of the budget? Of course, basic is in the eye of the beholder. Consider Henrico County, a district near Richmond, Virginia, that purchased a $19 million networking package that included 23,000 Apple iBooks that were handed out to every high school student at the start of school in 2001. With that kind of money available, the district still feels the need to insist that kindergartners bring in a lengthy list of supplies, including 10 glue sticks, scissors, a watercolor set, soap, baby wipes, and a box of tissues. By third grade, kids must bring in 36 pencils, index cards, folders, three packs of paper, antibacterial soap, and a check for $3.50 for *Time for Kids* magazine. By fifth grade, a dictionary, calculator, and plastic milk crate are added on to the basic supply list. Four-function and graphing calculators are added to the middle school list, along with books. Besides all this, parents receive a fee letter: $4.00 locks, $12.00 gym suit, $6.00 gym shirt, $1.00 gym lock rental, $5.00 computer support, $4.00 science, $8.00 Exploratory A, $3.00 Exploratory B, $10.00 art, $2.00 inventions and innovations, $7.50 technology foundations, $8.00 band, $8.00 chorus, $8.00 strings, $2.00 dramatic arts, $3.00 keyboarding, $3.00 teen living, $6.00 independent living, $3.50 newspaper, $20.00 yearbook, $12.00 Spanish workbook, $6.50 Latin workbook, $11.00 German workbook. Check that budget: Is milk money being spent for software?

The seventh-grade supply list has the usual materials—plus a stapler, audio headphones, a box of computer disks, and 5 BAND-AIDs. BAND-AIDs. Having taught seventh graders for 10 years, I know that with each kid armed with his own stapler, they definitely need BAND-AIDs. Even with these lengthy and detailed supply lists, these days teachers spend, on average, more than $600 out of their own pockets to supply their classrooms. One can wonder if any politician voting on tough new education accountability bills has ever had to lug in antibacterial soap and toilet paper to stock his place of work.

## SUMMER READING

Virginia is definitely on standards overload. Here's the required summer reading list for incoming ninth graders who have opted for the International Baccalaureate Program at Stonewall Jackson High School in Manassas, Virginia, *Time Magazine*'s 2001 high school of the year.

> During the summer, you must read the unabridged versions of Lewis Carroll's *Alice in Wonderland*, Harper Lee's *To Kill A Mockingbird*, and Michael Ende's *The Neverending Story* in preparation for class. Assignments for all three readings are due the first day of school; they are all to be written in ink in a "black and white" composition book.

Assignments are given for each of the novels. Here are some of the assignments for *Alice in Wonderland*:

> Various critics of Alice in Wonderland have interpreted Alice's troubles with her variations in size, her confusion and forgetfulness, her slips of the tongue, etc., as representative of the "problems of growing up." Argue for or against such an interpretation, using the following questions as guidelines:
> a.  Specifically, what types of problems in communication and self-control does she experience?
> c.  Do any aspects of these problems have symbolic overtones? (For example, what do Alice's troubles with the golden key, her struggles to get through the small door into the beautiful garden suggest?)
> d.  In what instances does she muse over or struggle with questions about her identity? How are these questions answered?
> e.  Does Alice seem to gain self-control as the story progresses? (Is she, for instance, more sure of herself, more socially adept, in her second encounter with the Duchess on the croquet field than when she first met her in the kitchen?)
> f.  Would you go so far as to say that *Alice in Wonderland* is primarily a story of "growing up?" Would you deny such a statement altogether?

The summer reading assignment for 10th graders in the IB program includes *The Count of Monte Cristo* by Alexandre Dumas and *Fahrenheit 451* by Ray Bradbury. Students are allowed to read the Bantam Classic abridged version of Dumas. Good thing. It is 441 pages long; the Modern Library edition weighs in at 1488 pages. Students are given questions to answer in their reading journals and then warned, "These journals will help to prepare you for the test on the novels that you will be given the first day of class."

Have a good summer, kids.

Maybe every adult who is screaming that standards should be raised should stop and take a breath. Or maybe stick his head in a bucket.

Stop and think about how you spent your 14th summer, that perilous period between eighth and ninth grade. *Alice in Wonderland?* I seriously doubt it.

## OKAY TO BE DIFFERENT

"Charles can be a little strange," his special education teacher warned me when I agreed to mainstream him into my third-grade classroom. At age eleven, Charles was three years older than the average third grader, and for the first week he was on his best behavior. One day, without warning, Charles vomited. After the mess was cleaned up, he cried and moaned, "I'm a weirdo and a retard. I never can do anything right." I was devastated, not knowing how to comfort this child who was indeed a bit odd. His classmates—who'd never really warmed up to him but didn't tease him either—came to the rescue. "Everybody vomits sometimes," they reassured Charles. Then each had a vomit story to tell. After about 15 minutes I announced, "Enough sharing." But as I pushed ahead with the lesson, the children worried over Charles and continued to sneak to his desk with another whispered "My Most Embarrassing Vomit."

Charles stopped sobbing, but he kept his head down on his folded arms. I couldn't tell whether his classmates' messages were getting through. But the next day, he came to class carrying a bright yellow poster, asking me to tack it up on the bulletin board. It was a note to the class, listing each child's name and concluding with "I love this class very much." Opposite the message was a large, smiling face that I recognized as myself—the red hair and glasses being a giveaway. Charles' special education teacher told me he had told her the names of all the children; he asked her to help him spell them correctly, insisting that it was very important to get them "just right."

In a school that rigorously grouped children according to reading ability, our group of "low" readers had a variety of difficulties: a deaf child, a severe stutterer, an asthmatic, and a child who was alternately hyperactive and zonked out by medication. Several children had failed a grade; most started the year thinking they hated both reading in particular and school in general. For all their difficulties, these children were normal third graders; they laughed, they cried, they pestered, they hugged, they complained, they rejoiced. And when someone had a personal crisis, they gathered round as one and offered consolation. You might call caring for each other our highest classroom standard.

Another important standard in our classroom was that children chose their own books and they read silently for half an hour, a time span that increased to a full hour by January. Charles read *Rumpelstiltskin* 17 days in a row. And then I stopped counting, because I know that when a child reads the same book over and over, he's not wasting time; he's getting something he needs from that book.

In May, Charles told me he didn't want to move on to fourth grade. He asked me if he could stay in my classroom, as my aide. "I know where all the books are," he said. This was definitely no small feat in our overstuffed room.

Charles's suggestion had a lot of appeal. I thought, "Why not?" He'd come so far in a year. One more year might be just the trick. His special ed teacher and I were seriously considering the idea when Charles's mother sent in a note, asking us to have a little sex ed talk with him. Reality set in. We couldn't have a twelve-year-old in third grade.

During the last week of school, I asked the children to choose a favorite book and write me a note about what made it so special. "I know which one I want!" Charles exclaimed. I thought to myself, "Yep, I know too."

But as children are wont to do, Charles surprised me. He didn't reach for an omnipresent dinosaur book, or *Rumpelstiltskin* either, but went to a bookcase and dug out a book he had hidden behind several others. It was *The Ugly Duckling*.

Charles, who had never written more than six sentences on any topic all year, wrote nine pages. He told me he hoped I'd send his report to the newspaper so that everyone would know about this important book. Here is the opening sentence in Charles's report: "The ugly duckling found out it is okay to be different."

This is what every child in America deserves. Children should not have to pass a test on a college prep curriculum to prove they are okay. I can tell the bean counters that Charles scored at the 3.8 grade level on a standardized reading test. Not bad for a third grader. Not good for a twelve-year-old. But the real point is that the numbers reveal neither the richness nor the deficiencies of our year together; they don't tell us a whole lot about what Charles can and can't do. A longer test, the kind that overwhelms schools these days, would not be any more informative, and would not help Charles or his teachers do a better job. As the old Scottish proverb advises, "You don't make sheep any fatter by weighing them."

The ugly irony about Charles's story is that today, he probably would not be allowed to be mainstreamed. I have in my hand a note from a teacher in Virginia who wishes to remain anonymous. "The Developmentally Delay classes don't even want us to send kids to them—unless these kids are "smart enough" to do the SOLs. They worry these kids will bring the scores down in the classes in which they are mainstreamed. If they can't do those SOLs, we have to place them in classes for the mentally retarded. The real meaning of SOL is not Standards of Learning; it's S---Out of Luck!"

Third graders in the high reading class in our school were astounded when Jessica brought home the prize for outstanding science project in the citywide Edu-Lympics competition because, after all, Jessica was a low reader. Sadly, not even this award convinced Jessica's parents that maybe her low standardized test scores were deficient in labeling their daughter's potential. I wondered if they heard me when I told them that their child was outstanding: Jessica was resourceful, hardworking, persistent, reliable, humorous, helpful, and kind.

A lot of children in my class started an independent project for the science fair; Jessica finished it. She had a friend draw a life-sized outline of her body as she lay on a large piece of butcher paper. Then, consulting encyclopedias and other books, she drew in all the organs, writing a short description of the function of each. On the back side of her "body," she carefully drew in all the bones, labeling them with both their English and their Latin names. Not bad for an eight-year-old low reader! The whole class had learned to sing "Dry Bones" with the Latin names (astounding local pediatricians); Jessica saw a way to incorpo-
this fun into her science project.

Leslie, Jessica's best friend, would say that Jessica deserved high marks for teaching her to read knock-knock riddles. This was a skill that eluded Leslie for months as her classmates delighted in the tomfoolery. Jessica sat with Leslie, reading with her, explaining and giving her hugs when Leslie moaned and wept that she "didn't get it." Severely hearing impaired, our classroom was Leslie's first experience with public school. Until third grade she had gone to a school for deaf children.

I had my doubts that knock-knock riddles were appropriate reading matter for a deaf child, but I respected Leslie's determination. And one day she jumped up and shouted, "I get it! I really get it! Let me read it to the class."

And she did.

The class clapped its approval. Leslie burst into tears, and I was also blowing my nose. Then Leslie shouted, "Let me read another one!"

And she did.

Where does this fit on a school's report card of excellence? Where does it fit on Leslie's achievement record? And on Jessica's?

Such triumphs are not objective. They don't appear on standardized printouts, so no high-powered committee on excellence will pay attention. But I insist that even if one anecdote is just that—a story—two anecdotes are data. And so I persist with stories. As a teacher, my stories identify who I am. I believe in the children in my classroom. The rest is hearsay.

When, at the end of the year, Leslie scored six months below grade level on the standardized tests, my colleagues insisted I should admit failure. Not bloody likely. Why should I admit failure when I could document that Leslie had a strong interest in books? She read orally with accuracy, enthusiasm, and drama; she also read silently with concentration and comprehension. Leslie memorized poems and recited them for the principal; she participated in class dramatizations of fairy tales. And she loved books. Her year in third grade was a triumph.

Five years later, Leslie wrote to invite me to her eighth-grade graduation. She told me she was on the honor roll. I checked it out with her eighth-grade English teacher, whom I knew to be a very tough grader. She told me that Leslie was an excellent student, a delight to have in class. Years later, Leslie phoned me from college. She wanted my opinion on whether she had the "right stuff" to be a good teacher. "I'm majoring in architecture," she confided, "but it doesn't seem people-oriented enough. I think I want to teach. I want to help kids who have a hard time in school."

Teachers, while careful about the minutiae that fill the classroom life, teach for the future, and only at great peril do we allow the state to distract us from this reality. Every third-grade teacher knows that in the long run knock-knock riddles are more important than apostrophes. And if the testocrats persevere with apostrophes, that's their loss. We must not let it be the children's.

## COUNTING WHAT COUNTS

The Venetian monk and friend of Leonardo da Vinci, Fra Luca Pacioli, is credited with being the father of our modern obsession with counting things. Pacioli popularized double-entry bookkeeping, making assets and loss clearly measurable. In *The Sum of Our Discontent: Why Numbers Make Us Irrational*, David Boyle points out that Pacioli had his critics, who "feared he had abolished quality altogether. All that you could put down in the double entries was quantities—numbers of sheep, amounts of wool: There was no column for qualities like good or bad. The numbers had taken over, simplifying and calculating the world in their own way."

Surely our educationist bean counters are Pacioli's direct heirs, measuring the children but not appreciating them. Standardistas think that only physicists can appreciate a rainbow. Parents must not kowtow at the throne of standardized test results, dismissing their own knowledge of their children as meager. In Spanaway, Washington, Juanita Doyon says she's given up running the band fundraiser and baking for the kindergarten class. "Now I'm running for state superintendent, and working hard at buttoning up the tests." Juanita asks, "If not me, then who? Who will fight this takeover of the lives of our children? Who will tell the education government to get off our backs?"

To count things, you have to define them in measurable ways. That means narrowing your definitions. Take the measurement of children's language skills. Politicians and corporate CEOs, whose books are most often ghostwritten in the "as told to" format, insist that the nation's youth must be interrogated, ranked, and sorted on state tests containing such fine grammaticality as this one asked of California third graders:

Is a raindrop *hitting* one's head more like the hit in:
- A dart *hitting* a target
- A storm *hitting* a region

Third graders. What is an eight-year-old to make of such a question? I haven't yet met any adults who can make any sense of it. I have asked 386 teachers, two priests, a rabbi, a poet, a physicist, a plumber, a postal clerk, and a French chef this question. Not only did nobody have a clue, nobody was willing to hazard a guess. Only third graders are required to commit themselves. Imagine how they feel: whether or not they pass to fourth grade could depend on the answer. Dave Barry says that if you clearly have no clue about grammar or vocabulary, you can become president of the United States. There you have it: it's tougher to pass the hurdle from third to fourth grade than to sit in the Oval Office.

Michael's story is one that parents and teachers should take to heart. My student in both seventh and eighth grades, Michael was personable, popular, and athletic. If dyslexia exists, Michael had it. When I gave seventh graders an open-ended question, "I'd rather read than ____; I'd rather write than ____," Michael wrote that he'd rather read than write; he'd rather write than die. Dying, for Michael, was the only thing worse than putting words down on paper. When I heard that students taking the high-stakes test for graduation in California in spring 2001 had to write about hummingbirds, I thought about Michael.

I lured Michael, if not into spelling, at least into writing. I wrote each of my students a letter every day, and I expected them to write me replies. No five-paragraph themes, but writing as communication every day. No excuses. After much initial grumbling, Michael did write me a note most days of his seventh- and eighth-grade years. He even took his notebook on vacation to Florida and wrote me a note most days. Our note exchanges were written in small 3" x 5" spiral-bound notebooks, and when Michael gave his mother permission to read his during Open House, she was awestruck, telling me, "Maybe he'll write you from the Senate some day."

When my notes were filled with complaints about the winter weather, Michael advised me, "I just take the months as they come." When I revealed to students that for me, the asparagus ads in the newspaper were a sure sign that winter was losing its strong grip, the kids, of course, thought that this was a hoot; only a teacher would care about asparagus. But they began to watch the newspaper, competing for who could find the best asparagus bargains for Mrs. O. They left ads on my desk. One day Michael walked in and typed this note:

Dear Mrs. O,

As you no I want to Boston firday. It was a lot fo fun. Wen I first got to Boston we drov aron looking for a parking plas. We fon one and then we got out of the car. We walkt to a fance market and had a bite to aet.

Than we went to the aquarium and that was eciting. There was a shoe with dolphins and seals. Wan we got out we want by a fruit markt. I thogt of you and chekt the pric of asprgus. It is $1.00 a lb in Boston and 3 heds of letis for $1.00. Boston is a long way to go for asprgus tho.

Your freind,
Michael

Not surprisingly, he asked me how to spell *aquarium* and *dolphins*. I share Michael's asparagus letter every time I give a talk to educators and to parents. I share it to remind them of what really counts in education. If you can look beyond the spelling, you see that Michael is employing the skills of a writer: He crafts the letter to suit his audience; his letter has structure, using telling details effectively; he ends with a humorous bang.

The week before his graduation from eighth grade, Michael's mother sent me a note. "I was going to phone you, and thank you for everything you've done," she wrote, "but Michael told me to write a letter. He says when you care about someone and you have something important to tell her, you write it in a letter. He learned that from you. He learned a lot. And we are grateful forever."

Fifteen years after Michael wrote the asparagus letter, I showed it to a university audience. Afterwards, a teacher came up to tell me that she was Michael's first-grade teacher and that she still knows his parents. Michael is now a big-time chef in an upscale restaurant in Connecticut, making more money than any of his teachers. I figure I can claim partial credit for Michael's success: after all, I introduced him to an interest in asparagus. Kids learn many things from teachers. I happen to think that one of the most important things they learn is the possibilities of who they can be and how they can behave.

If Michael were in school today, he'd be denied a high school diploma, and then he couldn't get work as a chef. Or a plumber, beautician, auto mechanic, bus driver, draftsman, and so on and so on. You can't work in the warehouse at UPS without a high school diploma. We travel down a very dangerous road if we continue to allow the Standardistas to impale our young people on stakes that are impossibly high. Everybody doesn't need to go to college; algebra mastery doesn't determine the worth of a person or his ability to lead a useful and productive life and contribute to our communities. I would remind Standardistas of Jean Anthelme Brillat-Savarin's observation: "The discovery of a new dish does more for human happiness than the discovery of a star." No Standardista blather about workers for the global economy will convince me that this maxim is any less true today than when it was uttered in 1825. I like to think of Michael creating happiness.

But Michael wouldn't flourish in today's schools. In fall 2000, the superintendent of schools in Boston sent a letter to all city principals, warning that students who don't pass the state's mandatory tests shouldn't receiving passing marks in their courses. The assistant superintendent in the New York district where I taught Michael and Charles sent a similar letter to every principal in the district, demanding that every teacher defend and justify every passing grade given to a student who didn't pass the CTB/McGraw-Hill test required by the state. The state rules. A teacher's role is reduced to that of petty functionary—getting kids ready for someone else's exams. Students are known only by their numbers. Some call this *No Excuses*. I call it *No Sense*. It signals the destruction of childhood.

And for what? Noted researcher Gerald Bracey points out that in the long run, test scores don't count for much. "They don't predict wages. They don't predict success on the job. Even tests designed to predict success in college don't do a good job of it. The SAT only predicts about twenty percent of what goes into college freshman grades. Eighty percent of what determines who makes the dean's list and who gets slapped with academic probation comes from other qualities. And that's just for the freshman year. The SAT loses predictive power for each additional year of college."

Bracey continues, "All of the above makes sense when you consider even an incomplete list of personal qualities that tests don't measure:

Creativity
Critical thinking
Resilience
Motivation
Ambition
Persistence/perseverance
Humor
Attitude
Reliability
Politeness
Enthusiasm
Civic-mindedness
Self-awareness
Self-discipline
Empathy
Leadership
Compassion

If a person ranks high on these qualities, what does it matter if they do or don't remember certain dates or events or how to factor a quadratic equation?"

"What does it matter?" is a crucial question for parents to ask every time the state tries to rank and sort and define their children. If we want to predict how children will do in college and in life, let's scrap the tests and try chiromancy. An ancient art dating back to the Assyrians, Egyptians, and Hebrews, palm reading focuses on the four lines and seven mounts on a person's hand to analyze character and predict destiny. It's a whole lot easier on kids than undergoing 17 hours of filling in bubbles for the state's high-stakes tests.

The Business Roundtable Plan for Education Reform.

## Chapter 5

# The Global Economy Smokescreen and the Rest of the Story

READING COMPREHENSION: Read this passage.
   "Schools are lousy! Schools are lousy!"
DIRECTIONS: Select the best answer.

This phrase was most likely *not* uttered by:
1. A politician
2. The Business Roundtable
3. Chicken Little
4. The media
5. Parents of kids on your block

In *Adventures of the Screen Trade*, William Goldman lists, alphabetically, the seven people who are crucial to a film:

Actor
Cameraman
Director
Editor
Producer
Production designer
Writer

These days, the media parrots the message designed by the Standardista-corporate-politico consortium that the crucial elements for educating your child are:

Accountability systems, including money incentives
High-stakes testing
Homework overload
School choice
Standards based on the APEC agenda (see below)
Scripted, teacher-proof curriculum
Teacher as deliverer of skills
Vouchers

Here's an interesting question for sixth graders taken from a famous national high-stakes test.

Most decisions concerning public schools are made by the:
a) Students
b) Parents
c) Local businesses
d) School board

There should be an e) "None of the above." There is a business agenda in the schools, but it comes from organizations such as the Business Roundtable, not from the local butcher, baker, or candlestick maker. Karen Canty reveals, "Since I sit on a school board in California, I can say unequivocally that school boards did not, either individually or collectively through our state association, have anything to say about the SAT-9's being adopted for all of our kids. We tried to have input, but the legislature passed a bill, the governor signed it, and the state department of education had to find a test by a certain date, give it to all second- to eleventh-grade students, and create an Academic Performance Index score based only on SAT-9 scores. Of course, local boards and school districts will be held accountable for the results of this test the legislature and the governor have forced upon us."

A clamorous chorus of millionaire CEOs, politicians, and assorted pundits is waging a preemptive strike on public education. Employing a psychobabble lexicon for the New Millennium, overlaid with prophecies of global economy servitude if the nation's schools don't follow their lead, this disingenuous crew chants, "I'm terrific, you're OK, but those guys in the schools stink." The Business Roundtable, assorted state governors, members of the U.S. Congress, and newspaper editorialists across America seem to think that their repeated denunciation of teachers and schoolchildren will distract the public from noticing the downsizing and outsizing of middle-class America. The words this crew uses to describe what they want to happen in schools are significant: *raise the bar, high-stakes testing, targeting students.* When did it become acceptable to talk about children as though they were racehorses or high hurdlers? As targets with bull's-eyes on their chests? This imagery is deliberate. In Jane Smiley's *Horse Heaven*, a trainer explains, "These horses are here to race and win." This is not why parents entrust their children to schools.

Schools used to be responsible to parents. Now it's *stakeholders.* Increasingly, our politicians, institutions such as the Business Roundtable, and the news pundits who trail in their wake talk of the *knowledge industry.* Thus learning, like children, becomes just one more commodity, and teachers mere functionaries in an accounting system. The corporate/politico Standardistas call for data-driven decision-making. Parents and teachers must continue to call for kid-driven decision-making.

Standardistas claim the nation's position in the global economy is at stake. Parents must not yield up their children to the business agenda.

George Schmidt is an English teacher of 30 years who is being sued by the Chicago Board of Education for over $1 million because he published six city tests—after students had taken them—in *Substance*, the education resistance newspaper of record he has been publishing for 25 years. When Schmidt is asked about "stakeholders," he doesn't mince words, observing that such "barbarisms [were] invented in some Orwellian alternative space to deflect from the fact that in the real world there are no 'stakeholders.' There are only parents, children, business people, teachers, doctors, and so on."

Writing in the *School Administrator*, Jonathan Kozol pleads, "Schools should not go down on bended knee to the world of business, as if to say, 'We are prepared to serve these children to you on a platter, so they may be of use to you.' That's not why God created children. It ought to be the other way around. Business ought to be serving the needs of children."

## SCHOOLS FOR GLOBALIZED BUSINESS

The agenda for globalized education is no secret: It is available in documents published by the Business Roundtable and the Alliance for Business. It is laid out clearly in a paper published in May 1997 by the Ministry of Labour of the Republic of Korea for a meeting of the APEC Human Resources Development Ministerial Meeting. This latter paper is instructive, as it shows the degree of consensus among the international elite of corporate executives.

APEC is the Asia-Pacific Economic Cooperation, 18 "economies" with borders on the Pacific, both in Asia and in the Americas. It describes itself as economies rather than countries. Global economy, get it? One of the themes of the Korean paper is that globalization is inevitable and education must prepare workers for the business needs of this globalization. Once school's purpose is defined as preparing future workers, then it follows that business should have a central role in determining the content of schooling. The APEC paper could not be more explicit, stating that "decisions must be taken by a school system for good business reasons with maximum business intervention." APEC sees schooling as "a transition from school to work." For parents who wonder why high-stakes testing has been imposed on schools, APEC explains that the governments "create a complementary educational environment and system" for "industrial restructuring due to technology advancements, a new international order with increased competition, and a distinct world trend of globalization."

The paper attacks "the emphasis on education for itself or on education for good members of a community." Further, children should not grow up to think that "work is only an instrumental part of one's life." Instead, "students should acquire a breadth of knowledge, skills, and attitudes necessary for adjustments into [a] work environment. Academic achievement should correlate with potential for ample job opportunities."

For APEC, "the work ethic" is what is important, not learning for learning's sake. "Schools should provide a comprehensive skills-based achievement record." APEC touches on the need for teacher education institutions to prepare future teachers to teach this way, subsuming any love of learning into an awareness of the needs of the marketplace. We see daily evidence of this pressure as newspaper articles scream that teacher-education colleges are falling down on the job, failing to prepare the sort of teachers the business community wants. APEC calls it "need-based education." Not children's needs, but the needs of big business. APEC complains that some people respect general high schools more than vocational schools. That's because "curricula have been traditionally developed by intellectual elites with emphasis on learning for the sake of learning without much emphasis on outcomes."

Such thinking must be stamped out. And the way to do this is by insisting that "decisions must be taken by a school system for good business reasons with maximum business intervention. A government should actively support or facilitate links with business." APEC explains that this is important so that they can build "a positive training culture to ensure that education and training meet the needs of business, labor markets, and changing economic environment." No more frivolity like learning for learning's sake, no siree, Mable.

Bill Clinton, in partnership with Lou Gerstner, tried to institute a national test that would push a de facto national, marketplace-oriented curriculum. Bush, Jr., may succeed.

Perhaps cooler heads have decided they shouldn't tip their hand with the dissemination of this paper. Formerly available on-line, it is not listed in the papers available at APEC's Web site or available for purchase from its bookstore. A query to the headquarters in Singapore brought vague summaries but not the real thing. But globalists who want to mastermind our children from cradle to grave beware: once something has been on the Internet, it doesn't disappear.

## BENCHED

There are lies, damned lies, and benchmarks. Benchmarks. What a word. Intoned by school reformers to invoke the legitimacy, even sanctity, of their operations, the benchmark was originally a surveyor's mark that served as a reference in topographic surveys. The mark was pressed into some durable material such as a rock or a wall to indicate elevation. These days the mark is used as a brand of educational excellence. No one in the school community dares admit that his benchmarks aren't lined up in a row, ready to be compared with those in the miracle state of Texas, where every child soon will be above average in everything but housing, health care, and books-per-capita. Benchmarks are also supposed to be international, so the business imperative is that every school in the country rate how its benchmarks measure up to those in Japan, Singapore, Germany, Burkina Faso, Cameroon, Maldives, Côte d'Ivoire, and Mauritania. That's just for starters. Get one thing in place, and the emperors of excellence will be back with another list.

The term *benchmark* comes to education from the business world. Surprise, surprise. Benchmarks are software tools used to measure the performance of a computer system. In business, these ostensibly objective measures enable manufacturers to distinguish themselves from their competition. Now, on the theory that what's good for IBM must be good for America—and for the nation's schoolchildren—benchmarking has become the educational imperative of our time. Achieve, a nonprofit group created after the 1996 Educational Summit of governors and business leaders meeting to firm up their curriculum regulations for the schools, hires out its "benchmarking services" to individual states.

These services are pricey, but Achieve is quick to point out that states don't have to pony up the money for educational overhaul. In a cozy rob-Peter-to-pay-Paul arrangement among business brethren, Achieve helps states find funding to pay off the consultants Achieve sends in. The Illinois Achieve Review, for example, was cosponsored by the Illinois Business Roundtable, the Ohio Review by the Ohio Business Roundtable, and so on. There you have it: big business hires big business to pronounce judgment on the work of teachers. Big business hires big business to pronounce judgment on what children need. In Illinois the roving consultants announce that the state's children need more intensive phonics; in Ohio they call for children to learn about native son William Dean Howells; in New Jersey they call for a beefing-up of academic writing. Yes, if Achieve has its way, students who don't measure up in academic writing will be benched. Permanently. No high school diploma.

In South Dakota they explain that benchmarks "provide targets for student performance and are an essential and critical component for local school districts to use in designing district and classroom assessments aligned with the goals, indicators, and grade-level standards." Still not clear? South Dakota uses the "education as a journey through learning" analogy to clarify things. Goals are the final destination, indicators provide targets and guideposts, benchmarks "serve as mile markers and weigh stations along the way, and the grade-level standards represent the turns, hills, traffic signs, and the white lines along the road."

Point of information: The cochair of Achieve is Louis V. Gerstner, who in 1993 went from being CEO of RJR Nabisco to being CEO of IBM, with a signing bonus of $4,924,596 and a stock package that *Business Week* listed at more than $21 million. Soon after signing on with IBM, Gerstner fired 90,000 of IBM's 270,000 employees, the same sort of highly trained workers he now insists the schools aren't producing.

Writing in the *New York Times*, Peter Schneider points out that "in the global economy, you don't get points for character."

In its reports to individual states, Achieve explains that benchmarking is a highly respected practice in the business world, an activity "that looks outward to find best practice and high performance and then measures actual business operations against those goals. Benchmarking in education follows the same principle. It is appropriate at a time when state education reforms are focused on raising student and school performance, as states want and need an external yardstick to gauge their efforts." That's the repeated cheerleading slogan that seems to appear in every Achieve report. Achieve has set itself as that yardstick, proclaiming which states have good benchmarks and which states don't. Gone are the days of the teacher holding sway in her classroom. Today, corporate benchmarks rule. This is why students cannot receive a high school diploma unless they can pass an algebra test and produce an academic paper. Or get out of third grade if they stumble over a schwa.

But benchmarks are of very limited value—even in the computer industry. As Keith Diefendorff, editor-in-chief of a semiconductor-industry newsletter told the *New York Times* in 1998, "There's the hype factor." Diefendorff advises customers to ignore most of the benchmark blather, warning that "benchmarks themselves are not very accurate. Even objective, methodical benchmarks, the best and cleanest job you can do, seldom represent reality. There is certainly no one benchmark that provides a single number that represents what you are going to see." And remember, he's talking about computers. Computers are different, so using a benchmark disk to test different computers makes the results questionable. Imagine that.

If computers are different and therefore difficult to compare by some universal yardstick, how about children?

If benchmarks can't give definitive information about computers, why are the people who work in schools being forced to bow at the benchmark shrine? Parents in Akron, Ohio, for example, need to ask, "How is this benchmark going to help my child tomorrow?" Here's what the Akron Public Schools Web page announces:

Akron uses benchmarks to show what a teacher must teach and what students should learn in order to ensure their progress.

What teachers *must* teach? At least they have the grace to say "what students *should* learn." Parents must ask, "What happens if my child doesn't learn on schedule? What happens if he's a day late?" Not to mention a dollar short, as so many schools are when it comes to funding.

The fact that benchmarks seldom represent reality isn't the real point. After all, benchmarks are just smokescreens to sweet-talk the fact that children are being treated as commodities in the global economy, pawns of a knowledge industry that has been taken over by corporate America. We shouldn't be measuring—or even talking about— children in terms of profit growth and market capitalization. We shouldn't be training children to feel insecure and unworthy, training them from kindergarten and even preschool to worry that they won't measure up, won't make the grade. Think of the eight-year-old in Texas who started crying. When his mom asked what was wrong, he said he was afraid he'd fail the infamous TAAS and then his teacher would lose her job and her children would starve because she couldn't buy them food.

That said, here are three (of nine) South Dakota Benchmarks in Social Studies for Grades 6 through 8:

a)  Determine the impact cultural diffusion has had on various civilizations.
b)  Describe various ways cultural diffusion takes place over time.
c)  Explain the importance of preserving and sharing culture.

The sixth-grade standards accompanying these benchmarks declare that STUDENTS WILL

1.  Analyze the geographic, political, economic, and social structures of Mesopotamia and Egypt with emphasis on the location and description of the river systems, the physical settings that supported permanent settlement and early civilizations;

the development of agricultural techniques that increased production which led to economic surplus; the emergence of cities
as centers of culture and power; the relationship between religion and the social and political orders in each civilization; the
origin and influence of Judaism; the significance of Hammurabi's Code; the art and architecture of Egypt; the impact of
Egyptian trade in the eastern Mediterranean and Nile Valley;
the evolution of language and its written forms; and cultural
contributions; and their effect on modern everyday life.

2.  Analyze the geographic, political, economic, and social structures of ancient China and India with emphasis on the location
and description of the river systems and the physical setting
that supported the rise of these civilizations; the geographical
features of China that made governance and movement of
ideas and goods difficult and served to isolate that region from
the rest of the world; the significance of the Aryan invasions in
India with emphasis on the social structure of the caste system;
the major beliefs and practices of Hinduism; the major beliefs
and practices of Buddhism and how it spread to other regions,
especially during the Mauryan Empire; the fundamental teaching of Confucianism and Taoism; the policies, achievements,
and political contributions of the Qin and Han dynasties in
China; the locations and significance of the trans-Eurasian
"silk roads"; and cultural contributions and their effect on
modern everyday life.

3.  Analyze the geographic, political, economic, and social structures of the early society of this civilization; the connections
between geography and the development of city-states, including patterns of trade and commerce; the transition from
tyranny and oligarchy to early democratic forms of government and the significance of citizenship; the differences between Athenian, or direct, democracy and representative
democracy; the significance of Greek mythology to the
everyday life of people in ancient Greece and its influence on
modern literature and language; the similarities and differ-

ences between life in Athens and Sparta; the rise of Alexander the Great in the north and the spread of Greek culture; and the cultural contributions in the areas of arts, science, language, architecture, government and philosophy.

4. Analyze the geographic, political, economic, and social structures in the development of Rome with emphasis on the location and physical setting that supported the rise of the Roman republic; the significance of the republican form of government; the political and geographic reasons for the growth of the Roman Empire; the influence of Julius Caesar and Augustus in Rome's transition from republic to empire; the origin and spread of Christianity during the Roman Empire; and the cultural contributions in the areas of art, architecture, technology, science, literature, language, and the law.

Note: these are the standards for three of nine benchmarks. On May 13, 2001, Secretary of Education Rod Paige wrote in the *Washington Post*, "A good test—the kind the president and I support—is aligned with the curriculum so that schools know whether children are actually learning the material that their states have decided a child should know." What is a South Dakota parent to assume: that Secretary Paige is bonkers, or that he hasn't read their curriculum standards?

It is not our job to train eight-year-olds or eighth graders to be fearful. It is not our job to train them to grow up to be compliant workers, people who are so grateful for their jobs, they won't rock the boat. Or join unions.

Take Massachusetts. Beginning in 2003, all 10th-grade students will have to pass the state's high-stakes tests to earn a high school diploma. No matter how they do in class, students can't get a diploma without passing the MCAS. The MCAS is the brainchild of the Massachusetts Business Alliance. This test, and others like it in most other states, is not about education. It is about social control, training children to define their worth by how well they measure up to the needs of the corporations. Of increasing concern to parents in Massachusetts and elsewhere is the fact that students become discouraged about passing the high-stakes graduation tests and drop out of school in ninth or tenth grade. In Minnesota, when Jimmy Dressen was told that he had failed the state's math test, he dropped out of school, figuring, "What's the point?" He wasn't going to get a diploma, so why bother? As it happens, Jimmy had actually passed the math test in February and again on a retry in April. But by the time he was told, "Sorry, scoring mistakes were made," Jimmy, who had planned to become a pipefitter, was just another dropout statistic. As a dropout, the best he could do was get a job collecting shopping carts at Kmart.

Noted independent policy analyst and writer Anne Wheelock observes that by the Massachusetts Department of Education's own estimates, 33 percent of Latino students, 25 percent of African-American students, and 10 percent of white students in the class of 2002 will drop out before graduating. Fearing they won't pass the exit exam, they figure there's no point in continuing. Urban schools are hit the hardest. Cities contributing 15 percent of the state's high schoolers have 39 percent of the dropouts.

Other costs are more subtle. Wheelock tells of Sylvie, a 15-year-old member of the class of 2003. A B+ student whose plans include college and a job in the banking industry, Sylvie admits that MCAS scares her. "I'm afraid that I won't graduate. MCAS made me want to drop out." Sylvie observes that her MCAS scores cause teachers to see her in a new light, looking at her in terms of what she does not know rather than what she does know. "Teachers always liked me," she says, "but MCAS made us look stupid."

Wealthy parents can save their children from this misery: students in private schools don't have to take any state tests to pass from one grade to another or to receive the high school diplomas issued by the state.

Another horse trainer in Smiley's novel says you can tell a horseman by his willingness to wait. "A horse is no machine . . . but a living, breathing, opinionated beast. You got to wait for them, and then wait some more." This used to be the teacher credo: Give the child time and space to grow, to learn, to flourish. The Business Roundtable and their bedfellows insist that teachers must get out the rulers and see who meets the mark. And the Business Roundtable and its bedfellows as Education

Trust and Fordham Foundation, to name just a couple, are willing and even eager to discard those who fall short on implacable exams.

Eldon Lee, a retired principal in Milwaukee, observes, "The biggest damage standards do is establish time frames. If you don't answer on Monday for the test but know it on Wednesday, are you still stupid? And if you do memorize it on schedule, does that do you any good?"

## A ONE-EYED PLAN

Education critics like to use a medical metaphor for education, saying that competent teachers should diagnose children and then supply prescriptive teaching. Many teachers reject this metaphor, saying that children are not some disease to be cured. Nonetheless, the medical metaphor persists, and it is troubling to consider that educational benchmarks are following in the tradition of the medical cost-cutting plans that have become cookbook in their approach. Milliman & Robertson, a Seattle-based actuarial firm, has published a nine-volume set on utilization management, selling at $500 per volume. The firm also sells consultant services to help hospitals implement the schedules it publishes.

These guidelines amount to blueprints for a hospital's day-by-day treatment of a patient. There's a checklist—enumerating what tests, medications, and procedures should be used and in what order. In schools we call this "direct instruction." The assumption is made that teachers don't know enough to do the teaching. Instead, they need to follow a carefully scripted manual that tells them what to do. Chicago, for one, publishes day-by-day lessons for each grade level: No matter who the children are and what might be going on in their lives, here's what should be taught in every third grade on day 83. In California, philanthropist David Packard gave school districts up and down the state millions of dollars—with the stipulation that they must agree to use the scripted reading program of his choice.

It is a program that tells the teacher what to do each day; teachers are reprimanded for reading aloud to children when that activity is not in the script. Experienced teachers are ordered to leave their years of know-how outside the classroom door and stick to the script, using only the materials listed in the script as "approved." Life imitates art—but we must remember that "I've Got a Little List," sung by Ko-Ko, the Lord High Executioner in *The Mikado*, was a satire:

> You may put 'em on the list—you may put 'em on the list;
> And they'll none of 'em be missed—they'll none of 'em be
>     missed!

In Los Angeles, Houston, Chicago, and New York City, the prescriptive lists are not funny.

School districts establish checklists in the name of higher scores on standardized tests; hospitals use checklists to move patients out and save the HMO money. In both cases, institutional benchmarks shipped in from unknown experts-for-hire take precedence over local professional experience and judgment, not to mention student and patient well-being.

Some people insist that this rote teaching guarantees a certain curriculum rigor. Many teachers contend that it's more like rigor mortis. Take Donna Moffett. In September 2000, Donna Moffett answered the call by the New York City Schools Chancellor to fill chronic vacancies in troubled schools. "I was leading a pleasant life with very little risk," Ms. Moffett told *New York Times* reporter Abby Goodnough, who chronicled this new teacher's first year in an extraordinary series. Moffett gave up her $60,000-a-year job as a legal secretary near Wall Street to earn under $37,000 as a first-grade teacher in Brooklyn, reflecting, "This school and these children, they may take everything I have. But there's a really deep well in me, and it's time to draw on it."

Goodnough points out the tension between Ms. Moffett's instinct to make the most of children's experiences and interests, and the orders from her supervisor not to stray from the set curriculum. By edict of the Board of Education, teachers at low-performing New York City schools use a rigid, prescribed curriculum. The supervisor says, "The beauty of these types of programs is that you don't have to think about it. Everything is spelled out for you." A thick manual spells out what the teacher should say and do and how much time it should take. And Ms. Moffett tries to play by the rules, but there's plenty of evidence that she sees the children in her care as much more than skill units. Her frustration with the conflict between children and curriculum mandates becomes the *New York Times* Quote of the Day for May 23, 2001. Given a very hard time by her supervisor when she strayed from the curriculum script, Ms. Moffett said, "I don't think the call for help was to have people come into these schools and say, 'Open your book to page blah-dee-blah.'"

McDonald's has built a successful empire by ensuring that its hamburgers are the same size from Anchorage to Atlanta to Altoona. Some question that this formula should be imposed on children.

Milliman & Robertson also offers scripts and timetables, but M&R is quick to point out that the optimal times for drive-by maternity procedures and outpatient mastectomies are established not by actuaries but by medical professionals. M&R hires a team of doctors and nurses to read medical journals and textbooks and come up with the guidelines. The question remains: If the for-hire doctors and educators make their judgments about how hospitals and classrooms should operate while sitting in libraries and committee rooms, are they just bean counters? By the very nature of their task, have they forfeited a degree of professional credibility? Public outrage forced the revocation of the bean-counting guidelines stipulating that elderly patients with cataracts should be allowed surgery on only one eye because an old person doesn't need to see out of both eyes. More public outrage about the actuarial recommendations for drive-by maternity procedures provoked all 50 state legislatures to pass laws overriding the actuarial minimums.

Clearly, there are many parallels with education, with the opinions of consultants-for-hire dominating the curriculum decisions and teaching strategies in classrooms across the country. Get thirsty when you eat Fritos? So drink a Pepsi. It's the same thing in education. Standardistas relegate the teachers and principals who actually work with students to the delivery of services decreed by the bean counters. These teachers would do well to start each day by ignoring the actuaries and listening to e.e. cummings:

While you and I have lips and voices which
are for kissing and to sing with
who cares if some oneeyed son of a bitch
invents an instrument to measure Spring with?

In education as in medicine, goals become benchmarks, etched in
stone—or in hospital care protocols or state graduation requirements.
In both medicine and education, university complicity and private entrepreneurship go hand in hand. In medicine, a goal becomes a standard
that decrees an infant with bacterial meningitis should leave the hospital after 3 days instead of the customary 10 to 14 days. In education, a
goal becomes a benchmark, engraved in state statutes listing graduation
requirements so that a student is denied a high school diploma, no matter what the report-card grades accumulated in the 12 years of his required attendance may indicate.

In a little *New York Times* opinion piece, "When the Doctor Is
Forced to Fire a Patient," Howard Markel, M.D., insists that sometimes
teenage patients are just too obnoxious to keep on the books. Dr.
Markel relates that it is "common practice in adolescent medicine for
doctors and patients to make a contract on the services and behavior
each expects from the other."

And there you have a great example of why people should stop using the education-should-be-more-like-medicine metaphor. School
is the place where, when you show up, they have to take you. And so
it should be. First, do no harm. I'll take the Hippocratic oath. We
can't fire out students. I taught seventh and eighth graders and students in an alternative high school every bit as obnoxious and destructive as the one Dr. Markel described. And, by God, it was my job
to come back every day and try again. It was my job and my sacred
calling.

Acknowledging that is uncomfortable to fire a patient, Dr. Markel
maintains that "patients and physicians, after all, have mutual obligations." Oh my, ever try to tell a teenager this? Teachers try to help stu-
velop obligations to themselves. Occasionally we may try the
of Mom" ploy. It doesn't work, but we try it anyway. Of course

we hope to help our students become responsible citizens. But we can't fire them when they disappoint us.

No one would argue that we must keep schools safe, but policies such as Zero Tolerance are exaggerations rather than remedies. In my 20 years of teaching difficult students, I encountered only one student I felt should be barred from our campus. If teachers give up on a child, what's left? A teacher is someone who can't wash her hands of trouble/disappointment/despair/failure. She must come back tomorrow and try again.

## INTERNATIONAL BUSINESS MACHINATIONS

Historically, calls to reform public education have been as numerous as blackflies in an Adirondacks summer, but the education summits of the 1990s were blatant about who wasn't invited to the table. You didn't get invited if you weren't a governor, a Fortune 500 executive, or a proven lapdog of the Corporate/Conservative Think-Tank Standardistas. Special consideration seems to have been given to think-tank wonks who write op-ed pieces for the *Wall Street Journal* praising vouchers and denouncing public education. And one can't talk about those education summits without talking about Lou Gerstner—the fellow who has been known to refer to employees as "units" and sees children as "workers in global economy."

At a 1997 speech at the National Press Club, Gerstner applauded the "common agenda for improving our nation's schools" exhibited by the Business Roundtable, the U.S. Chamber of Commerce, and the National Alliance of Business. It is illustrative and rather mind-boggling to take a look at the way the National Alliance of Business, for one, describes children and teachers. In a document titled "'Knowledge Supply Chain': Managing K-80 Learning," we read of "relationships with knowledge suppliers" (formerly known as teachers); "greater business involvement in the knowledge supply chain" (formerly known as schools). Here's more from *Work America*, vol. 15, issue 5, May 1998, published by the National Alliance of Business and available at www.nab.com:

- I dream of the day when I can go to a knowledge systems integrator, specify my needs and have them put all the partners
  together to deliver the people I need.
- Applying the principles of the material supply chain to the
  process of lifelong learning is a cost-effective, efficient way
  businesses can ensure that worker knowledge is put to use to
  help companies' bottom line.
- Improved potential for individually customized K-80 education and training processes that balance the needs to prepare
  people for current and future work.
- Increased understanding by students and faculty at all levels of
  the education system of business and competitive needs of industry.

In the preface to his *Dictionary* in 1755, Samuel Johnson wrote, "I am
not so lost in lexicography as to forget that words are the daughters of
earth." The words of the National Business Alliance are sons of the
compost heap. I would suggest to the National Business Alliance and
others of their ilk that *teacher* and *student* are honorable words, that their
relationship is sacred; knowledge systems integrators and the competitive needs of society be damned.

It is of no small significance that *teacher*, a good, solid word dating
from the fourteenth century, contains just two syllables. The term
*knowledge systems integrator* not only quadruples the syllables, it at the
same time obfuscates and defames a noble endeavor. Knowledge systems integrators are, of course, servants of the global economy, people
on the cutting edge of the corporate takeover of the schools, people
who use sleight-of-phrase to make children feel unworthy.

In what George Orwell called a catalog of swindles and perversions,
we encounter these interchangeable pat phrases in the press releases issued by biz-whiz politicos, in the documents from corporate front-
group foundations, and in every government document about
reforming schools. Anyone can put together a Chinese menu of a
school reform press release by choosing one each from columns A, B,
and C.

| A | B | C |
| --- | --- | --- |
| Assessing | Clearly-articulated | National consensus |
| Producing | Best-performing | Accountability systems |
| Reforming | Technology-based | Global economy |
| Restructuring | Information-age | Education output |
| Competing | Twenty-first century | Academic standards |
| Networking | Cost-effective | Goals implementation |
| Investing | World-class | Business intelligence solutions |
| Initiating | Data-driven | Benchmarking initiative |
| Institutionalizing | Fact-based | Knowledge systems integrator |
| Implementing | Low-performing | Public accountability |
| Reinventing | Back-to-basics | Market forces |
| Assuring | Cutting-edge | Industry needs |
| Transforming | Data-warehoused | Information infrastructure |
| Facilitating | Teacher-proof | Instructional applications |
| Innovating | Blue-ribbon | Networked solutions |
| Disseminating | Needs-driven | Significant learning targets |
| Collaborating | Long-term | Reform process |
| Formulating | Step-by-step | Education stakeholders |
| Strategizing | User-friendly | Authentic assessment tool |
| Allocating | Rubrics-based | Advanced systems measurement |
| Benchmarking | High-stakes | Resource allocation |
| Validating | State-mandated | Goal consensus |
| Standardizing | Needs-assessed | Framework essentials |
| Rewarding | New-economy | Quality assurance |
| Targeting | State-of-the-art | Information dissemination |

Many words can be warped to fit into any column, so you have benchmarking/benchmark-based/benchmark essentials. Once you get the idea, you can choose two or three from each column to produce a numbing concoction of high-sounding tripe. With practice, you can produce something to rival the Mass Insight's "forum for best practices in standards-based education strategies." Mass Insight is part of the Business for Better Schools Coalition, whose members include Associated Industries of Massachusetts, the Greater Boston Chamber of Commerce, the Massachusetts Business Roundtable, the Massachusetts High Technology Council, the Massachusetts Taxpayers Foundation, and the North Central Massachusetts Chamber of Commerce.

Of course the writing is humbug, jargon talking to itself—celebrating a reunion, perhaps. But we must not forget that it is humbug with a dark purpose, offering up inflated words in defense of the indefensible. As George Orwell pointed out over half a century ago, such language is "designed to make lies sound truthful and murder respectable, and to give an appearance of solidity to pure wind. . . ."

Why are the corporations trying to impose high-stakes tests on the schools? They say it's because kids can't read the driver's license test or the voting ballot, never mind succeed in the high-tech jobs industry is proffering. They say if states standardize the curriculum around skills that the workplace needs, then kids who are successful at sticking it out and passing the tests will get a diploma that "really means something." Those who drop out along the way have only themselves to blame.
By corporate-politico rules, students who want to be butchers, bakers, beauticians, bricklayers, pipefitters, and plumbers need to meet college entrance requirements in order to earn a high school diploma.

Another agenda emerges.

In 1994, Congress passed the *Goals 2000: Educate America Act*, an initiative started by President Bush the Elder, and supported by Bill Clinton both as Governor of Arkansas and as President. The basis for the act was a report called "Reinventing Education: Entrepreneurship in America's Public Schools," which was coauthored by one Lou Gerstner. When Lou Gerstner took over the reins of IBM in 1993, a *Business Week* article speculated that his lack of high-tech savvy wouldn't be a hindrance. Gerstner had, announced *Business Week*, "the guts to slash and burn." Gerstner has brought this same take-no-prisoners spirit to school reform. He stands out among the crew that noted educational researcher Gerald Bracey terms the Education Scare Industry, out on the stump creating anxiety over test scores and the U.S. eight-year-old's place in the global economy. Bracey points out that they issue their dire warnings in the absence of any firm data. When Gerstner is not out on the stump scaring the public, he's leading a chorus line of cronies who insist that the "business" of schools is "the distribution of information," and advising teachers, "Know what your job is; know what your outcomes should be; know how you will measure output."

Is there any mom in America who wants her eight-year-old to be measured as output?

But the fellow is brilliant. Consider this: the former head of RJR Nabisco (the guys who make cigarettes and Oreos), where he presided over the Nabisco Dinah Shore Ladies' Professional Golf Association tournament, avid golfer Gerstner takes over the reins of IBM. There, he turns up the heat on education, inspiring and engineering politicians and business leaders into a couple of education summits proclaiming how lousy public schools are. Not naming specific schools, just proclaiming that public schools in general are in the toilet, rather in the spirit of Joseph McCarthy proclaiming that he had the names of communists who worked in the State Department in his briefcase (which he never opened) and President Reagan talking about the welfare queen driving a Cadillac. Don't name a school so the public can look at the problem—and fix it; just declare all public education a failure and all teachers incompetent. The truth of the matter is that plenty of U.S. schools are excellent, even more are good. Plenty are fair, and some are dreadful. And there reasons for the conditions of all of them, reasons having more to do with the zip codes in which they are located than the skill of the teachers who work in them. Or what kinds of tests they give.

In a July 2001 speech at the White House Summit on Early Childhood Cognitive Development, Assistant Secretary for Elementary and Secondary Education Susan Neuman stressed the importance of environment in a child's learning. It comes as no surprise that Neuman found more children's books available for purchase in middle-income neighborhoods than in poor. What is unexplainable as well as inexcusable are the vast differences in public elementary school libraries within the same city. Twelve books per child in middle-income school libraries; closed libraries in low-income neighborhoods. Librarians with master's degrees in middle-income; no librarians in low-income. In Neuman's words, "Children can't learn literacy without books."

USC professor and noted linguist Professor Stephen Krashen points out that in the summer of 2001, Chicago spent $29 million in an attempt to boost test scores of 29,000 students. "There might be an easier way," suggests Krashen. "The time spent reading for pleasure has a stronger impact on increasing reading-test scores than time spent on traditional 'skill-building activities,' such as vocabulary drill and reading-comprehension exercises." Chicago's own University of Illinois researchers found that picking up vocabulary by reading real books is 10 times as fast, in terms of words learned per minute, as vocabulary drills and exercises.

So, posits Krashen, drawing on Neuman's research, why not improve library collections, staffing, and hours open? "Twenty-nine million dollars buys a lot of books."

The politicians would do well to make some library book counts before they start counting standardized test scores. Take New York City. With a book budget for New York City school libraries of $4 per student, the Chancellor of Schools advised parents that their kids should read at least 25 books a year. Mayor Rudolph Giuliani's response was to cut $41 million from the city's public libraries (even as he was advocating spending $96 million on sports stadiums). Listen for Marie Antoinette in the wings, intoning, "Let them go to Barnes & Noble," where a children's hardcover costs, on average, $16.60.

At the same time I was digging out information on the funding of books for New York City schoolchildren, the *New York Times* was reporting on our society's experimentations with the limits of self-indulgence. In its pages I read about the $120 chef's tasting menu at Daniel's restaurant; I read about the $1,500 price tag for a regular-season front-row seat at a New York Knicks game at Madison Square Garden; I read speculation about whether the Clintons might join the just-opened Hudson National Gold Club in Croton-on-Hudson, where the initiation fee is $317,000.

Such figures reveal the obscene gap between the haves and the have-nots, between our private-economy boom and our public-sector bust, and this is what high-stakes standards and testing is all about. Once the high-stakes tests have driven a standardized curriculum into the schools, politicians and their corporate cronies can claim that they have equalized education—regardless of the shameful inequalities of facilities and resources.

Money talks. When Washington politicos holding the purse strings talk about "raising the bar," as though children were steeplechase horses, then educrats across the country tell kindergartners to forget finger painting, skip recess, and start jumping higher. When Goals 2000 business partners say they want to deny diplomas to high school students who don't pass tests, then educrats rush to fail fourth graders. Governors launch tactics harking back to Soviet panzer tactics right out of the Frunze Academy—feed your successes and starve your losses. They want to feed their successful schools with more funds and starve the struggling schools with a loss of funds. Writing in *The Nation*, Calvin Trillin suggested that if cutting funds doesn't help kids score better, "We could prohibit lunch, or take their shoes."

It's important to remember that corporate condemnation of public education serves a variety of purposes other than fixing the schools that need fixing. Some want to privatize schools; some want state support for religious schools; some want to get into the $700 billion-a-year schools run by for-profit corporations. People come to school-bashing from different camps, but they join in the same chant, repeating over and over that public education is broken.

Gerstner sounds the trumpets for standards and testing; he sets up Achieve, a nonprofit standards and testing consulting company; he gets his state governor cronies of all political stripes on board for mass testing. And then, IBM offers a dazzling array of for-profit services to school districts to organize and manipulate the mountains of data that the call for massive state testing has created. A killer bee swarm of high-tech jargon enters the language: everything from juried lessons to data warehouses to authentic assessments of every stripe. Who would have guessed that all the blather about high-tech information-age jobs for the global economy would come down to the way a teacher writes her lesson plans? At the National Education Computing Conference in Atlanta in June 2000, IBM announced IBM Insight at School, "a new business intelligence solution for the K-12 market, which provides schools with the technology, consulting and services that will help them make more informed decisions to improve the learning process." Network nirvana. Or maybe it's just a sales pitch.

Dateline Georgia, June 2000. At the National Education Computing Conference, IBM announces the launch of IBM Insight at School, "a new business intelligence solution for the K-12 market," providing "instant access" via computer to students' academic histories and to the "avalanche of data" that accumulate daily in a school, that will allow educators to "make strategic decisions to improve the curriculum and meet accountability requirements imposed by legislators and governors."

Dateline Georgia, July 2001. The *Atlanta Constitution* reports a serious security breach in the computers that run Georgia's HOPE scholarship program. The executive director of the Georgia Technology Authority confirmed that a technician's goof left confidential files vulnerable from April through June and that hackers might have gotten access to other state computers, such as those containing tax files and medical records.

This gives parents who are already unsure of how much data they want schools to collect about their families plenty to think about.

But at IBM, they call it "data-driven decision making." This term appears twice in the IBM press release launching IBM Insight at School. Ben Barnes, general manager of IBM Global Business Intelligence Solutions, enthuses, "In corporate America, putting business intelligence at an employee's fingertips has spawned a multibillion-dollar industry. And now we are seeing many implementations in public education."

"Schools gather an avalanche of data on a daily basis," said Rae Ann Alton, IBM worldwide K-12 segment manager, "and educators have made it very clear to us that they are looking for an integrated solution that puts accurate, easy-to-access data at their fingertips to help them make data-driven decisions."

Then it pops up again in a press release about the services IBM sells to Gwinnett County Public Schools, the creation of a "single source of key information that is readily accessible to classroom teachers, administrators, and other constituencies in fulfilling their educational mission." Katie Lovett, director of planning for Georgia's largest school district, is enthusiastic about IBM expertise. "The data warehouse has caused an overwhelming culture change in the GCPS organization. Now we are focused on data-driven decision making. As a result, we can more effectively anticipate and manage change."

Plenty of us longtime teachers remember the good old days of kid-driven decision making. As historian David McCullough observes, "Information is a wonderful thing, but it is not knowledge. You wouldn't be educated if you managed to memorize the entire encyclopedia. You would just be weird."

## CAPITAL, HUMAN AND MONEY

Lou Gerstner is not an educator with long years of experience in the public schools. He is the CEO of the IBM Corporation, which is why the report on which the nation is basing its school standards defines students as "human capital" and urges schools to compare themselves to each other as "Xerox compares itself to L.L. Bean for inventory control." Children as inventory control. Now there's an idea. Think of the board of education sitting in front of a huge computer screen, evaluating a teacher by tracking her inventory:

- Children underachieving
- Children overachieving
- Children's homework tread separating
- Children blow out
- Children whistling Dixie

- Children in need of rotation
- Children subject to recall
- Replacement children no good either
- Time to rotate blame for children's problems

All those little chunks of human capital (who used to be children) must be put into uniforms and standardized, like so many cans of lima beans. Timothy McVeigh referred to the children killed in the Oklahoma City blast as "collateral damage"; it's hard to see that the Business Roundtable are viewing children who don't measure up any differently.

Funny thing. International Business Machines, led by that friend of education Lou Gerstner, asked for $1 billion in reduced assessments in San Jose, California. Schools are mostly supported by local property taxes, and corporate America is unwilling to pay its fair share. They threaten to pack up their marbles if they don't get the exemptions and abatements they demand. Writing a front-page story in the *Wall Street Journal*, Robert Tomsho points out that at the same time Toledo business leaders are complaining that the "abysmal academic record" of the 38,000-student Toledo Public School District "hampers efforts to hire well-trained workers," these same business leaders are insisting on receiving hefty tax breaks that drain tens of millions of dollars badly needed by the school system. Tax breaks to business currently cost the district about $13.7 million a year. Tomsho reports that Memphis-area businesses have received so many abatements that school officials in surrounding Shelby County talk of eliminating high school athletics.

## AWARD-WINNING SCHOOLS:
## WHEN IS A ROSE REALLY STINKWEED?

In Tucson, Merle and Paula McPheeters were contacted by staff from their child's school, offering "reading-skill advancement." With the tests approaching, school officials were singling out students whose scores they thought they could boost—and thereby boost the school average. Paula recounts, "Of course we were outraged. We expect the focus of the school to be about meaningful, engaged learning, not about how test scores reflect on the school." By spring 2001, the McPheeters had had enough, and opted both their daughters out of the tests.

Massachusetts education writer and analyst Anne Wheelock sees this phenomenon of schools targeting which students should receive special intensive tutoring to raise school scores popping up around the country. In Birmingham, Alabama, they took the easy route and pushed out the low scorers; in Tucson they try to boost the scores of children already doing well. When one group of children is getting extra help, another group is being ignored.

Wheeler says parents should be warned about award-winning schools. Sometimes the scores are the zip code effect, but single-year score gains may be what in Massachusetts is being called "the Nauset effect." Nauset Regional High School boosted the number of students scoring in the "advanced" category, jumping from 9 percent to 19 percent in English and from 12 percent to 28 percent in math. A closer look at the scores shows that although the top is moving up, the "middle" is either remaining stagnant or dropping, and the "bottom'" is getting larger.

In Dallas, Deborah Diffilly, assistant professor at Southern Methodist University, warns of the "bubble" trend. "Directly related to the pressure of high-stakes testing is a new phenomenon—bubble kids. Teachers divide their students into three groups: those who will surely do well on *the* test, those who will not pass *the* test, and bubble kids. The bubble kids are the children who are 'almost' passing the practice standardized tests being administered. As time for *the* test draws near, many administrators demand that the first two groups of students be given work that will keep them quiet, and the bubble kids are given intensive test preparation. For weeks, teachers guide the small percentage of bubble kids as they repeatedly answer test questions. The rest of the children continue with their busywork."

The First Annual Building on Success Conference, held in June 2001 in Boston, looked like a who's who of corporate influence. Attending were executives from State Street Corporation, FleetBoston Foundation, Donahue Institute, Jessie B. Cox Charitable Trust, Pew Forum on Standards-Based Reform, Achieve, Federal Reserve Bank, and so on.

Kati Haycock, Executive Director of Education Trust, was the keynote speaker. Ted Kennedy was there. Among the schools lauded as a "Vanguard School" was the Nauset Regional High School.

Wheelock reports that students with disabilities at Nauset appear to be more at risk now than in 1998. She cautions that people need to keep track of "missing" students, "both because high-stakes testing can create pressure on schools to push out low-scoring students, pressure on low-scoring students to leave school, pressure on parents to remove vulnerable students from the testing pool." Whatever the reason, in 1998, Nauset's 10th grade lost 9.4 percent of 10th graders between October and May. Wheelock raises important questions:

- Who are the missing?
- Where did they go?
- Why?
- What impact does the loss of students have on test-score patterns?

When corporate Standardistas single out a school for commendation, they don't ask any of these questions. When the media report on the commendation, they don't ask any of these questions either.

## MEDIA WEIRDNESS

Too many newspapers provide education coverage that is mostly refried press releases from the Fordham Foundation, the Heartland Institute, the Education Trust, and other public-school-bashing enterprises. I have first-hand experience of the frustration of trying to get a newspaper editorial board to look beyond the corporate charts and chants and see real children. When an editor at *USA Today* phoned, asking me to write an op-ed piece about Goals 2000, President Clinton's refurbished version of Bush the Elder's plan for national standards and tests, I was elated at the idea of being able to show the difficulties these standards present to children and their teachers.

I'd written plenty of op-eds for *USA Today*. I knew their formula and followed the rules in writing a poignant little 800-word piece expressing concern that high-stakes tests based on a standardized curriculum gives nonstandardized students no place to go. I described the way Jack remade himself in our storefront high school—set up for kids too obnoxious to be allowed on the regular campus. Jack didn't learn quadratic equations; he didn't read *Hamlet*. But while studying his self-chosen subject of Scrabble four hours a day for six months, he began to acquire the skills he needed to change the destructive course of his life. I allowed Jack to study Scrabble as long as he curbed his filthy tongue and refrained from pestering other students beyond endurance. I use the word "study" quite deliberately. I'd shown Jack a *Harper's* article about New York street hustlers who made a living playing Scrabble, and suddenly Jack had a career goal. He pestered me into buying the *Funk & Wagnalls Standard College Dictionary*, the official Scrabble arbiter of that day. A teacher's dream: conferring with a youngster about the merits of one dictionary over another.

Jack had a history of carving out his own niche of self-selecting what he wanted to be best at. In seventh grade he gained districtwide notoriety by walking around the two-story school on his hands. Hey, there was no rule saying students had to walk on their feet. My hope as a teacher was that Scrabble would be a temporary fix, a way for Jack to earn respect while he pulled his life together. Although Jack did no conventional work in our school, as his Scrabble skills improved, so did his behavior. For those who think Scrabble skills might not be a life skill, I would point out that even as television and computer games dominate American leisure time, Scrabble sales remain solid. With next to no advertising, more than two million sets were sold in 1998 and 1999. In taking on this cultural talisman, and an intellectual one at that, Jack was preparing himself to become a solid citizen.

One of my school rules was that no matter what else they were doing, students had to read half an hour a day. Jack went on scouting raids with me for used paperbacks.

An inspector from the New York State Education Department complained about the quality of our reading matter—he wasn't satisfied with individual copies of *Macbeth, Call of the Wild*, and so on. He wanted to see class sets—every kid reading the same thing at the same moment. I wrote the State Commissioner of Education, telling him to keep his inspectors out of our school while classes were in session. I allow no one to sneer at my classroom when students are present. No one. Years later, I reflect on the fact that at least those auditors were willing to show up in person, willing to put themselves in our midst. These days the auditors sit in their corporate boardrooms, issuing their decrees on what unseen teachers and students must do

After six months of Scrabble immersion, Jack beat me by 200 points and began working his way through the teacher-created curriculum, completing the graduation requirements in two years. I could document in detail the tremendous personal and intellectual growth Jack made. Suffice it to say that he changed his career goal from Scrabble hustler to career man in the Marine Corps. This is what school should be about: Teachers and curriculum being flexible enough to meet the needs of one obnoxious kid, not pretending we can shove every kid through some distant committee's phantasmic pipe dream of a necessary curriculum for the global workforce. If my colleagues and I hadn't been certified competent to judge when Jack had earned a high school diploma, he would not have been accepted by the Marine Corps. What then? We rescued this young hoodlum from the streets. Do the ed-biz-politicos and their blue-ribbon commissions really want us to throw Jack back in the gutter?

The *USA Today* editorial board rejected my op-ed piece, telling me Jack's story was "too unique" for their readers. And so I wrote another piece, describing another nonstandard student. And another. Each time I pleaded for the need for schools to be able to come up with oddball plans for oddball students. Finally I caught on. The *USA Today* editorial board wanted a pro-national-testing piece that would give newspapers the tools to show how kids in Grosse Pointe measure up against the kids in Scarsdale and Palo Alto—something of interest to the business traveler reading his free copy of *USA Today* at the hotel breakfast table. One oddball teacher and her oddball students aren't on this corporate-politico-infotainment agenda.

Years later, *Word Freak*, by *Wall Street Journal* sports reporter and National Public Radio commentator Stefan Fatsis, reconfirms my conviction about supporting Jack in his Scrabble obsessions. Fatsis says Scrabble is about "mastering the rules"; it is a "balance between risk and reward." Scrabble is also about linguistics, psychology, mathematics. In the words of the book's dust jacket, "it throws light on such notions as brilliance, memory, competition, failure, and hope." Admittedly, at the national competition level, Scrabble is also about weirdness. Here's an exchange among some of the finest players, including a former bank manager and someone whose only steady job was as a paperboy ("I was a good paperboy"), and Fatsis, the *Wall Street Journal* reporter.

"Maybe he's just weird," Fatsis says.
"We're all weird," G.I. Joel replies.
"He's weird enough to be called weird by the weird," Matt says.

Weirdness is an important concept in schools as well as in life. Not on the charts of excellence issued by the corporate-politico-infotainment battalion chiefs, those emperors of excellence who know no shame when it comes to issuing edicts about educating the nation's youth, weirdness must nonetheless be considered. I don't much care about a teacher's score on the national teacher exams; I want to know, when face-to-face with weird kids, how she behaves.

There isn't a teacher in America who doesn't already know which kids are performing on or above grade level and which ones aren't. We look at their performance day in and day out. We have plenty of standardized assessments to help us fine-tune our professional hunches. We don't need to inflict yearly 17-hour exams on kids to know how they're doing.

Concurrently with running periodic editorials advocating educational excellence and high-stakes national tests, *USA Today*, like many news organizations, has gotten into the education delivery business. On July 17, 2001, when I punched "education" on their Web site, up popped a *USA Today News Challenge*:

To which actress has Tom Cruise been romantically linked? (*Life*, 2D)

    Penelope Cruz
    Rosie O'Donnell
    Gwyneth Paltrow
    Meg Ryan

Mind boggling. These are the fellows excoriating the nation's teachers for not being excellent enough. These are the fellows who say Jack's story doesn't meet their standards.

Next an article popped up: "Ten Reasons to Work at McDonald's." After giving the pitch of why work at McDonald's is so terrific, the employee qualifications are listed. A McDonald's employee should:

- Be a team player, have the ability to work well with others.
- Have pride in themselves, outwardly and inwardly.
- Have the ability to adapt to various situations.
- Have an understanding that many others, customers and employees, rely on them to be at work when scheduled and give their best while there.
- Maintain mature behavior while at work.
- Be honest, dedicated and loyal.

Funny thing: there's no mention of algebra skills or writing a persuasive essay. No quiz on whether the person for whom Constantinople was named was a pope, a scholar, an emperor, or a poet. Kids in California need to know this bit of esoterica to pass sixth grade, not to work at McDonald's.

The characteristics any organization says it wants from employees run counter to the way teachers are being directed to run their classrooms, where competition must rule, where even kindergartners are put under the factoid gun and made to see how inadequate they are, where school makes them cry because they fear failure. Plenty of parents are crying too.

## THE NEW STRIKE ZONE

In July 2001, the baseball umpires' union filed a grievance challenging major league baseball's decision to use pitch-count averages "as a yardstick by which to measure the performance of major league umpires." Citing an average of 270 pitches a game as ideal, Sandy Alderson, head of baseball operations in the commissioner's office, complained that umpires were averaging 287.3 pitches per game. He contacted some players, telling them to call more strikes. The World Umpires Association contended that "pitch count pressure threatens the integrity of the game." Larry Barnett, longtime American League umpire with 31 years' experience, and now a supervisor, had to call a young umpire, advising him to call more strikes. Then Barnett resigned, telling the *New York Times*, "it was time for me to leave because there were things I didn't believe in, didn't fit with what I was taught. I just walked totally away from it."

The umpires' union stepped forward, insisting that focusing on pitch counts "interferes with an umpire's duty to exercise independent judgment on each pitch." In addition to the fact that the teachers' unions have backed the corporate-politico push to undercut the teacher's duty to exercise independent judgment in her classroom, there are other interesting contrasts with the teacher "strike zone." Sports columnists were quick to mock the owners' attempt to define and manipulate the game, insisting that umpires must be allowed to do their jobs. In contrast, few members of the media elite seem to trust teachers to do their jobs. For teachers, 30 years' experience counts for nothing.

Editorially, *USA Today* is consistent with their Standardista approach to education, grumbling about umpires taking a "cavalier approach" to their job. *USA Today* also plays the high-tech card, warning that technology exists to check out whether individual umpires are calling the full strike zone and not their own idiosyncratic preferences. We learn that electronic systems developed to track missiles have been installed in six ballparks. These devices create a three-dimensional video image of each batter's strike zone. The editorialist concludes, "But umpires have long resisted accountability or management-imposed standards.

If umpires persist in not calling strikes according to the rules, baseball could threaten to give the job to its electronic eyes."

This sounds chillingly similar to the way reading teachers are replaced by scripted curriculum and computerized reading delivery systems used in Los Angeles and elsewhere. Funny thing: the fans weren't complaining about the umps' calls—not any more than is traditional. The players weren't complaining—not any more than usual.

Professor Thomas DiBacco weighed in, "Get this straight: Umpiring is like my profession, teaching. You call—or grade—as you honestly see fit. Any attempt to interfere with that responsibility violates integrity."

Amen.

News coming out of schools today sounds more like stockyards quotes from grains futures. Or pork bellies. Maybe it's past time for parents to stop putting up with their children being rated as though they were so many slabs of beef. Steve Orel was an adult-education instructor at the World of Opportunity (WOO) in Birmingham, Alabama. When 522 Birmingham high school students were pushed out of school for "lack of interest" just before the administration of the SAT-9 test in the spring of 2000, Steve set out to rescue them. Fired by the city school system for rocking the boat, Steve joined up with the local Catholic community and members of the Birmingham Human Rights Project, and created the World of Opportunity. Teachers and students from around the country have sent books and supplies. Steve notes that "Especially gratifying is that a lot of the support came from the very pockets of this country where test resisters are under attack. Just short of their one-year anniversary, the WOO enrolled their 504th student and saw their 4th student earn his GED. This young man didn't skip a beat, but came in the next day to begin studying the Windows 98 operating system and to enroll in the Health Care class and begin a career in nursing. Steve has provided an item analysis of President Bush's blueprint for education. Politicians call this plan "No Child Left Behind"; parents and teachers call it "No Child Left Untested."

## What's Missing?

Item analysis of President Bush's blueprint for education: "No Child Left Behind"[1]

| Code | Term | Frequency |
|------|------|-----------|
| 1 | Student | 87 |
| 2 | Education/educate | 87 |
| 3 | Fund(s) | 68 |
| 4 | Teacher | 45 |
| 5 | Achievement | 39 |
| 6 | Assessment | 30 |
| 7 | Parent | 27 |
| 8 | Standards | 21 |
| 9 | Reward | 15 |
| 10 | Sanction | 11 |
| 11 | Bonus | 09 |
| 12 | Test | 09 |
| 13 | Learning | 09 |
| 14 | Community | 08 |
| 15 | Private | 08 |
| 16 | Failure | 06 |
| 17 | Consequence | 04 |
| 18 | Study | 01 |
| 19 | Fundamental | 01 |
| 20 | Standardized | 01 |

*(continued on next page)*

Item analysis of President Bush's blueprint for education: "No Child Left Behind"[1] *(continued)*

| Code | Term | Frequency |
| --- | --- | --- |
| 1 | Creativity | 0 |
| 2 | Curiosity | 0 |
| 3 | Democracy | 0 |
| 4 | Esteem | 0 |
| 5 | Fun | 0 |
| 6 | Happiness | 0 |
| 7 | Imagination | 0 |
| 8 | Independence | 0 |
| 9 | Joy | 0 |
| 10 | Laughter | 0 |
| 11 | Love | 0 |
| 12 | Peace | 0 |
| 13 | Pleasure | 0 |
| 14 | Pride | 0 |
| 15 | Soul | 0 |
| 16 | Spirit | 0 |
| 17 | Tolerance | 0 |
| 18 | Virtue | 0 |
| 19 | Whimsy | 0 |
| 20 | Zeal | 0 |

[1]http://www.whitehouse.gov/news/reports/no-child-left-behind.html
This "What's Missing?" item analysis is based on a research method found in *One Size Fits Few: The Folly of Educational Standards* (Heinemann 1999) by Susan Ohanian.

Tom Meyer © The San Francisco Chronicle. Reprinted with permission.

## Chapter 6

# Ask the Experts: Should the Fox Be in Charge of the Henhouse?

Shall we, then, thus lightly suffer our children to listen to any chance stories fashioned by any chance teachers and so to take into their minds opinions for the most part contrary to those that we shall think it desirable for them to hold when they are grown up?

By no manner of means will we allow it.

*The Republic,* Plato

Lining up solidly behind Plato's assertion that any chance remarks from any chance teachers must be eliminated from the schools are: Keith E. Bailey, Roy Barnes, Craig R. Barrett, William J. Bennett, Teresa Bergeson, Frank Brogan, Wilbert Bryant, John E. Chubb, P. M. Condit, Christopher Cross, Gray Davis, David Driscoll, Eugene W. Hickok, Denis P. Doyle, John Engler, Bill Evers, Sandra Feldman, Chester E. Finn, Jr., Lou Gerstner, Jay P. Greene, Eric A. Hanushek, Kati Haycock, E. D. Hirsch, Caroline M. Hoxby, Frank Keating, Lisa Graham Keegan, Kurt Landgraf, Gary Locke, Robert L. Linn, Jaime Molera, William J. Moloney, Mark Musik, Jim Nelson, David Packard, Rod Paige, Thomas Payzant, Diane Ravitch, Lauren Resnick, S. Paul Reville, Edwin B. Rust, Jr., Arthur F. Ryan, Linda C. Schrenko, Robert Schwartz, Bob Taft, Abigail Thernstrom, Tommy Thompson, Marc S. Tucker, Paul Vallas, Herbert J. Walberg, Charles Zogby. And a host of others.

Materials shoveled into schools to prevent teachers' chance stories are too numerous to list, but the reading programs that treat teachers as mere clerks in a corporate one-size-fits-all system of skills delivery include: *Accelerated Reader, Corrective Reading, Lexile Framework for Reading, Open Court, Reading Counts, Reading Mastery*, and *Success for All*. Parents whose children are subjected to these materials should be aware that their children are losing out on the wit and whimsy and the deeply personal experiences of what reading is all about.

Take the Sylvan Corporation's Book Adventure management program. It offers a second grader who punches in what types of books she likes nearly 300 titles. To their credit, one of these titles is a riddle book, *Batty Riddles*. One out of three hundred is paltry, but let us praise any ray of hope we can find. In its kindergarten–Grade 2 selected titles list, the New York State Education Department offers only 90 titles, and not a riddle book in the lot.

For a child like my friend Gracie, who loves poetry, neither Sylvan Learning Systems nor the New York State Education Department offers satisfactory recommendations. Even given their very loose system of categorizing any rhyming book as poetry, Sylvan offers only nine poetry possibilities (one of which is Ludwig Bemelman's *Madeline's Rescue*, a fun read but not poetry). Of New York State's 90 recommended K-2 titles, just eight are poetry, and these include Mother Goose and the *Eensy Weensy Spider: Fingerplays and Action Rhymes*, slim pickings indeed for Gracie. Gracie was lucky, though. Lori Perlman, her second-grade teacher, offered a classroom library of chance encounters with about 70 poetry titles, books containing the play and profundity of Ciardi, McCord, Florian, Lewis, Hoberman, Aldis, Basho, Coatsworth, Esbensen, Farber, Fisher, Worth, Smith, Singer, O'Neill, Nash, Moore, Merriam, Hoban, Holman, Kennedy, Prelutsky, Silverstein, Kuskin, Stevenson, Dakos, Updike, George, and many, many more. What a list: it beats the Standardista schedules and timelines into mush.

With Sylvan, Gracie can take the on-line quiz on Bill Grossman's *My Little Sister Ate One Hare* and win points to qualify for a free game of miniature golf at www.putt-putt.com or win a coupon for $3 off on any regularly priced footwear at Kmart. If she doesn't like these prizes, she can hope her teacher will buy her something from Scholastic's *Reading Counts!* Web site: T-shirts, baseball caps, trophies, mini-footballs, squeeze bottles, key rings, beanbag toys, and lots, lots more. And thus, a child's love of poems is reduced to one more item in the education of the American consumer.

But Gracie's teacher offers her books, not frippery. Exploring the shelves, Gracie discovers a book of sea poems, and her teacher finds her reading aloud to herself,

> I must go down to the sea again, for the call of the running tide
> Is a wild call and a clear call that may not be denied.

John Masefield is hardly standard fare for seven-year-olds. And that's the point. In a nonstandard classroom, one devoted to the teacher nurturing that grows from the chance encounters so disparaged by Standardistas, a child like Gracie becomes expert at something she loves. On February 21, 2001, President Bush the Younger said, "You can teach a child to read, and he or her will be able to pass a literacy test." There's the tragedy: The man driving Congress to pass regulations about testing and teaching reading thinks the reason to teach reading is so kids can pass tests. A second tragedy came home to me when I obtained beautiful posters to celebrate Poetry Month—a short poem for every day of the month. Gracie's teacher loved the poster. Three other teachers to whom I offered them expressed regret, "There's no time in the test preparation curriculum to 'do' a poem a day." Not even two minutes to read a poem out loud.

## SPEEDING UP THE THREE-MINUTE EGG

M. F. K. Fisher once pointed out that a three-minute egg took about the same length of time to boil in 1922 as it did in 1722. And things are no better in 2002: still three minutes. Eggs can dawdle, but kindergartners can't. As soon as they walk in the door, they are on the no-frills, high-skill conveyer belt to college. Out with the blocks and paints; in with math workbooks. Standardistas shriek that kids are getting dumber and dumber, but facts show differently. I learned the difference between sedimentary and metamorphic rocks in a college geology course. Today, third graders encounter such niceties in their science text. A fifth grader encounters more new vocabulary words in science than do students taking introductory French in high school.

While studying in Aix-en-Provence, I found occasional work typing up manuscripts penned in M. F. K. Fisher's almost indecipherable handwriting. Unfamiliar with the *New Yorker* and raised on Kraft's macaroni dinner and roast beef cooked until it came up burnt umber clear through, I found it astounding to be working for someone who cared so much about food, most often food I'd never heard of. But even in the green days of youth, I understood expertise when I met it, and I understood that Mary Frances was talking about more than food. I wonder what Mary Frances Kennedy, with her disdain for the obsessive weighing and measuring of foodstuff, would make of our national fixation for rating students like so many slabs of beef. Speaking of the "ghastly good balance" nutrition fanatics tried to bring to eating, Fisher insisted that people are different. Some feel better with two meals, others with five. Some need more proteins, others more broccoli. I wonder why it is so difficult to convince Standardistas that different children have different curricular needs. It seems so obvious. But to understand this principle, one has to understand teaching and learning at more than a behavioristic checklist level. Teaching is a lived occupation, not an abstraction. Like eunuchs in a harem, Standardistas can see the action performed but can't do it themselves.

Take Sarah. She was one of a group of high schoolers so obnoxious and troubled they were denied access to the regular campus and sent to our storefront school. My teaching partner and I were officially on the books as public-school employees, but everybody left us alone—just so long as we kept control of the rejects. On probation for various infractions of the law, Sarah was sullen and uncooperative. Showing up because the law required it, she spent as little time as possible on academic pursuits. Then we discovered her ambition: Sarah loved to cook. When we held out a promise to help her continue her studies at a culinary institute once she earned her high school diploma, she began to work seriously for that diploma. When Sarah graduated, she prepared and served an elegant meal for her teachers. I was definitely in the presence of an expert—and she hadn't even set foot in a culinary institute yet.

The Standardistas who might sneer at the idea of high school teachers encouraging a student to become a cook would do well to read *Haute Cuisine: How the French Invented the Culinary Profession* by Amy Trubek.

> In the first semester at a leading culinary school in the United States, students must master the fundamentals of stock preparation and learn the five mother sauces of French haute cuisine as well as their many derivations. In "Knife Skills" class they learn to hold the French chef's knife and perfect the transformation of raw vegetables into precise mirepoix, brunoise, julienne, and bâtonet. They also learn the biographies of French chefs Antonin Carême and Auguste Escoffier. . . .

Surely just as rigorous as studying algebra or Shakespeare's sonnets. And maybe a whole lot more beneficial to society. William Bennett, Lou Gerstner, members of the U.S. Congress and their designated, for-hire experts insist they know what's best for the Sarahs in our schools. Parents and teachers must hold the line, resolving never to betray a single child to dogma. The global economy should crumble before we sell out children to the Standardistas.

Eileen McNamara, *Boston Globe* staff writer, gets to the heart of the matter when she asks, "How can we argue that what we expect our children to know is not arbitrary?"

Ask a dozen people for a detailed list of information that kids should know, and you'll get a dozen different lists. We may well agree on fundamentals, but as soon as you try to get to the details, things get messy. And in the end they are arbitrary, which is why the Code of Hammurabi appears in sixth grade in some standards and high school in others. Only William Bennett puts it in second grade. Education Trust trumpets that "College Begins in Kindergarten." On the topic of the failures of African-Americans and Hispanics taking the New York Regents exam, Education Trust CEO Katy Haycock made one of the most outrageous, cruel, and asinine statements imaginable: "At least they failed something worthwhile." That one is worth reading again: "At least they failed something worthwhile."

Pushed by a corporate agenda for producing the kind of docile workers big business finds profitable, our politicians and their state boards of education functionaries are determined to turn all kids into cooked squash. Summarizing the revolt against testing by Scarsdale, New York, parents, *New York Times* columnist Gail Collins commented, "Those who can't, test."

Executives of the Fortunate 500 and their political and media lackeys, for whom schoolrooms are terra incognita, have never met Gracie or Sarah—or heard their stories. They are scornful of me and my teacher colleagues; they are disdainful of principals and superintendents who don't cozy up to the idea of raising the bar and targeting students; they are disdainful of people who doubt that a sixth grader's knowledge of the treaties between the U.S. and the Soviet Union in the 1970s and 1980s should determine their advancement to seventh grade or whether a high schooler's knowledge of the third-string metaphysical poet George Herbert determines his worthiness for a high school diploma. Standardistas proclaim that test scores are expert, and students' classroom performance and teachers' training, experience, and good judgment be damned. Like Plato, they don't want "chance stories fashioned by any chance teachers" to infect students and perhaps lead them to stray from the established agenda. Parents beware: Never eat at a place called Mom's. Never play cards with a man called Doc. Never trust your child to a man who has a plan that works for all children.

## TWENTY PERCENT EXPENDABLE

Washington State Superintendent of Public Instruction Terry Bergeson said that if the state continues to see increases on test scores, the goal of 80 percent of Washington students meeting the standards in 10 years is within reach. Treating 20 percent of our children as expendable seems to be common throughout the high-stakes-testing states. In the days of Vietnam, people of the same ilk spoke of "acceptable losses" and "collateral damage."

Professor Don Orlich says what too few academicians dare speak aloud, "The WASL (Washington Assessment of Student Learning) has a disturbing moral dimension. Is it moral to use the police powers of the state to coerce all fourth-grade children to experience a test they have little chance of passing? How moral is it to watch children and teachers spending between 8 and 20 days to prepare for and administer the WASL?" Don Orlich insists, "If you're going to have a test that has anything fair about it, children must have a decent chance of succeeding." If the state of Washington imposes a test on its children knowing that 20 percent will not pass it, shouldn't they be held accountable to that 20 percent and their parents?

Orlich is a curriculum expert. None of the Standardistas in Olympia will answer his questions.

Rosemary Fitton, the Washington Assistant Superintendent for Assessment Research and Curriculum, said that the state is still working out some bugs in the tests. Bugs in the test? These are nine- and ten-year-olds we're talking about. Have these testocrats considered what it means to a fourth grader to be labeled a failure? How are the two-thirds of the fourth graders who failed the math test in 1999 doing now? Fitton calls it "bugs"; I call it bats in the belfry. And worse. Soren Kierkegaard said, "Life can only be understood backwards; but it must be lived forwards." That's for adults. Children only live forward. They have no notion that maybe a few decades hence they will be able to look back in tranquility on the present misery that school offers.

Tumwater schools superintendent Nick Broissoit doesn't talk about bugs or 20 percent. He told an *Olympian* reporter, "The test is too damaging. Kids don't function that way. They need to have hope." Broissoit has the guts to admit that some students will never pass the test. Some don't test well; others don't learn enough—often through no fault of their own or the schools either. It's the dirty little secret that few people in the country will admit: All kids can't achieve at high standards, all kids can't pass the state tests, no matter how many $50-an-hour test tutors the state hires. In Broissoit's words, "Public school is not like a dry cleaner, where you drop them off, then pick them up all starched and pressed."

But the other problem is whether the tests are fair about how they rate students. In Washington, 88 percent of the students who finished 10th grade passed math class; 28 percent of them passed math on WASL. And 89 percent passed English classes; 53 percent passed reading WASL; 27 percent passed writing WASL. Parents must decide: Either the students are stupid, lazy, and irresponsible, or the teachers are stupid, lazy, and irresponsible. Or the test is whacko. Parents must decide: Whom do you trust? Your neighborhood teacher or the corporate-political cabal?

In Boston, they have a way of dealing with whacko tests, enshrining them as the only thing that counts. On May 1, 2000, Superintendent of Schools Thomas Payzant sent this memo:

To: Principals, Headmasters, Directors of Instruction, Program
    Directors, Chief Academic Officers, Teachers
ME (memo) From: Thomas Payzant
Re: Standards-Based Instruction and Assessment
Date: November 1, 2000

As the first marking term comes to a close, I wanted to reaffirm the system's focus on standards-based instruction and assessment, and its impact on students' grades.

The standards included in the BPS Citywide Learning Standards define what every student should know and be able to do, year by year and course by course. Teachers are expected to use the standards, and related course guides, pacing documents, and assessment instruments, to guide and assess their instruction, and students' learning, throughout the school year. Teachers' assessments should align with the standards and assess students' mastery of the content and skills included in the standards. Students' grades should accurately reflect their level of mastery.

Last year, many students' grades did not reflect their mastery of the content and skills included in the standards. For example, many students who scored at level 1 on the MCAS received passing or exemplary grades in English language arts, math, science and history. Further, many students received passing grades in these same subjects even though they failed to meet the district's minimum competency reading benchmarks. I recognize we are only beginning to implement the standards in some subjects and grades (e.g., elementary social studies). I also recognize that some students' strong in-class performance and poor test-taking abilities may explain the difference between a failing test score and a passing grade. However, the gap between the scores our students receive on the district's and state's assessments, and the grades they received, remains far too great. This gap must close. This is a multifaceted problem that requires a multifaceted response. Teachers who are not closely aligning their instruction with the standards, and setting an appropriate pace, must do so immediately. Principals and headmasters must help teachers understand how to do this, hold them accountable for doing so, and call upon central support services for assistance as needed.

Teachers must also hold students accountable for their performance and assign grades based on academic performance. Students not meeting standards should not earn passing grades.

Grades should not be given to students on the basis of attendance, attitude or effort.

In addition, if students are going to meet the standards we have
set, they must read grade-level materials with fluency. All teachers
must help students learn how to search for main ideas, supporting
details, key vocabulary, and other critical information; to capture
their findings in well-constructed notes or organizers; and to dissect
and answer thoughtful, MCAS-like questions on a regular basis.

This work is nonnegotiable. We are in our fifth year of standards based instruction. Teachers' instruction, assessments, and
grades must be closely aligned with the standards, and students'
grades should accurately reflect their mastery of the content and
skills included in the standards. When students are attending
regularly, working hard, but performing poorly, we must make
sure they have access to every available resource to remedy their
problems, support them every step of the way, and give them the
grades they have earned.

If teachers teach to the standards, students are provided with
appropriate supports, and students continue to work hard, I am
extremely confident our students will meet the standards and
earn passing grades. Thank you for all the energy, hard work and
emotional investment required to do this work well.

Just call him Yoda. "Do or do not. There is no 'try.'" The orders
Payzant issues might work in the movies, but in the real world not all
kids grow up to be Luke Skywalker.

You can wash your hands after handling Payzant's memo, but it's
hard to wash the stain from your mind. When the state rules, teacher
expertise counts for naught, while test writers' expertise rules the king-
dom. Payzant specifically orders teachers not to count attendance, attitude or effort, and he specifically orders them to run their classes as
test prep factories. Surely this must be a knife in the heart of parents
who know how different each of their children is; how nonsensical it
is to treat them all the same; nonsensical, also, and vicious, to expect
the same from them. Equal educational opportunity cannot mean

treating everybody the same. William Cala, superintendent of schools in Freeport, New York, says that *all* really doesn't mean *all* when it comes to providing support, instruction, caring, compassion, and opportunity. "*All* simply means *all* when it comes to testing. *All* means *only those left standing* after an assault of narrow, biased, bigoted tests." Those left standing receive the state's diplomas. Everybody else becomes collateral damage.

What Payzant is ordering all Boston teachers to do is even more damnable when you realize that the MCAS tests students on materials significantly beyond their grade level, so of course the test scores are low for many.

Dave Stratman, a Boston parent and organizer of MassRefusal, pointed out to the Boston School Committee that Payzant's position is even worse than arbitrary support of MCAS. "Aligning grades with MCAS means erasing the professional, day-to-day judgment of teachers as a factor in judging children's development." How do Payzant and crew spell Machiavelli? By eliminating the obvious mismatch between the teacher's assessment of a student's accomplishments and his MCAS score, authorities erase any evidence that there might be anything wrong with the MCAS. With only its own loony assessments of students' abilities left, the state rests its case. When they can ignore and erase all expert dissension, the state will win every time.

Teachers have disputed the readability of the MCAS fourth-grade reading test from the beginning. Pitched at an average seventh-grade level of difficulty, some selections range as high as the eleventh-grade reading level. When this problem was brought to the attention of the Department of Education (DOE) in 1997, the DOE promised to make adjustments in subsequent tests. "The DOE has not kept its promise," observes Linda Sarage, a sixth-grade teacher and member of Western Massachusetts CARE. The resistance group points out that third graders receiving Iowa test scores placing them higher than 50 percent of all third graders in the country received "failing" marks on the MCAS. The answer from school districts is to stop giving the Iowa test and rely solely on the MCAS. Researchers at Boston College have shown that many students who score in the higher percentiles on the TIMSS science test in the eighth grade or the PSATs in the tenth grade have scored in the "failing" or "needs improvement" categories on the MCAS.

This kind of state manipulation of schools for their own unacknowledged agenda gives rise to revolution. Sarage told a *Salon* reporter that resistance to the test has become her passion. "Working on MCAS is the only way I can walk into my classroom and hold my head high. This whole standardized testing movement is like being on a moving walkway. Working actively against it allows me to keep my sanity."

Community dissent grows. In January 2001, the Massachusetts chapter of the American Association of University Women resolved that the group does not support the use of MCAS as the sole requirement for graduation from high school. Former Judge Sumner Kaplan of the American Jewish Congress says, "Businesses may have the money, but we have the people and the power." Her comment refers to the fact that big backers of the MCAS include BankBoston, Federal Reserve Bank of Boston, Hewlett-Packard, IBM, National Alliance for Business, Pioneer Institute, State Street Corporation. In late February 2001, a coalition of business leaders, led by William Edgerly, the retired chairman of State Street Corporation, launched an advertising blitz to support MCAS. "We operate in a globally competitive economy, and we are accustomed to the unforgiving accountability of the marketplace," Edgerly wrote in the *Boston Globe*. He also wrote, "Without the high-stakes element, neither schools nor students will be motivated." He is repeating the same old party line: assume the worst of teachers and students.

The next day, *Boston Globe* reporter Eileen McNamara wrote, "Forget 'we.' What about 'them,' the children?" McNamara is one of the few reporters in the country who consistently asks about the children.

## FINDING PATTERNS

In a letter to the editor in the *New York Times*, Catherine Gardner put a child perspective on testing results. Her daughter scored very poorly on the fourth-grade standardized test. "Years later, I learned why. She understood how to darken the appropriate square on the answer sheet. But after a few answers, she became intrigued with the pattern formed and used that pattern to complete the entire test." If Catherine Gardner's daughter were in fourth grade in Boston, she'd be repeating the grade.

This child's test performance is one reason child psychologists caution against putting too much emphasis on the results of bubble-in tests given to young children; they caution that such tests shouldn't even be administered to children in the lower grades. Some children find it very difficult to line up the answer sheet with the questions; some lose track of the task and, like Catherine Gardner's daughter, daydream a little, inventing their own task. Some are just too frightened by all the pressure to be able to perform well. What about the San Jose third grader that bilingual expert Stephen Cary saw struggling with a SAT-9 practice test on English reading comprehension? "The girl spoke maybe a dozen words of English, max. She looked at the first page of incomprehensible text, shook her head slowly, and began chewing on her pencil. Her eyes filled with tears and before mine followed suit, I left the room to compose myself."

Stephen continues, "Here's a kid who needs some nice comfortable visual text, maybe a Gon book or a Looney Tunes comic. And I actually think her teacher would use those materials if he could. But he's got to meet the standards, got to give the practice tests, got to raise the test scores, got to keep his job. Almost makes me angry enough to quit education and run for the state legislature."

If all this weren't troublesome enough, then there was the snafu on the WASL in Washington, proving, perhaps, that item writers get as bored as students. In a math logic question, 10th graders were asked to figure out a bus driver's route through four imaginary towns. The right answer was: Mayri, Clay, Lee, Turno. When students pointed out that this name sequence, when said out loud, sounded very much like "Mary K. Letourneau," Washington's most notorious teacher, jailed for child rape after having two children fathered by a former student with whom she began a sexual liaison when he was 12, the state Office of Superintendent of Public Instruction ordered high schools to direct students who hadn't yet taken the test not to answer that question. Riverside Publishing, a unit of Houghton Mifflin and developer of the WASL, employer of hundreds of item writers, says the person who wrote that item no longer works for them.

Speaking at the Virginia Forum in July 2000, Dr. Lawrence H. Cross, professor of educational research, evaluation and policy studies, titled his remarks "Virginia schools need accountability for the tests as well as the tested."

> ". . . there is good reason to challenge the validity of SOL test scores as measures of student proficiency and their use in awarding diplomas and rating schools for accreditation. . . . But even if the SOL tests were beyond reproach, the use of test scores as the ultimate criterion for graduation decision violates professional standards for test use. Test scores should inform professional opinion, not override it."

## STUDENTS PERFORM POORLY BECAUSE THEY ARE ASKED TO DO THE WRONG THING

The one good thing about the Massachusetts Comprehensive Assessment System questions is that they are not secret. Questions are made public after the tests are given. So the public can see how truly goofy they are. Here's a question asked of fourth graders:

> Monique is taking a train to Boston. Her train is stopped at the station.
> She is facing the direction the train will be moving. All she can see from her window is the train next to her. That train is also going to Boston and leaves first. As the other train leaves, it seems to Monique as if:
> a) She is moving forward.
> b) She is moving backward.
> c) The other train is moving backward.
> d) The train station is moving.

No law of physics will help a student answer this question. You can only answer it if you've been on a train. And you have to have been in a position where you saw only the other train. If you saw people stand-ing on the platform, you wouldn't have gotten that motion sensation. How many Massachusetts 10-year-olds are seasoned train riders? And what global economy skill will getting the right answer demonstrate?

Here's another MCAS question:

Which of the following people was the first to serve as a United States president?
a) Andrew Jackson          c) James Monroe
b) James Polk              d) John Adams

Most kids know that none of this crew was first.

Experience tutoring in MCAS math forced John E. Cawthorne to denounce MCAS on the WGBH educational television site. Assis-tant dean for students and outreach in the School of Education at Boston College, Cawthorne worked for an hour a day with high school students, helping them prepare for the MCAS tests in May 2001. Cawthorne used released items from the MCAS and Kaplan's SAT review to teach students. In Cawthorne's words, "This decision led to a remarkable discovery. The MCAS is more difficult than the SATs. The test that is given by the Commonwealth to students at the end of grade 10 is more difficult than the test that first-semester sen-iors take for college admission. The test used to determine whether one will graduate from high school is more difficult than the test that predicts how students will fare in their first semester in college." Cawthorne, clearly stunned, asks, " Am I the only one who recognizes the absurdity of this finding?"

Cawthorne says students found the SAT math difficult but easier than the MCAS math. "They often found the MCAS linguistically con-fusing; they would often give up, feeling frustrated and inadequate."

Cawthorne concludes that the MCAS math "would likely be too difficult for all but the top achievers. It is patently unfair, on a test re-quired for graduation, to use items that only a few can answer cor-rectly." He opines that if the other sections are like the math, the MCAS is irreparably flawed. "In its present form, the MCAS is more demanding than the admission test colleges use. It seems that we have entered into a Kafkaesque world. Slogans such as 'our children deserve nothing less' masquerade as reality. When reality does not reflect the slogan, it is summarily dismissed. Slogans cannot change that fact that the MCAS is tragically flawed. It is immoral to use a flawed instrument to decide the future of our young people."

There's that word again—spreading across the continent from Washington to Massachusetts: Immoral tests.

Acknowledging that the MCAS exam is "widely regarded as one of the nation's most challenging state tests," the *Boston Globe* noted that students taking the 2001 MCAS got their lowest marks on the data and probability questions. What the paper, a supporter of the MCAS, doesn't acknowledge is that the questions are both flawed and inappropriate for high schoolers. Eugene Gallagher, an oceanographer and associate professor in the environmental science program, teaches the graduate applied statistics courses at the University of Massachusetts, Boston. He wrote a letter to the Massachusetts Commissioner of Education and the MCAS staff, offering a detailed explanation of why three of the six questions on the 2001 10th-grade MCAS in math that deal specifically with probability and statistics are "too badly flawed to be used in deciding the overall grade." Gallagher pointed out that "versions of one of the questions can be found in several college-level probability texts, but the MCAS testers phrased it improperly, so that the only correct answer is not among the four choices."

Gallagher's graduate classes at the University of Massachusetts have met the calculus requirement for admission. When he asked a select group to answer the six MCAS probability and statistics questions, the students, most of whom had GRE math scores above the 90th percentile, only four of nine got it right. Gallagher summarizes, "Not one of the graduate students could provide a statistically based answer to the open-response Question 40c. Four of the nine left the question blank or with large question marks indicating that they didn't know what was being asked. As I suspected, this question is nearly unanswerable." Gallagher says that those who answered would probably get 0 points on the MCAS open-response scale.

There it is: In order to be eligible for a high school diploma, Massachusetts students must answer college-level questions (that even graduate students in a statistics course can't answer).

## ALGEBRA OR ELSE

Algebra, once the cauliflower of the curriculum, now rules the roost. "Algebra equals empowerment," Tamara Henry announced in *USA Today*, parroting the easy jingoistic phrase of the day, one supporting her newspaper's editorial scream for a national test. Others, people with the advantage of having more savvy about education than a turnip, tell a different story. Noted researcher Gerald Bracey says the nation has been "algebra-scammed." Writing in *Education Week*, Bracey says, "Quick, given $(ax2 + bx + c = 0)$, derive the formula for solving quadratic equations." Bracey concludes, "Although algebra is all about finding values in equations, it has no value for most people." Worse, cramming algebra down all kids' throats "is more likely to turn kids off math, and even off school altogether, than to identify hidden talent." Bracey insists that the people in charge of schools need to pay attention to the correlation between forcing kids to take algebra and increased dropout rates.

When a *Milwaukee Journal Sentinel* headline screamed, "Only 1 in 4 students moves beyond basic math," Dennis Redovich, longtime educator and director of the Center for the Study of Jobs & Education in Wisconsin and the United States, retorted that math testing results in general and NAEP scores in particular are "much ado about nothing." Redovich notes that although testocrats insist that all students must be prepared for the high-skill jobs of the complex high-tech global economy, "The facts are that technology makes jobs simpler, a worker more productive, and everyday tasks easier. A majority of jobs require only short-term training. Only about four percent of jobs 'might' require advanced math or science skills. What is the problem? Where is the crisis? The United States has more college graduates than it needs for most jobs."

Traditionally, the real use of algebra has been as a screening device for some colleges. Now Standardistas want to make algebra not just a gatekeeper to college, but a high hurdle to a high school diploma. They do this at great peril. As Redovich reports, 40 percent of Milwaukee ninth graders fail algebra, and ninth graders constitute more than 40 percent of Milwaukee's dropouts. As a consequence of the algebra hurdle, the ninth-grade class in Milwaukee has been getter larger each year. "The kids fail algebra, sit around in ninth grade until they're 16 or 17 and then just disappear." Writing in *The Oklahoma Observer*, Jim R. Slater, president-elect of the Oklahoma Association of Secondary School Principals, says there are two reasons to raise the bar for high school graduation by requiring algebra for every student:

1)  To make good jumpers jump higher;
2)  To make not-so-good jumpers fail.

Slater adds, "Requiring every non-special education student to pass algebra to get a high school diploma makes as much sense as requiring every student with two good legs to run a 12-second 100 meter dash as a graduation requirement."

## GLIMPSES OF REAL-WORLD MATH

A few years ago, inspired by all the hoopla about the mathematics crisis in U.S. schools, I sent out several hundred letters to famous people, asking them a few questions about mathematics in their own lives.

1.  What did you like about math in school?
2.  What did you hate about math in school?
3.  Can you think of some incident, in or out of school, that made math seem interesting and maybe even awesome to you?
4.  Describe the importance of mathematics in your professional and/or personal life.
5.  Do you have any math advice for students today?

For starters, I wrote the editors-in-chief at the *New York Times*, the *New York Post*, the *New York Daily News*, the *Washington Post*, the *Boston Globe*, and *USA Today*, all of which have run plenty of editorials bemoaning the lamentable math education children receive in our schools. No one answered.

Next, I wrote people with interesting jobs at zoos and people who work for various wildlife, ecology, and preservation agencies, desert museums; I wrote poets, psychologists, museum curators; I wrote an undertaker who had recently published a lovely little book about his trade; I wrote cartoonists, long-distance runners, professors of medicine, epidemiologists, astronauts, George Bush the Elder, and the Postmaster General. Busy people all, none responded, not even in the name of giving advice to teachers and students. I'd say the real disappointments among the no-shows were the Car Guys, Famous Amos, Debbi Fields, and Ben & Jerry. I know the Car Guys can be depended on to denounce algebra, and I do wonder about the math involved in cookies and ice cream. My letter to Mario Cuomo bounced back—no forwarding address. Too bad: I'd love to hear him temporize about "algebra for all."

Some people extended the courtesy of responding that they weren't going to respond: FAME, subtitled Management Enterprises, wrote, explaining that Patrick Ewing "believes mathematics is very important in succeeding," adding that his busy schedule "does not allow him the luxury of taking part in surveys." Bill Gates sent his regrets from his e-mail address, askbill@microsoft.com (Askbill Questions). Go ahead, ask him. According to his public relations manager, he appreciates questions. He just doesn't have time to answer them, not if they're about math, anyway. Lou Gerstner's office at IBM phoned, expressing his "so many regrets," and explaining that "pressing business" prevented his participation in "this very worthy project." Hearing that Gerstner was busy, I watched the news for more downsizing. Allen Greenspan's office sent his regrets, and sent along a long profile of the Federal Reserve Board Chairman from *Dow Jones News/Retrieval* that indicates a bookish teenager Allen liked playing the tenor saxophone and reading the novels of Ayn Rand. Miss Manners sent her regrets. Maestro Zubin Mehta sent his regrets. Mr. Rogers sent his regrets.

Mary Kay Ash, at home recovering from a stroke, sent word that when she was at the helm of her Dallas-based company, she did not handle any of the financial aspects. She says she is "the first to admit that her son, Richard, has always balanced my checkbook."

Julia Child penned brief answers on the questionnaire—and wrote a letter besides. Her 75-year-old math trauma fairly jumps off the page.

Q: What did you like about math in school?
A: Nothing.
Q: What did you hate about math in school?
A: The teacher and the subject.
Q: Can you think of some incident, in or out of school, that made math seem interesting, maybe even awesome, to you?
A: NO!!
Q: Describe the importance of mathematics in your professional and/or personal life.
A: Simple math for metric/U.S. translations; recipe portions, etc.
Q: Do you have any math advice for students today?
A: Find nice, warm, fun teachers!

Julia Child added, "I hated every minute of math when I was in school 75 years ago, and I hope the methods of teaching it have improved."

Will Shortz, the *New York Times* crossword puzzle editor as well as the puzzle guru on National Public Radio, also answered every question—in pencil. Geometry was his all-time favorite subject in school, and he didn't hate anything about math, though in retrospect, he doesn't think calculus was particularly useful. Will loved proving theorems, insisting, "It was like having a class in puzzle-solving every day." He reflects, "I grew up solving the mathematical puzzles of Sam Loyd. He was my childhood hero. At one time I even considered making a career in mathematics. I eventually realized, though, that it wasn't so much the mathematics that excited me as the puzzle aspect." As for the importance of mathematics in his professional life, Will says, "Mathematics is great training for the mind. It's indirectly useful in almost any career. As a professional puzzle maker and editor, of course, I use math all the time." He advises students, "If you can, approach mathematics as a game, with real-life connections. That makes it more fun and relevant."

Federal Express CEO Frederick W. Smith's reply was delivered by the U.S. Postal Service. Fred confesses he didn't like much about math in school and particularly disliked calculus. Nothing in school made math seem awesome, but over time, the use of statistics, especially in business, has fascinated him. He rates statistics as "a key factor in building Fed Ex," and advises students that math "is the key to all business activities and the effective management of any type of organization. Study hard!"

Hizzoner New York City Mayor Rudy Giuliani says, "As a young high school student, I loved the challenge of a long complicated calculus problem and the feeling of accomplishment when all the pieces fell into place and the equation was finally solved."

He confesses, "As a young high school student I hated the challenge of a long and complicated calculus problem and the feeling of frustration when none of the pieces fell into place and the equation remained unsolved!" Rudy can be forgiven for bragging a little, "In my role as mayor of New York City—the largest and most complicated city in America—math has proved invaluable to my understanding of an ability to produce a $33 billion balanced budget—with a surplus. Of course, it comes in handy in balancing my checkbook too. My advice to young math students in particular is to rely on brain power rather than computer power. Solving complicated math equations without the assistance of a calculator or computer will lead not only to better arithmetic skills but to clear and logical thinking and ultimately to better problem solving abilities in other areas of life."

Michael Crichton confesses he hated the earlier rote work of math facts. "But what can you do? Gotta have it." He liked algebra and geometry: "The more abstract it was, the better. But then I disliked spherical geometry and calculus—I think because I had a lousy teacher. Teaching really matters!" Crichton reflects, "I always say that when I finished high school, the two things I was certain of was that I disliked running, and I disliked mathematics. Then in my thirties I found myself programming personal computers (which did not exist when I was in high school) and relying heavily on math; and in my forties, my preferred exercise was running. So you never know how things will turn out."

Thomas Monaghan says, "During school in the orphanage that I lived in for a time, I didn't enjoy math a whole lot, but I worked hard in it anyway. I have never been 'math-minded' in the algebra or calculus types of math. However, it was my dream growing up, and into college, to become an architect. In my studies, I sure did use my geometry skills! That is the part of math that I love—the structure of it—the perfect exactness of it that makes it possible to build beautiful buildings and homes. Without math we would not have the buildings that are around us today."

Monaghan continues, "As president of Domino's Pizza, I constantly work with percentages—percentages of daily sales, weekly sales, yearly sales. We base what we do or don't do on these mathematical percentages. There are frequently cheese price increases, or pepperoni decreases due to different events in the economy or ecologically. I work with a Finance Advisory Board. This board advises me on the money market of Domino's Pizza. We are constantly looking at money, budget, marketing ploys, spending allowances, and the economy. Math generates this information. Without it, companies could not possibly survive." As far as advice to students, Monaghan says, "You may be able to let your quadratic equations slide, but don't forget the basics and the cores of math."

Popular children's author Jon Scieszka always "loved the patterns and connections numbers made in math. . . . I really loved the nine times tables. I figured them out by making the first digit one less than the number I was supposed to be multiplying. What a pattern. Plus I always felt like I was getting away with something." Jon admits he didn't love everything about math. "Logic problems and really stupid word problems always did (and still do) drive me crazy. I never cared who lived next to the girl with the brown dog and the red hat but not next to anyone with a black dog or a white hat. I guess math hell for me would be a really stupid logic word problem." Jon admits, "As a writer, I don't have to do a lot of number calculating every day. But already this morning I used mathematics to compare the cost of B-1 bombers and books in a newspaper story, estimate the number of bricks in a wall, and marvel at the self-repeating fractal shape of a broccoli stalk. Math is mental music for me. I couldn't imagine living without it." Jon advises students, "Forget about finding the 'right' answers all of the time. Find the right questions. Play with problems. Make connections. Use your mathematical sense to understand the world."

Standardistas claim that high-stakes math tests cover "things a group of people, including parents, teachers, and community members, decided all students should know." Funny thing: nobody seemed to have asked Julia Child, et al. Real-world experts, people of repute in their lines of work, don't offer any ringing endorsements for algebra, but rather a strong advocacy for helping people find math connections that make sense in their own lives. Dave Barry reports that "for a period of approximately 15 minutes back in 1962" he knew how to do square root. At least he thinks it was square root. Who could tell? It might have been something else. Tom Magliozzi, one of the NPR "Car Talk" duo, went to his son's math class for back-to-school night. Written on the board was "Calculus is the set of techniques that allow us to determine the slope at any point on a curve and the area under that curve." Tom's reaction was, "So who gives a rat's patootie?" On "All Things Considered," Tom observed that he had almost no occasion to use any of the mathematics he had learned beyond long division. Tom says the purpose of higher math is to prepare us for even higher math, none of which we will ever use. Tom went home and made a list of the courses he wished he'd been exposed to in place of algebra, not to mention geometry, trigonometry, and calculus. He concluded, "Education really ought to help us to understand the world we live in. This includes flora, fauna, cultures, governments, religions, money, advertising, buildings, cities, and especially people. Then it should help us to cope with that world. And in the process, it would be nice if it helped us to become good, kind, empathetic people. Algebra doesn't do any of these things."

Garrison Keillor says you can go through life never using mathematics, but if you learn to tell a joke right, this skill will serve you well throughout life.

## FACT CHECKING

Alex Molnar, director of the Center for Education Research, Analysis, and Innovation at Arizona State University, worries that the media is rather loose in their designation of the title "expert," readily quoting private think-tank functionaries who don't subject their research to external peer review before sending out glossy press packets. Case in point: In February 2001, Jay P. Greene's report on Florida's "A-Plus" education reform program, released by the Manhattan Institute, received lots of positive press attention. The report, written under a contract with Florida State University as part of a grant from the Florida Department of Education to evaluate the A-Plus Program, concluded that the threat of vouchers increases public school performance. *USA Today*'s story about the report read like a Manhattan Institute press release. Even though the topic of Greene's research is hotly debated, the *USA Today* article contained no dissenting opinion. Research articles published in a refereed academic journal challenging Greene's statistical methodology and conclusions received no play in the mass media.

These days, private policy organizations play an increasingly important role in shaping education policy, but the public hasn't a clue about either their agendas or the incestuous ties among them. In April 2000, for example, the Thomas B. Fordham Foundation issued *The State of State Standards*, giving every state a grade, but the casual reader doesn't have a clue about the particular bias behind the D+ for Vermont and the B for Texas. And to get more bang for the buck, a Fellow at one conservative think tank promotes and praises the work of Fellows at another. One advantage of this system is that they can keep a very small address book. Here's how it works: Marci Kanstoroom, director of research at Fordham, publishes an article on the miracle of Texas in *Education Next*, a publication of the Hoover Institution. *Education Next* is sponsored by the Thomas B. Fordham Foundation, Manhattan Institute for Policy Research, and the Program on Education Policy. Funny thing, Chester E. Finn, Jr., senior editor at *Education Next*, is the president of the Thomas B. Fordham Foundation, former James M. Olin Fellow at the Hudson Institution, founding partner of Edison Project, now designated "scholar" at the Manhattan Institute, and, along with Newt Gingrich, a "Distinguished Visiting Fellow" at the Hoover Institution, where Ronald Reagan, Alexander Solzhenitsyn, and Margaret Thatcher are Honorary Fellows. Whew! Vertigo sets in when you try to follow that. Simply put, when Finn writes a paper at Fordham, he can act as outside reviewer at Manhattan, and then get it published at Hoover. Neat trick! Not that Finn has any trouble getting mainstream newspapers to print his words. They treat him like a legitimate scholar, rarely warning the public of his ideological bias. "Why We Need 'Straight A's,'" issued by Fordham, is the text of testimony Finn gave before the U.S. House of Representatives Committee on Education and the Workforce, and the basis for op-ed pieces running in the *New York Times*, the *Los Angeles Times*, and the *Washington Times*, among others.

When a newspaper runs an article about a report published in the *American Journal of Medicine* or *Educational Researcher* or *Physical Review*, the reader knows that report was subject to external review before it was published. With all the inbreeding and crossbreeding in the private policy operations, maybe the newspapers that cover the goings-on at these organizations should include a truth-in-disclosure statement.

Certainly such a needed declaration was absent from the PBS National Desk episode *Education—A Public Right Gone Wrong*. Hosted by Larry Elder, a Los Angeles hot-button drive-time radio talk show host trying to wear a journalistic hat, the show's version of investigative reporting was to posit 38 conservative foundation wonks, for-profit and religious-school employees, and assorted voucher recipients speaking in favor of privatizing public education against four people defending public schools. Of these four, one is the president and another the chief counsel of the NEA, the largest teacher union. So the viewer gets the impression that only an organization that puts its own bread-and-butter interests at the forefront of educational policy-making has anything good to say about public education.

Surely journalism ethics reaches a new low when the viewer must examine the annual reports of the underwriters to figure out why the program is so long on unsubstantiated accusations about public education and so short on facts. A truth-in-disclosure statement would have revealed a web of financial entanglement that touches every public-school-basher who was handed the microphone. To name just one entanglement: the arch-conservative, Milwaukee-based Bradley Foundation is the nation's leading champion of school privatization and vouchers. Bradley is sustaining a voucher system in Milwaukee until the state can be bullied into subsidizing the privatization scheme with public tax dollars. Of the 38 guests testifying against public schools on the show, 33 had links to Bradley, Scaife, and/or Olin monies. As does PBS itself, with the Bradley and Olin Foundations listed in its 1998 annual report as major underwriters. One comes away with the conclusion that if you donate in the neighborhood of $500,000, you can say anything you please on PBS.

Larry Elder insists this National Desk show is about an "unsalvageable government system." There it is—using government the way right-wing extremists are wont to do, as a code word for evil. "Public" is used the same way, as a term of scorn and derision. Perhaps someone should remind the folks at the Public Broadcasting System what the "P" in their name represents. Here are a few of the many distortions and downright lies offered by experts that went unchallenged.

- Thomas Sowell (Rose and Milton Friedman Senior Fellow in Public Policy, Hoover Institution): "The state of American public education is one big disaster."
- Clint Bolick (Vice President and Chief Litigator for the Institute of Justice): "Public education has been in serious decline in the U.S. over the last several decades."
- Milton Friedman (Senior Research Fellow, Hoover Institution, cofounder of The Milton and Rose D. Friedman Foundation for School Choice): "We have a higher level of illiteracy today than we had a hundred years ago."

Anyone who follows education in the news can see 5862 front-page headlines in every allegation. And then the facts, if they are ever published, appear in section B, page 47.

- Standardized test scores are at record highs.
- Scores on the National Assessment of Education Progress (NAEP) for all ethnic groups are at all-time highs.

- The proportion of students scoring above 650 (the 92d percentile on the SAT mathematics test) has risen to a record level.
- The number of students taking Advanced Placement tests has soared from 78,000 in 1978 to 704,000 in 1999.

Advocates for vouchers, choice, charters, high-stakes testing, and any other notion certainly have a right to be heard. One might even suppose they have a right to try to establish an educational marketplace that ignores any obligation to improve education for all children. But the media has an obligation to label truth-in-promotion, to label propaganda as such, to separate the experts from the chaff. The conclusions of a Chester Finn or a William Bennett should not be given the same weight as the conclusions of a Jerry Bracey or a Linda McNeil, not because of their ideologies, but because of the respectability and the peer review of their research. At the very least, the media has an obligation to indicate which research is juried, and if they ever get really courageous, the media might also point out think-tank incest when it occurs.

## PARENT EXPERTS

Columnist Clarence Page asserts, "Parenting makes education experts of us all." Page says his own parenthood makes him suspicious of President Bush's proposal, as reiterated by Education Secretary Rod Paige, for "a system of high standards, annual testing against those standards of every child in third through eighth grade, and a system of accountability that makes schools responsible for results." Page draws on his experiences when his own son was a second grader to know that the President's call for high-stakes decisions about children is "wrongheaded and destructive."

Washington mother activist Juanita Doyon is a gadfly as well as an expert. She writes letters to the editor, appears on TV interviews, and stands on street corners handing out anti-testing buttons. She probably mutters "We won't WASL!" in her sleep. Always ready with a snappy rejoinder, ever ready to counter Standardista assertions, Juanita is also a passionate advocate for both public schools and for children. "Children are not accountable to the system. Neither are parents, for that matter. The last time I checked, this country was supposed to have a government of the people, by the people and for the people. Some of the people in power seem to be afraid of this. Government in the form of tests will never rectify the situation. So they might as well give up now, and save us all a lot of time, money and indigestion." Juanita continues, "I don't want some $10-an-hour temp worker grading anything my son or daughter might write. After their papers have been scanned and shredded, what remains is my trust in myself and in my children's teachers. I do not trust any testing company to do the right thing."

Juanita argues that a student who has jumped through the hoops of some 50 certified teachers for 13 years should not be blocked from the certificate of the rite of passage by one test written by a testing company in Iowa or Monterey. "We're not talking brain surgery here. We're talking about young adults getting on with their lives. We're not telling this kid who fails this one math test that he can't get into the Harvard math program; we're telling this kid who fails this one math test that he can't get out of high school with a piece of paper that says he traveled through 13 years of public school and passed his classes." Juanita notes that if her children were two years younger, they'd probably fail the WASL. "So, thank the good Lord that the WASL isn't required until 2008." Her own kids safe, Juanita is fighting for "all those other kids."

Some communities in Vermont still honor parent experts, and student experts, too. Vermont has not yet totally succumbed to the lure of state control over local variety—not quite, anyway. In May 2001, graduating seniors at Champlain Valley Union High School presented their challenge projects to the public. With the guidance of a community consultant and a faculty advisor, each student had to complete a 30-hour community experience, write a Tri-Search paper, and present his efforts in a formal setting before a panel of community and faculty members. This is the very sort of project emphasis that Richard Mills, the former Vermont Commissioner of Education, will not allow in New York State, even though some schools have been using student portfolios and community presentation for decades. Now, Mills insists, every student must pass the New York State Regents tests to earn a high school diploma.

What strikes me about the list of projects from the students in my village of Charlotte is the wide variety of projects, covering many of the skills and knowledge actually needed by a community, as contrasted with the knee-jerk "Algebra for all" fiat.

- Teaching a middle school Shakespeare appreciation class
- Homelessness in Vermont
- Cooking with regional products
- African drum construction and playing
- Rebuilding transmissions
- Portrait photography
- Coaching youth track and field
- Music recording
- Learning the art of Ninjutsu
- Investing in the stock market
- Sports science
- Creating the video
- Desserts prepared in bakeries
- Restorative justice
- Bioethical issues concerning the end of life
- America's parks
- Teaching the game of golf
- What is a radio?
- Self-defense
- Child abuse prevention
- Children with emotional disabilities
- WKA kart racing
- Designing a therapeutic garden
- A closer look at dentistry
- Organization structure
- Art of collage
- How Visual Basic works for me
- Baby signing
- World of small business
- Functional Web design

- Sports photography
- Emergency medicine
- Noise
- History of Maine schooners
- Designing a police station
- Creating a guitar song

The "Teaching Shakespeare appreciation" project flopped. The senior who proposed this for his project had lofty goals, planning to teach "meaningful scenes" from *Much Ado About Nothing* to appreciative middle schoolers, who, after hours of dedicated practice, would appear in front of the graduation-challenge judges as a proficient acting troupe. Middle schoolers being middle schoolers, the ambitious senior was left "with broken dreams and no tangible product." But since he needed a "product" to present, he tried to learn from his failure. He took bits of raw video he'd taken of his students and set it to a Phish song, with the title "I Would if I Could, But I Don't Know How."

Standardistas would do well to come to this same realization: I Would if I Could, But I Don't Know How. Alas, sitting in their conference rooms, they can maintain their expertise. Standardistas avoid putting themselves in the position of dealing with real kids. It is a delicious thought: Members of blue ribbon education commission shut up with 28 seventh graders for an hour, teaching *Much Ado About Nothing*. Fifteen minutes would probably do it. It's probably more daunting than the one faced by data storage giant EMC. Over six years, they paid Insight Development $650,000 to inspire more than 5000 new hires to walk across 1500-degree coals. The theory goes that once employees face the fear of such an endeavor, they will find nothing impossible in the workplace.

## CHOOSING SIDES

Experts are in the eyes of the beholder. Both sides in the testing wars can line up plenty of people with impressive degrees to declare Truth. In the end, parents must choose what they want for their children.

Dickens offers Thomas Gradgrind. With a rule and a pair of scales, and the multiplication table always in his pocket, sir, ready to weigh and measure any parcel of human nature, and tell you exactly what it comes to. Andy Rooney advises, "Don't take a butcher's advice on how to cook meat. If he knew, he'd be a chef." Perhaps it's time to stop taking the President's advice—or the governors', legislators', or members of the Business Roundtable, on how to educate our children. If they knew, they'd be teachers. At least butchers know what a slab of beef looks like. But there's the rub. Knowledge of children is not on the Standardista list of what schools need.

I asked parents around the country to respond to a text-based writing assignment for fifth graders based on a technical passage found in the Delaware Student Testing Program. On the test, students are given a recipe for Bacon-Tomato Sandwiches, a recipe that indicates the need for a serrated knife and a table knife. Students must write an account explaining why two different kinds of knives are used. I asked moms what kind of knife they used to slice tomatoes for a bacon and tomato sandwich. Here's a sampling of the responses:

- I use a serrated edge knife because that's all we have—and they cut refrigerator boxes quite nicely as well. But we'd never eat bacon and tomato sandwiches. Cooking bacon for my brood would take forever.
- I use a paring knife to cut tomatoes. But if you're from East Texas you wouldn't eat a tomato unless you peeled it first.
- To slice tomatoes, I use a very sharp, red-handled paring knife made by Victorinox, the Swiss Army Knife people.
- I only use a serrated knife when I cut bread. That's what they were made to do, not slice tomatoes: rough exterior = serrated knife; smooth exterior = paring knife.
- I use a serrated knife after first trying every paring knife in the drawer and discovering they are all dull.
- I use a one-size-fits-many Chicago Cutlery butcher knife I have honed to perfection.

- It's not a culturally valid or fair question. I, of course, would never cut a bacon anything. It would also be repugnant for kosher Jews and Moslems too.
- This is repugnant to us nonsectarian vegetarians.
- I don't make sandwiches. That's why God made delis.
- Is it developmentally appropriate to expect a fifth grader to know what a serrated knife is—and to let him loose with tomato-slicing? Not my kid!
- I've never known a kid who would touch a bacon and tomato sandwich. Does anybody eat them anymore? This is an item left over from "Leave It to Beaver." Get real. Now kids pop all those instant pizzas into the microwave.

But the serrated knives question, with a scoring rubric from 0 to 2, was just a warm-up. Here's the writing prompt, with a scoring rubric ranging from 1 to 4 and requiring an extended answer:

Your class has decided to ask the school cafeteria to add a "Make Your Own Sandwich" section to the school lunch line. Write a letter to the cafeteria manager explaining why the Bacon-Tomato Sandwiches recipe would be a good one to use in the new section.

The state of Delaware indicates that to receive a top mark, a response must reference the benefits (simple ingredients, many variations, liked by most students, easy to assemble, requires very little cooking, etc.).

Maybe the state of Delaware should talk to a few expert cafeteria cooks before writing their high-stakes questions: For starters, has anybody on the writing committee tried cooking bacon for 650 kids? If the state of Delaware doesn't have time to talk to a few orthodox Jews, Muslims, and vegetarians before writing their high-stakes questions, they could just try for themselves to write in praise of something they find morally/ethically/socially repugnant.

Not all experts sit at the Business Roundtable or in state departments education. The official, self-proclaimed experts would do well to get ir heads out of the sand occasionally and talk to a few gabby moms.

*Chapter 7*

# Mad as Hell and Doing Something About It: Parents Taking Back Their Schools

Suzie did not have time to finish her math in school today, so I have sent it home with her to finish; please give her time to do it.

— Mrs. Teacher

We did, but that did not give her time to do all her household chores, so we have sent some laundry to school with her to fold; please give her time to do it.

— Mrs. Mom

This apocryphal exchange appears in an on-line essay by Birmingham, Alabama, philosopher-photographer Rick Garlikov (www.garlikov.com). Dr. Garlikov makes the point that parents just might decide that they have better things to do with the time they have with their children than following a blueprint sent home by the school. Prize-winning author Sharon Creech's new book, *A Fine, Fine School*, touches this same nerve. In it, a well-meaning but over-zealous princi-pal does away with weekends, holidays, and summer vacations so stu-dents can carry around books with titles called *Really Hard Math*—and learn lots more. Tillie, who formerly spent her free time teaching her little brother to skip and climb trees, begins lugging a giant briefcase off to class to do the serious work that now fills her life.

The New Jersey department of education makes its homework ex-pectations clear. Similar instructions to parents appear on school dis-trict sites and advice columns throughout the country:

- Schedule daily homework times.
- Find a quiet spot in the home for your children to work.
- Turn off the television or music to make it quiet.
- Pick a location that is close enough for them to ask you for help.
- Ask to see the finished homework.
- If your child often seems confused or unsure about homework assignments, contact the teacher yourself.

"Do this. Do that." One can wonder if the New Jersey department of education has any idea of the pressures on the modern family. One can wonder if the New Jersey department of education has any idea of how obnoxious this list of imperatives sounds. The New Jersey de-partment of education might do better to investigate the relationship between homework and children's test scores. The New Jersey de-partment of education might do better to investigate the relationship between rich playtime activities and children's test scores. The New Jersey department of education might do better to stick a banana in its collective ear.

It could be worse. Parents could live in Chicago, where the Chicago Public Schools Systems issues report cards on parents. One of the categories in which parents are graded is their children's home-work production.

## FIRST THE HOMEWORK,
## THEN THE WORLD

In Texas, Carol Holst says homework is intrusive. "The school has my child from 8 a.m. to 3 p.m. If he stays there all day but still comes home with two hours of homework that I have to teach him, then why should I send him to school?" She continues, "I work, Dad works. We try not to let our work interfere with our family time together. We resent the school taking family time away from us."

Minnesota mom Teresa Saum admits, "I couldn't stand to sit at the table and supervise homework every night. We try to help him struc-ture his time, but refuse to handhold. Come to think of it, maybe I'm just refusing to do the same things he's refusing to do! I wouldn't sit still for this endless fill-in-the-blank stuff every night. In second grade, my son brought home huge packs of multiplication worksheets. Not only did he have to answer the problems, he had to do a color-by-number thing for every sheet. He cried sometimes because he didn't see the point of the coloring. But neither did I." Teresa said the col-oring made the whole family crazy. "He saw the point of the prob-lems, but rebelled at the color-by-number." She adds, "He's hated math ever since."

Teresa observes that her son is obsessed with toys, and he draws in-tricate scenes featuring his toys. "Cartoons go on for pages, but when he draws pictures of miners with tiny headlamps and pickaxes over their shoulders besides his social studies notes on the miners of Virginia, the teacher writes 'NO!' in red ink and tells me that it distracts him from his serious studying."

Teresa comments that inane homework distracts him; drawing in-tensifies his understanding, adding "I would love to live in his mind, in the elaborate worlds he weaves every day to have a place for his toys to live and play."

"I hate the sheets labeled proficiency test garbage, hate worksheets, and am infuriated by middle school projects where four or five kids have to work together outside school. Just try getting all five together at the same time," says Ohio mom Mary O'Brien. "And I'm not even wound up yet." Mary acknowledges that "Maybe my finding homework a waste of time and intrusive on family life might have something do with the fact that I have five kids. I go through the homework, separating out the Ohio Proficiency Test preparation garbage, because my kids don't do that. I hate worksheets, don't see much value in hours of mindless repetition, and am infuriated by middle school projects."

Mary was annoyed enough about an overly simplistic ditto questionnaire on multiple intelligences that she wrote to the teacher. "I told her I have corresponded with Dr. Gardner and the project Zero folks and that I was sending them the ditto, asking their take on the assignment."

Mary's husband suggested that she overreacted. She laughs. "My son complained that the next day his teacher was overly attentive. He hinted that he hoped that I would limit my notes to his teachers this year. I'm having a negative effect on his 'cool factor.'"

In Spokane, Washington, Galen Leonhardy puts excessive homework in a larger context, "Until my wife and I spoke with our daughter's teacher, it took one and a half to two hours for our nine-year-old to finish her homework. Before that, we stopped the piano lessons. And homework kept Sarah up until after 10:00 p.m. on ballet nights. Even with the late nights and long hours, Sarah had a hard time keeping up with the workload. When she did not turn her homework in on time, she was punished. So we did what rational parents do. We met with the teacher.

"Our daughter's teacher, as it turned out, was responding to the pressures associated with a high-stakes testing process that will be used not only to judge our daughter's progress in the public school system but also to determine the teacher's standing in relation to other teachers across the state. So the teacher's position is directly affected by our daughter's performance on the fourth-grade test."

Every parent has a homework horror story. In 2000, the school board in Piscataway, New Jersey, took a strong stand against homework invasion, voting unanimously to set a limit of 30 minutes for children in elementary school, two hours for high schoolers. They also "discouraged" homework on weekends.

Jane, a mother who lives in a suburb of Cleveland, took on homework head-on. She recounts, "I finally had enough of the homework interfering in my time with my family, and decided to give them a taste of their own medicine. I walked into each of my children's classes this morning and told their teachers that I needed to take my children home for a little homework. I told them, 'It won't take very long. I just need to reinforce our home values.'"

Jane laughs, "You should have seen the looks I got. Of course my daughter was eating this up. She lives for confrontation! I took them out for breakfast, and we had a great time."

Jane said that her son's teacher gives homework on weekends. When Jane said she'd contact the teacher at home with some questions, the teacher answered, "I'd prefer that you wait until Monday—I'm off on weekends."

Jane replied, "So is my son. We do not do homework on weekends at our house." Jane now wonders if parents could start an anti-homework movement.

Kids sometimes take the homework problem into their own hands. Here's a call to arms written by a sixth grader in Massachusetts:

Dear Fellow Students:

Do you feel like I do and are you very frustrated about how much time it takes to do homework? Do you do not have enough time to play or do other things for fun? Please write a letter that looks something like this and send it to all the people on the address list. Add or take out anything that you need so the letter fits you. If we all work together, we can make changes happen. Don't forget to get your parent's permission.

The young protester provided a sample letter, names and addresses for the governor, the commissioner of education, the superintendent of schools in Barnstable, the middle school principal, the editor of the *Cape Cod Times*.

## OH, MY ACHING BACK

It's 10 p.m. Do you know where your child's homework is?

In the spring of 2001, members of the California Assembly voted 59 to 1 on a bill asking state school and health officials to study whether heavy book-bag weight causes spinal damage. Assemblyman Rod Pacheco, author of the bill, said his six-year-old daughter carries a book bag that seems to weigh as much as she does. It's a start. First get politicians worrying about book bags; next thing you know, they might start worrying about the kids. And as an observable, weighable fact, book bags are something our political leaders can understand—in a way they don't seem to grasp the hearts and minds of our young.

Virginia mom and cofounder of PAVURSOL (Parents Across Virginia United to Reform SOLs), Mickey VanDerwerker reflects that her son's book bag was so heavy it caused her son, a sixth grader, to fall backwards off the bus. "He weighs 62 pounds; the book bag is 41 pounds. He does homework from 5 to 9 each night, with a 25-minute break for dinner. He has gone to bed crying twice this week because he is doing a 1000-word research paper on what the walls of the U.S. Capitol would say (from 1800 to 1900) in addition to everything else. We are definitely speeded up around here." Mickey criticizes the need for state educational standards that drive tests to pose questions like "What is a cartouche?" to measure a student's knowledge of "the contributions of ancient Egypt and China, which have had an impact on world history, with emphasis on written language, laws, calendars, and architectural monuments such as the Pyramids and the Great Wall of China," and feed the homework frenzy.

Don't people in charge realize that the nation has reached a state of homework meltdown when the American Association of Orthopedic Surgeons (AAOS) issues guidelines on recommended weights of book bags? They say 20 percent of the child's body weight is the point at which book bags become a clinical problem. Maybe parents need to ask for a consult from the American Psychiatric Association. What's all this homework overload doing to kids' psyches?

The *Florida Times-Union* weighed the book bags of 385 students at 11 schools and published a chart in the paper. Education-data analyst

Gerald Bracey matched up average book weights from each school with the schools' ratings in the Florida testing system, and determined that the high and middle schools with the heaviest loads were both rated A. Those with lighter burdens were rated C. Of the two elementary schools listed, the heavier school was rated B and the lighter C. Perhaps a modest proposal for ending testing insanity (and saving a lot of money) would be to skip the tests and just rank schools on the weight of students' book bags.

But the physical problems are real. According to the U.S. Consumer Product Safety Commission, some 12,000 kids age 17 and under suffered backpack-related sprains and strains last year—up from the 3900 in 1999—costing an average of $11,000 per injury. Homework should come with a warning label: WARNING: The Surgeon General has determined that prolonged use of this product may cause bodily injury.

In late August 2001, the *Wall Street Journal* weighed in with a parent consumer report of the durability, kid appeal, and prices of the wheelie backpack, a daypack with suitcase-style wheels and retractable handles added, pointing out that "even the American Academy of Pediatrics is recommending them." Prices range from the $40 Target model to REI's $75 Class Act.

And then the AAOS came up with a different solution. Noting all the above statistics about book bag injuries, the AAOS wants kids to do 15 minutes of back-conditioning exercises—bridges and crunches—two to three times a week. Plus stretching exercises every day. As a back-to-school service in August 2001, the *Washington Post* published directions for doing the Plank Start, the Back Bridge Start, the Prone Bridge Lie. The article concluded with this advice, "Sit on a fitness ball, if you have one." Or, lacking that, stick a banana in your ear, if you have one.

An easier solution would be to ease up on homework.

The book bag problem and the testing craze creep out of the same primordial ooze. Standardista commissions and committees are advertising for a new model of kid, as though children were toasters or SUVs, consumer goods needing constant redesign. The Fortunate 500, whose members sit on high-level commissions, demand an upgrade in kids at the same time as they systematically downgrade the U.S. standard of living. In a kick-the-dog chain of events, the Standardista demand for ever-increasing scores on high-stakes tests filters down to individual classrooms as an increase in homework. The worst thing Standardistas have stolen from us is trust: trust in parents and teachers to work hard and do the best job they can. They've also stolen our trust in children to work hard and do the best job they can. Meanwhile, Standardistas work hard and do the best job they can to convince the public that schools are filled with laggards. Laggards who don't know anything.

## WHO'S ASKING THE QUESTIONS?

The Association of American Publishers (AAP), the trade association for the publishing industry, conducted a Nationwide Survey of Parents on Standards and Testing and then trumpeted the conclusion that parents want tests. "A clear majority of American parents reported that standardized tests provided them with important information about their children's progress in school," said Michael H. Kean, chair of the test committee of the AAP. Kean is also vice president for public and governmental affairs at CTB/McGraw-Hill, one of the biggest test-makers in the country. Public Agenda headlined their poll: "Survey Finds Little Sign of Backlash against Academic Standards or Standardized Tests." The Public Agenda poll was funded by the Thomas B. Fordham, George Gund, John D. and Catherine MacArthur, and John M. Olin Foundations. For people savvy with the education wars, some of these names jump out as leading bashers of public schools and staunch supporters of vouchers.

The Business Roundtable found the Public Agenda poll useful when, in spring 2001, the Roundtable brought out a 27-page booklet, *Assessing and Addressing the "Testing Backlash."* The Roundtable used its own polls and those of Public Agenda to "prove" that the public really want children to be subjected to standards and testing.

Skeptics observe that Education Testing Service (ETS) conducting a poll on public attitudes about testing is rather like the National

Cattleman's Beef Association conducting a poll on attitudes about tofu. The headline to the ETS poll results read, "Benefits of Testing Outweigh Concerns." The question was: "Based on concerns/values you have heard about standardized testing, do you support or oppose greater use of testing as part of a broader education initiative?" When the question is asked that way, 68 percent of the people polled are counted as favoring testing. ETS is sensitive about criticism of their poll, insisting, "As the nation's foremost educational assessment and research organization, ETS has a unique role, opportunity and a special obligation to help inform the current Congressional debate over educational reform." Truth in disclosure: ETS, a nonprofit company, formed a for-profit subsidiary called K-12 Works, which, in May 2001, won a many-million-dollar contract to write the high-stakes exit exam in California. There is speculation that ETS offered California their services on the cheap—as a big foot in the door to getting similar contracts nationwide when Congress votes in the test-'em-til-they-drop legislation, a bonanza for the testing outfits.

People who put a lot of stock in polls should remember the V-Chip polling. You remember the V-Chip, the device that the FCC said had to go in all television sets with picture screens 33 centimeters or larger, a device that can block specified television shows. The Henry J. Kaiser Family Foundation polled a "nationally representative sample" of parents and then announced that 77 percent of parents wanted the V-Chip. A PTA poll claimed 98 percent of its respondents wanted the chip; a poll commissioned by the *Hollywood Reporter* showed the public to be "overwhelming in favor of the V-Chip technology." All this polling convinced Congress that there oughtta be a law, and in 1996, they passed one. An estimated 50 million television sets now have the V-Chip, and one-half of the people who have it don't know they have it; seven percent of the parents who have the chip use it.

Maybe it depends on how you ask the question. Public Agenda says that "Only two percent of parents who know their school district is implementing higher academic standards want to stop and go back to the way things were before the standards were put in place." Not wanting to "go back to the way things were" is far removed from wanting to implement higher standards. Admittedly, on-line polling does not have the stature of more traditional polling, but here are the results of an Internet CNN QuickVote poll conducted on April 17, 2001. Note how differently the question is posed.

> Are teachers spending too much time preparing students for stan-dardized tests?
> Yes   86.1%
> No    13.8%

The national poll of the American Association of School Administra-tors, conducted by Jennifer Laszlo and Frank Luntz, shows that people believe that "high parental involvement" and "children who are happy and like school" are the best indicators that schools are providing a high quality education. Only 18.8 percent of those polled selected "high scores on statewide tests" as the best indicator. Not surprising, these poll results did not make the front page of any newspaper. Somehow, the fact that people think children's happiness is important is not news.

A *Washington Post* headline for June 27, 2000, showed what happens when you change the question: "Virginia Parents Don't Trust Exam, Poll Finds." A George Washington University professor and his grad-uate students asked parents several questions about the Virginia Stan-dards of Learning (SOL) exams.

> The Virginia Standards of Learning exams are an accurate meas-ure of my child's achievement.
> Agree         17%
> Disagree      61%

> The SOLs are more politically than educationally motivated.
> Agree         70%
> Disagree      9%

> Teachers spend too much time teaching to the test rather than teaching other important materials and topics.

Agree          65%
Disagree       13%

The SOLs are not needed and the testing program should be eliminated.
Agree          49%
Disagree       29%

State education officials questioned the poll's credibility, saying the wording of the questions may have skewed the results. Maybe it's tit for tat. Officials didn't complain about the way ETS worded its poll. Maybe the pollsters should try asking parents whose children have failed a test required for high school graduation how they feel about standards and measures.

## ORGANIZING TO WIN BACK THE SCHOOLS

The spirit, the passion, and the indefatigable hard work of high-stakes test resisters, mostly moms, calls to mind 200 women in Burlington, Vermont. During the Civil War, this group adopted a resolution: "We further resolve that we will consider *all* our time and *all* our energies [to knitting blankets]." A growing number of women in this country consider themselves on the brink of a new civil war, a war centering on the control of children. To protect their children these women consider *all* their time and *all* their energies sacred to the cause of test resistance.

Politicians, take heed.

Parents don't want their children to be held hostage to state tests. Insisting that state and federal rule-makers must consult with the governed if government is to be legitimate, these parents won't settle for the pro forma seat on a showcase committee. These parents are determined to help teachers take back the schools. They are quick to announce that this isn't your old PTA-room-mother sort of deal. As Susan Misenheimer wrote on an activist-parent listserv, "I don't mean to brag or be arrogant, but I do have something between my ears besides a recipe box for chocolate chip cookies for the PTA bake sale." A Minnesota mom reflects on the same issue, "When I served on a parent panel, our function was figuring out how to bind the Campbell soup labels—the benefits of string versus tape versus rubber bands. Week after week. I thought I would lose my mind."

Tucson mom and PTA president of her school Adriana B. de Rincon organized a boycott of the SAT-9 test. Alarm bells went off for Adriana when, about a month before the SAT-9 was to be administered, "The teacher began sending homework that resembled a test. I asked her about it and I found out that for the first time, first graders would be required to take the test." Adriana shared concerns with other parents about subjecting such young children to standardized testing; they organized a boycott, and 70 percent of the first grade did not show up for the week of testing.

The group wrote letters protesting the test to the superintendent of the district and the state, to our local elected officials, and even to the White House. Although these fell on deaf ears, Adriana says, "This is a mandate from the State Superintendent of Public Schools. We are fortunate that our school truly looks out for the well-being of students. My impression is that our school administration and staff are sympathetic with our stand, but they are caught in the middle.

"Both my children are bilingual and biliterate, and they enjoy school immensely. I think they would have performed well on the test, but I do not consider it a valid measure of their ability. I especially object to the State imposing this stress on such young children. Our family puts a high value on education. Already we have family conversations about college and which one our children might attend."

Also in Tucson, Merle and Paula McPheeters decided they'd had enough. Their sixth grader talks about the test. "We were put into a special classroom to get directions to take the SAT-9. Our teachers seemed petrified that we were going to cheat or something, so they made cardboard dividers. The teacher would say, 'Go!' and I felt like we were starting a race—like this was a marathon. 'Watch out for trick questions,' they'd say. 'The test is trying to trick you!' I felt such pressure, I asked to be excused to go to the bathroom. I leaned against the wall and cried."

The McPheeters decided this is not why they send their children to school, and opted both their daughters out of testing in 2001.

First they ignore you.
Then they laugh at you.
Then they fight you.
Finally, you win.

— Gandhi

This quotation is a favorite among parents organizing against nutty standards and high-stakes tests. In Gilbert, Arizona, Gabie Gedlaman used it as the opening for a notice of a working meeting to "Stop the April Foolishness." This Arizona mother confesses that she was once afraid to speak out in public. Now she's leading rallies. Her story is similar to that of many parent-led resistance groups. First the Web page, then public demonstrations. The Web becomes a way for parents to find each other, to find out that they aren't alone in their discontent, to cheer each other on as they make their first tentative steps in public engagement: leading public forums, confronting the establishment, and cultivating the media.

Gabie's group challenged the Arizona State Board of Education and the local board to take AIMS, the state test—and have the scores published. "Arizona State Board of Education members, as powerful members of the educational system in Arizona, should be models for students and should take the AIMS to demonstrate their confidence in AIMS." Students presented over 1500 letters to the board, urging them to take the test.

Asked if he would take the test, the local superintendent replied he "wouldn't fall prey to that stunt." But the buzz was out there, talked about in local call-in and interview shows. The focus had taken a sharp turn: Should public officials prove they can pass the tests they are requiring of students?

Public officials in Virginia are not ignoring Mickey VanDerwerker anymore. The former Virginia Teacher of the Year, mother of five kids, three dogs, four cats, one hamster, and two fish, says watching her own perfectly capable son panic over the third-grade SOL test in Virginia turned her into an anti-SOL activist. Mickey and two other moms decided to have a meeting, each of the three bringing one more mom. That small group has grown to the 5000-strong Parents Across Virginia United to Reform SOLS (PAVURSOL). Mickey, a former teacher, advises, "It must be parents who drive this movement; teachers will get called whiners and naysayers if they do it. But parents need to hear that professionals back them up, in private at first maybe, but publicly when push comes to shove." She adds, "I can't tell you how many times superintendents, principals, and teachers have told me privately how important the PAVURSOL work is, urging me to hang in, fight the good fight. They tell me the children are counting on me."

Mickey notes that "Virginia is a very polite state, and demonstrations and civil disobedience acts will be a hard sell until enough children are hurt badly enough for people to put aside politeness." She adds that this time will come, but it's a pity that it won't come until children's suffering is more obvious.

Mickey urges people to write letters to the editors, not letting them get away with supporting the tests; she practices what she preaches. Here's her letter to *Teacher Magazine*:

> As a parent, I worry about the effects of high-stakes standardized tests on teaching and learning. I am even more deeply troubled by the view of test prep as legitimate educational work. It's wrong to surrender precious classroom time and money to help kids bubble in the same answer to a multiple-choice test. . . . Educators should not prostitute themselves to the test-prep companies. Test prep will never substitute for real learning. There's so much in the world to learn about; don't waste my kids' time.

Mickey offers practical advice to fledgling organizers. Unsure about the protocol for distributing materials at conferences? "Leave business cards in the bathrooms, on tables, in chairs in the session rooms." She also urges organizers to capitalize on every opportunity. "When I careened off the highway to call a talk show host to complain about the

Deputy Director of Education lying about SOLs, I lost my slip and signed up several gaping onlookers. Another time I went to testify at the Senate, forgot my clothes, and had to talk to salespeople at Dress Barn to let me in and to dress me (they even pressed the pants). Signed them up too. We call this Adventures in SOL Reform."

In Alvin, Texas, Carol Holst went back to college in 1995 to get a Texas teaching certificate. "As part of a course requirement," recalls Carol, "I observed classes. Much to my surprise, I didn't see science lessons, math lessons, history lessons, or literature studies. What I saw was something called "taas[1] practice." It was worse than strange. I complained to my professor and thanked my lucky stars that my family lived in a district that didn't do that kind of crazy stuff. After all, my son went to a *good* school."

After Carol earned her teaching certificate, she worked as a part-time substitute teacher in her local school district. "What an eye-opener! It was so painful—as though my eyelids were stuck open and I wasn't allowed to blink. There it was in all its ugliness: my district was just as taas-practice crazy as any I'd ever seen.

"There was the teacher who, in a fit of exasperation, told her class, 'If you don't settle down, we will do taas practice for the rest of the day.'

"There was the day my son came home from school, frightened, telling me how difficult taas would be. My son was a first grader. Supposedly, taas doesn't begin until third grade.

"I saw taas writing practice begin in October, though the test is not administered until February.

"There was the teacher, looking over her shoulder, showing me thick packets of test-formatted worksheets handed out by the district."

Carol became aware of a command from administration, "Don't talk to parents about TAAS." Carol relates, "That statement really stuck in my craw, pissed me off, infuriated the bejeebers out of me, and provoked me to start thinking about putting my son in a private school." But the proverbial straw that broke the camel's back—and drove this

---

[1]Carol belongs to a group of activists who are determined not to dignify state tests by using the capital letters commonly used in their acronyms.

mother into action—was the day her son came home from school with one more writing sample for homework, same rigid formula-writing as all the others. "Sitting at the kitchen table, he put his head on the table and cried and cried and cried."

What does a mother do? Time to organize. Carol asked her son to finish the school year. He is now a home-schooler, and Carol is out on the activist trail. She got on the Internet and met "a wonderful dynamo of a mom named Cindy Waltmon." Cindy created a Web page; Carol created a Yahoo! Groups discussion list. They were in business. Cindy and Carol testified at a state board of education meeting in Austin. "When we got a little newspaper coverage, we cackled like happy hens." Since then, they have picketed school districts, passed out "no mas taas" and other anti-testing buttons, testified at the state legislature, written letters and articles. Carol adds, "Best of all, we've found other people who are also sick of what's being done to our children's education. The gabby moms in my town have kept me going when I wanted to quit. Our numbers are still too small, but we will grow. There's no stopping us."

Carol reflects, "I can't teach in public schools right now because I refuse to teach to a state-mandated test. I also have concerns about the data collection aspect of the accountability system. Until the powers-that-be give us easy-to-find, detailed but reader-friendly information about where student data goes and what's done with it, I want nothing to do with it." So the state has lost a teacher, but children and their parents have gained an advocate.

In Michigan, the Rouge Forum launched a campaign against the Michigan Educational Assessment Program (MEAP). "Sleep Through the MEAP," informing the public, "Nobody has to take the MEAP, and no tenured teacher should be forced to give it." The Rouge Forum is a group of educators, students, and parents seeking a democratic society. On-line, parents can find a flyer: Opt Your Children out of MEAP Abuse, which includes a sample opt-out letter for parents to send to schools. The site also offers critical analysis of the MEAP and other resources with information about standardized curricula.

Cambridge parents in the Massachusetts parent group CARE (Coalition for Authentic Reform of Education) distributed a "Suspend

MCAS" petition, asserting that the high-stakes MCAS test is undermining children's opportunity for quality education. They note that the "test was introduced by a small group appointed to the State Board of Education by Governors Weld and Cellucci, unrepresentative of the parents, teachers, and students in the Commonwealth's public education system." They attack the test head-on with these charges:

The MCAS test:
- Violates the 1993 Education Reform Act, which calls for "a variety of assessment instruments."
- Narrows and restricts curricula.
- Burdens teachers and students with an extremely lengthy test regime (longer than the Massachusetts Bar exam).
- Devalues technical, linguistic, musical, athletic, and vocational skills.
- Introduces obstacles to disadvantaged students.
- Will force high schools to deny diplomas to deserving students.
- Discriminates against public school students, since private and parochial students are exempt from the MCAS requirement.

Parent activism takes a variety of forms. In North Carolina, Parents United for Fair Testing challenged the chairman of the State Board of Education's insistence that holding children to high standards means the state gets to decide who moves from fifth to sixth grade. The group marched on the General Assembly, insisting that a student's class participation, daily work, and report card grades should be part of promotion decisions. In Chicago, PURE (Parents United for Responsible Education) works at trying to force the public school system to stop using the Iowa Tests of Basic Skills illegally, that is, to make promotion decisions. They have also filed a discrimination complaint with the U.S. Department of Education's Office for Civil Rights, citing problems with the intent and operation of the Academic Preparatory Centers, which segregate students and provide a substandard curriculum.

The Coalition for Common Sense in Education (CCSE) is a grassroots coalition of parents, teachers, and educators in Rochester, New

York. One of the leaders, William C. Cala, Superintendent of Schools in Freeport, wrote Chancellor Carl T. Hayden, "As a lifelong educator and child advocate, I can say without reservation that the current reform movement in this state is the most harmful and destructive plan I have ever encountered. Every day, I, along with our teachers, principals, and parents, live with the 'collateral damage.' We watch children vomit, cut themselves, abuse alcohol and drugs, and hang their heads in shame and fear of not being able to jump through the 'one size fits all' scheme of the state."

Cala and others point out that CTB/McGraw-Hill (New York State's principal contractor) has clearly stated in its testing guidelines, as do all test providers, that no one test should be used to gauge educational progress and that none of the tests is to be used as "high stakes." These resisters then take the next step, making a modest proposal: "Since all CTB/Mc-Graw-Hill's standardized tests are being misused in New York, it would seem appropriate that they stop selling their wares to New York State."

While staking her tomatoes, California parent and teacher Susan Harman came up with a slogan that has swept the nation and become the title of an article in the *Atlantic Monthly*: "High Stakes Are for Tomatoes." Susan asked Sam, a fifth-grade Mien whose family's nomadic past make it uncertain whether he is from Laos or Cambodia, to draw a spectacular tomato vine. Susan's computer-graphics-expert son did the layout, and Susan's "High Stakes Are for Tomatoes" T-shirts are advertised on resistance Web sites across the country. Susan and Sam's teacher took his class on a field trip to the T-shirt factory, and saw Sam's design being put on the shirts. The front has the tomato imagery and the slogan "High Stakes Are for Tomatoes." The back reads, "Stop High-Stakes Testing: Go to www.fairtest.com." The proceeds go to CalCARE, the California test advocacy group.

FairTest, The National Center for Fair & Open Testing, is an advocacy organization working to end the abuses, misuses, and flaws of standardized testing and to ensure that evaluation of students and workers is fair, open, and educationally sound. ARN (Assessment Reform Network), FairTest's listserv, is a meeting place for test resisters seeking information and strategies for dismantling the oppressive testing system.

What started out as mostly an academic conversation on ARN has taken on a distinctly grassroots quality. Allen Flanigan, member of the Virginia resistance group PAVURSOL, father of children aged eight and five, and a government patent examiner, describes ARN as "the gabby moms, warrior moms, bad girls and good girls, mensches and nebbishes, recalcitrant teachers, outspoken parents and students, lapsed and practicing psychometricians, talking heads, ivory-tower types, union reps, and other unrepentant reprobates, as well as assorted test peddlers, lurkers, and others unheard from."

Thousands of parents are still suffering in relative silence. A Virginia parent, who wishes to remain anonymous to protect his daughter, speaks of how devastating the high-stakes test is for a child with specific learning disabilities. "She is a barely average student gradewise, and is horrible on the multiple-choice tests used in the SOLs. The SOL regulations are especially harsh on students like her for whom a college education may not be a goal. Kids such as these have been exiting high school with diplomas for decades, entering the workforce, raising families, and doing just fine." This father is well aware that "the dropout rates for students with various disabilities are already fantastically high. What happens when the students who do stay in school hit the SOL roadblock and have no 'payoff' for their efforts?" He is aware that his daughter could opt out of the SOL testing but worries that she would then not receive a standard diploma, worries about how that would affect her future ability to enter the workforce. "So we keep her in the SOL testing mill and hope for the best."

Eugene Garcia, dean of UC Berkeley's School of Education, is California's high profile critic of the SAT-9. As he travels around the state, Garcia repeats his message to parents and teachers, "We have created a monster and the monster is loose." Emphasizing that "the only way to escape the monster is in parents' hands," Garcia urges parents to exercise their right to keep their children from taking the test. In San Jose, an elementary school parent posted a sample opt-out letter on the Web, encouraging parents to protect their kids from the testing.

Seventy-five percent of the students in the four affected grades at the Mission Hill School in Boston opted out of the MCAS test in April

2001. Deborah Meier, who gained fame and admiration for the creation of Central Park East in East Harlem and is the principal of Mission Hill, makes it clear that Mission Hill did not boycott the tests. "The decision as to whether or not a child would take the MCAS tests was the parents' and theirs alone." Meier acknowledges that parents in her school know that she feels the tests conflict with the values of the school, but the decision was theirs.

"We won't WASL!" declares Juanita Doyon, mother of four in Spanaway, Washington, and founder of Mothers Against WASL as well as Washington coordinator of FairTest's Assessment Reform Network. "We're the gabby moms (and dads)," announces Juanita. "I'm just a parent, and I can say anything." Juanita has turned this motto into a battle cry for the entire 16 years she's been a public school parent. "They can put me down, but they'll never shut me up." Energetically pro-public schools and the teachers and principals in them, Juanita says, "To date, I figure my kids have experienced the teaching of 90 great teachers, and, as everything from popcorn chairperson to site council chair, I have worked with many more."

State interference is another matter. An inveterate researcher, Juanita can cite chapter and verse on funding mechanisms, legislative policy, codes, and so on. Although her twins took the fourth-grade WASL, they opted out of the seventh-grade WASL, and Juanita urges other parents to do likewise. "Any child who takes the test is encouraging the state to continue down the wrong path." When the A+ Commission claims that the WASL (Washington Assessment of Student Learning) is high stakes for teachers and schools but not high stakes for kids, Juanita counters, "A test is high stakes when it decides the fate of a child, an employee, a project, or a school. Any time you tell a fourth grader he is substandard, how can that not be high stakes?" She adds, "When they tell us 80 percent of our children are substandard, the stakes are pretty high. And they insist the test is valid. The operation was a success, but the patient died. The test is valid, but the children failed." She laughs, "I say button up the tests!"

Juanita, known as the button queen of ARN, produces custom-made T-shirts and anti-testing buttons for protesting parents and teachers across the country. Nationally, she's adding a growing number of superintendents to her mailing list; locally, she leaves buttons in restaurant restrooms, on store counters, and any other place she thinks a parent might pick one up.

Juanita has decided to give up her "just a parent" label. She is running for Washington State Superintendent of Schools in 2004. She's doing it because she objects to the attitude of the state, sending "The Music Man" to town with his supply of snake oil. "When the people who hold the purse strings demand ideological lockstep support from parents, unions, professional associations, teaching colleges, and on and on, well, we've got trouble in River City, my friends!" Juanita adds, "We don't need some day trading of standards, curriculum, and methodology imported from the Business Roundtable telling us what our kids need." Poking fun at the jargon of the Standardistas, Juanita says, "They want 'world class?' We're going to give them a 'world class' fight!"

## THIS IS NOT BACKLASH;
## IT'S A POLITICAL MOVEMENT

Writing in the *Washington Post*, Michael Powell says they are unlikely revolutionaries: women from Scarsdale, a wealthy New York suburb, who are "leading a rebellion against the drive for more and tougher standardized assessment tests." In a move that strikes at the heart of President Bush's education plan, 6 mothers led 200 eighth graders—60 percent of the total—in a boycott of the more-than-13-hour-long state-mandated tests. "The state is utterly disingenuous when it says the tests won't drive education," said Melanie Spivak. "We're law-abiding and we love process, believe me. But we're a bunch of fed-up mothers!" Deborah Rapaport, protest leader, asked, "What could be less productive academically than eighth graders spending 13.5 hours taking tests—especially when it's not even clear just what these tests are designed to do?"

The Scarsdale parents formed STOP, State Testing Opposed by Parents. Officially, Michael McGill, Scarsdale superintendent of schools, doesn't support the boycott, but as he told the *Washington Post*, state tests do encroach on local curriculum. "When the President of the United States and the business council say, 'Test, test, test,' who wants to be bothered with subtleties. The attitude is 'just cover the damn basics.'" Talk is that Scarsdale will defy the Regents and issue their own high school diplomas. If they go this route, there isn't a college in the country that will shun their students. And parents know it. As the *New York Times* noted, their schools "enjoy a reputation as golden as the price of the surrounding homes." Parents want to keep the schools that way, refusing to yield to the state standards and testing. Scarsdale parents didn't argue about who was in charge. They just took charge—and kept their eighth graders home on test days.

In May 2001, the Chicago NPR station WBEZ hosted a town hall meeting, also shown on public television. A representative from the Illinois Business Roundtable offered some pro-testing comments, as did a representative from the Illinois State Board of Education and the head of Chicago Public Schools Accountability Council. But the audience voiced strong disapproval of standardized testing in general and the Chicago Public Schools' misuse of tests in particular, namely its policy of using the Iowa test to flunk kids.

Julie Woestehoff, executive director of Parents United for Responsible Education (PURE), reports that "when they opened up the mike to the general audience, it was one hard-hitting comment against testing after another, with strong statements by parents, teachers, and students. Lots of people were left standing in line at the mike when they ran out of time." Commenting on the powerful audience response, Julie observed, "This is not a backlash, folks—this is a political movement. What struck me the most was the political implications of this passionate outpouring. Up until now, the high-stakes, tough-guy testing talk has seemed to come across pretty well politically, but this town meeting really called into question the viability of high-stakes testing as a popular movement. I'm quite sure Mayor Daley will be taking note."

In August 1997, Mary O'Brien was parent rep for her elementary school's building/planning team. As she listened to the teachers complain about the detrimental impact that the Ohio Proficiency Tests were having on the curriculum, Mary recalled a recent item about how Ohio rated on the FairTest assessment of state tests. She asked the principal why Ohio came out so low. He suggested that Mary "check it out."

So she phoned Monty Neill, director of FairTest, and "drove him nuts with my questions." Mary notes, "I always knew that I lived in an upper-income community known for its good schools, but, naive me, I thought other schools were like my school, that the whole country, or at least the whole state of Ohio, had evolved into this kinder, gentler model of education."

On her road to discovering the state of education in Ohio, Mary read her husband's course work for his graduate studies in education. She started calling his professors, asking questions. She also called the authors of his textbooks, asking more questions. "Life became a bit surreal. The authors of my husband's textbooks began calling our house to answer my questions." Mary was relentless. "I had to learn about how kids learn, about assessment, and about all the psychometric crap." Mary notes that at the same time she was launched on this campaign of high-stakes testing discovery, she was also president-elect of the school PTO. "My family was hooting and hollering and taking bets on how long it would take me to be impeached,"—and, sure enough, Mary was booted out that winter.

But nobody could stop Mary from focusing her energy and intrepid spirit on the Ohio Proficiency Tests. Mary heard about the shockwaves at the Ohio Department of Education and the legislature when an Upper Arlington parent had opted her kids out of the testing. While pondering this, Mary met Teri Zeigler, a fellow volunteer in YES, the Youth Education For Safety program. Mary was the parent who had opted her kids out of the test. Mary summarizes this meeting, "Woohoo!"

Let the resistance begin. Mary and Teri were experienced at teaching children to "Say No to Bullies." They decided adults could learn the same lessons. In Mary's words, "We became known as the moms from hell in our district and at the statehouse."

"Moms from hell" is a badge of pride claimed around the country.

Mary and Teri began writing op-eds against the test; they staged "very lonely statehouse protests," and attended Ohio Department of Education forums on assessment. "We wore out one ODE mouthpiece. She couldn't out-talk us because we did our homework." Mary feels that the press contacted them at first because "it was a novelty that two moms from a wealthy suburban district would protest testing that benefited their district." Mary became the Ohio state coordinator for ARN, and organized a symposium for the prestigious AERA (American Educational Research Association) annual convention.

The campaign "Be a Hero! Take a Zero—Say No to the OPT!" was launched to encourage parents to opt their children out of the OPT (Ohio Proficiency Testing). "That sure made us popular with superintendents around the state," Mary laughs. "But we also wanted to educate the public about the bogus practice of awarding a zero to the children whose parents opted them out of testing."

The group's Web site (http://www.stopots.org) acknowledges that lots of parents aren't quite ready to hit the streets with protest banners, and offers practical suggestions for what "the accidental activist" can do. "If picketing is not for you, that's all right. Write a letter, tell a friend. The important thing is just to spread the word." Mary points out that this Ohio group has done another very smart thing. "I think our best move was joining up and working with the religious right and conservatives. There is mutual respect and we have so much fun lobbying. The legislature can't play both sides of the fence with us." The group packed the Ohio Senate for weeks in 2001—hundreds of parents, students, and teachers testifying against the Senate bill that proposed the use of the Ohio Proficiency Test scores to rank students into one of four educational tracks starting in kindergarten. Mary's group formed an alliance with Christian homeschoolers to defeat the measure; she notes that people who find common cause for the sake of children learn how to avoid discussing other issues.

In June 2000, Lynn Haven, Florida, resident Gloria Pipkin launched a Web site to focus on resistance to high-stakes tests. A year and a half later, she reflects that she'd thought of this site as a repository of information: an essay from *Phi Delta Kappan* here, an analysis of the readability of the SAT-9 there. "But," says Gloria, "It's not enough. To build a dynamic site, you have to use it, change it, tweak it, promote it, and spend half your life keeping it current. I'm not willing to do that, and the site suffers." Even so, the site contains a provocative mix of strategy and support for individual acts of courage: news articles about Florida teachers who snubbed the bonuses proffered by the governor, the story of Steve Orel's unremitting struggle to rescue the 522 Birmingham students whose expulsion from high school occurred suspiciously close to the time when the district was desperate to raise its SAT-9 scores, organizing tools for fledgling groups, resources for school advisory councils, state media contacts, news stories about FCAT, and so on. Of special note is the Committee to Recognize Courage in Education site. Here one finds the Emperor's Clothes Award, awarded to George Schmidt in Chicago for courage in education; there are also stories of teachers and administrators around the country who have made extraordinary efforts to protect and support students from the ravages of high-stakes testing.

For Gloria, though, the heart of FCAR, Florida Coalition for Assessment Reform, Inc. (www.angelfire.com/fl4/fcar), has been the e-mail list. Set up a few weeks after the launch of the Web site, it started with an exchange of information among a few friends Gloria knew personally or met on ARN. The list now includes educators and parents in all corners of the state. A grassroots group with six directors, FCAR is incorporated as a not-for-profit. Gloria refers to one of the directors, retired teacher and administrator Marion Brady, as "the godfather of FCAR," pointing out that Brady was writing about the ills of FCAT in newspaper op-eds before most Floridians knew what it was.

In the summer of 2001, FCAR stepped beyond the virtual realm. Members hit the streets, launching a series of rallies around the state, beginning at Courthouse Square in Tampa. Test resisters wore "Spay the FCAT" buttons supplied by their Washington state mentor Juanita Doyon. Gloria Pipkin made a splash in various newspapers around the state with her summary of the FCAR position: "FCAT cannibalizes the curriculum, diverts scarce resources, discriminates against those who don't test well, and turns schools into giant test prep centers." A real plus of this effort was the birth of FCAR West, formed out of the response to the Tampa rally. "They are really going great guns," reports Gloria. She sounds ready to give up her allegiance to the virtual realm and keep to the streets. Let the Standardistas beware: this woman has already debated the deputy commissioner of education on public radio and pinned Governor Bush to the mat in an e-mail exchange.

FCAR takes action in individual schools as well as in more fundamental issues. As this book goes to press, FCAR is preparing to join school finance litigation being brought by the Florida Education Association against the state. At the same time, FCAR keeps an eye on individual schools, and is there with brochures when one principal asks:

> Gloria,
>
> My school SAC recently sponsored a panel discussion for parents. Teachers, parents and a former school superintendent who writes guest editorials in the local paper about education and testing were on the panel. We had only about 30 people, but they were very interested. They came expecting to hear a pep talk about FCAT and were amazed at what they heard. I believe we created a couple of zealots who are now writing impassioned e-mails to dialogue with Betty Coxe [deputy commissioner of education]. It's quite inspiring.
>
> As a result of the panel discussion, the parents want the SAC to organize another meeting with local legislators so they can tell them what they think. All said they will bring at least three more parents with them.
>
> Please send me some brochures. I think they'll have an impact now.
>
> Thanks.
> Cathy Kitto

Cathy is an extraordinarily thoughtful and courageous principal in Sarasota, Florida. She and four teachers from her school made a media splash when they traveled to Tallahassee to return the governor's "bribe money" they had received because their school's test scores gave them the label "high-performing." Cathy confides, "The worst thing they can do is fire me, and that doesn't sound so bad anymore."

Hard as it is to believe, this seems to be the intent of the Standardistas: drive good people from the schools.

## LOSING TEACHERS

Molly Ivins wrote about an excellent teacher she knows, someone very talented at teaching kids to read. "Then the Arizona Legislature had one of those fits of faddishness to which the political world is so prone, and passed a law saying the only method that can be used to teach reading is phonics." Molly continues, "My friend says, 'Phonics is a very good way to teach reading. But not all kids learn the same way. Some kids have to learn by sight and you need other methods to help them. I have been teaching for 30 years. There is not a single teacher in the Arizona Legislature. Why are they telling me how to do my job?' So she quit."

A veteran teacher in Texas was asked to resign because she was mainstreaming too many of her special-ed kids. Teachers were complaining that this mainstreaming would affect their TAAS results. The principal was so upset that he resigned too. Another Texas teacher admits, "If we talk about the TAAS, we can be fired; they tell us we'll be involuntarily transferred or fired if our kids don't succeed on the test. I can barely look at myself in the mirror."

More than a million teachers are nearing retirement—at the same time when we will see 11 percent more high school students. We need 2.2 million new teachers over the next 10 years. So why are we beating up on the ones we have? It would make a whole lot more sense to give every one we have a hug. What a switch: How about thank-a-teacher instead of bash-a-teacher editorials in the nation's newspapers? Think about how the world would change if people at the Fordham Foundation, the Hoover Institution, the *New York Post*, and in John Stossel's outfit decided one morning to be on the lookout for something good about schools and the teachers and kids in them.

In *Feasting the Heart*, Reynolds Price recalls that from the time that he entered school at age six until the time he quit at twenty-five, he "encountered only one bad teacher. Some were better prepared than others, some more inexplicably endowed with the sorcery that makes great teaching an unteachable art and elevates every master teacher into the guild of genuine magic—those rare magnetos who transmit vital skill, the tease for civilized joy, and the very essence of hope itself: the highest gift from one generation to the next." Teachers need to hear words like these occasionally.

Of the 33,000 members of the Colorado Teachers Association, Donald Perl, a language arts teacher at John Evans Middle School in Greeley, where he had taught for 19 years, was the first to refuse to give the Colorado Student Assessment Program (CSAP), a test required by the state. For his refusal, Donald was given a six-day suspension. His theory is that "school officials fear that if a teacher refuses to administer the tests, next students will refuse to take it."

Donald witnessed a senator standing up in a hearing and insisting that teachers "teach to the test"; he endured faculty in-service training orienting teachers to the tests. "We read test excerpts and answered the multiple-choice questions. Most of the questions had more than one answer."

Something else provoked Donald's revolt. "Thirty percent of our students speak Spanish at home. Since my room was across the hall from the principal's office, I was often summoned to translate. There, I saw another world: I saw intimidated, lost parents who obviously wanted the best for their children, but lacked resources and therefore had no voice in their children's education. I began to see the tests as more than ridiculous; they are also discriminatory and oppressive."

Donald asserts that the Colorado Senate Bill 186 is unconstitutional. His thoroughness is typical of test resisters. "Article IX of the State Constitution states that 'the general assembly shall . . . provide for the establishment and maintenance of a thorough and uniform system of free public schools throughout the state.' Section 15 declares that 'the general assembly shall, by law, provide for organization of school districts of convenient size, in each of which shall be established a board of education to consist of three or more directors to be elected by the qualified electors of the district. Said directors shall have control of instruction in the public schools of their districts.' Section 16 adds that 'neither the general assembly nor the state board of education shall have power to prescribe textbooks to be used in the public schools.'"

Donald reflects, "This last section is a reflection of Jeffersonian democracy, which asserts that the people themselves are best suited to making decisions that most directly affect their lives. Jefferson also maintained that public education had to be off-limits to private interests. The passage of Senate Bill 186, which extends high-stakes standardized testing, corrupts both Section 16 of the State Constitution and the essential concepts of democracy, and certainly threatens democracy, which requires a well-educated, broad-thinking populace."

"This is not about me," insists Donald. "Rosa Parks refused to get out of her seat in the bus, and that wasn't about her."

Donald Perl was a language arts teacher at John Evans Middle School in Greeley for 19 years. "Was" is the operative word here, because even though he survived the act of civil disobedience with a six-day suspension, at the end of the school year Donald made the decision to leave public school teaching. CSAP took the heart and soul out of teaching for Donald, and he's decided he must find other ways to work for social justice. In taking leave, he cites his favorite quote from Thoreau: "Must the citizen even for a moment, or in the least degree, resign conscience to the legislator? Why has every person a conscience, then?"

An English teacher at Cherry Creek High School in Denver, Bruce Degi resigned rather than participate in the Colorado Student Assessment Program (CSAP). Bruce brought outstanding credentials to teaching. As a Senior Fulbright Scholar, he taught at the University of Veszprem in Hungary as well as at the Air Force Academy, where he was a tenured associate professor of English. He became a Denver teacher after retiring from the Academy.

Bruce takes strong exception to the governor's determination to label schools based on students' performance on the state test. "I saw myself as part of public education in Colorado, not just as a part of the [Cherry] Creek District. I find it unacceptable to celebrate a 'victory' (if that is what it is) that causes needless pain and suffering to my colleagues in other districts." Bruce talks of the bribes offered to students to show up during the testing period—drawings for prizes and so on. "I could not be a part of that." He adds, "Schools are now just another business; teachers are simply assembly-line workers who produce a product that we have to 'quality control' during the manufacturing process. The business metaphor subverts and perverts everything I believe about education, every reason why I became a teacher."

Bruce explains the roots of his resistance. "Perhaps I just taught Gandhi and Thoreau and Martin Luther King, Jr., for too long. I guess I actually started believing that when something is wrong, seriously wrong, that you don't compromise, you don't quibble, you just say no. That, in a nutshell, is what I found myself having to do in the face of the CSAP."

In July 2001, the front-page headline of the *Washington Post* read, "SOL Tests Create New Dropouts." This time the dropouts are the teachers. Liz Seymour reported that ace math teacher and nominee for teacher of the year Bruce Snyder left public education to teach calculus at the private Georgetown Day School in the district. Why? "The Virginia Standards of Learning tests."

Snyder, a former calculus teacher at Park View High School in Loudoun, received a number of offers from private schools. He liked Georgetown Day's mission statement: "We encourage our students to wonder, to inquire, and to be self-reliant, laying the foundation for a lifelong love of learning." That sounds like the reason most teachers enter the field.

## SORRY, WRONG NUMBER

Just call it "Dial M for Measurement Meltdown." On June 6, 2001, Mark Spivack's mother received a recorded telephone message from Schools Chancellor Harold O. Levy telling her that Mark was at risk of being held back a grade unless he attended summer school. Note: it was June 6, not April Fool's. Mark Spivack is a 40-year-old financial planner living in New Jersey. He graduated from the New York City public school system 23 years ago. Rising to the occasion, Mark's mother said maybe he'd have to cancel his plans to play golf and attend summer school instead.

As reported in the *New York Times*, the phone calls were not so humorous for 237,000 other families who received the automated messages. With the call coming in at 6 p.m. on a Friday, the family of twelve-year-old Kendall Goodman, a student with a 3.0 grade point average, had to wait on pins and needles through the weekend before finding out on Monday morning that the call was a mistake and that Kendall wouldn't have to attend summer school. Her father said, "Whether you have a flunking student or a B-minus student, it is not nice to call someone at 6 o'clock on a Friday night. Who are you going to speak to? You have three days of sheer pain and agony. If you are going to do something like this, you should at least do it during business hours. Somebody should be held responsible for making an irresponsible phone call like that."

Welcome to the bizarre world of data storage. In Chicago, when one-half the children were slotted for summer school as a result of their test performance, it definitely depended on who was reading the numbers—and which numbers they were reading.

Parents worry about test data snafus, but they also worry about the other data schools collect on their children. Take the mistake made at the Air Force Academy: A confidential list of 40 or 50 cadets with criminal, discipline, and medical problems was mistakenly e-mailed to all 4400 cadets in the Academy instead of to the intended receivers, the school administration. The list included cadets suspected of stealing, credit card theft, drunken driving, making fake identification cards, and downloading pornography. It also included cadets being counseled for emotional problems and others who may be leaving the academy because of emotional or medical problems.

A security breach in the computer system that stores data for the Georgia HOPE scholarship program had all sorts of ramifications. The Georgia Student Finance Commission inadvertently released personal data about thousands of students, and at the same time passwords allowing access to computers at the agency were exposed on the Internet. This meant hackers could have used the passwords and code to gain access to any file in the commission's computers. Any file. Hackers could have fiddled with the value of the scholarships received by thousands of Georgia college students. Or, reported the *Atlanta Journal Constitution*, "they could have used the doorway into the commission's network to enter other state computers, such as those containing tax files and medical records."

The error allowed Google.com and perhaps other Internet search engines to copy confidential files that were on-line from April to late June 2001.

Schools claimed ignorance of the fact that the Web filtering software they were using—and encouraging parents to use at home—was collecting and selling lists called "Class Clicks," which detailed the Web habits of 14 million school kids and their families. According to the *Wall Street Journal*, N2H2's Bess filtering system "knows where the students go on the Web and how long they spend there." N2H2 sold the data they collected to marketers and to the Department of Defense, who wanted it for "recruitment purposes." Recruiting third graders? For $15,000 a year, fast-track entrepreneurs could get monthly reports detailing where kids were going on the Internet. First you gather the data; then you sell it. It's called capitalism. Ralph Nader calls these outfits "corporate predators," and Phyllis Schlafly agrees, proving that progressives and conservatives *can* hold hands for the good of children.

N2H2 agreed to stop selling the results of its schoolroom snooping, but this does not mean they aren't still snooping, just that they aren't, for the moment, selling info. Apparently, the Defense Department has also backed off from its prying. In a letter answering the advocacy organization Commercial Alert's complaint, the Pentagon's director of accession policy responded, "At this point, we are delaying our decision about participating in the 'Class Clicks' project, indefinitely." The Electronic Privacy Information Center filed a Freedom of Information Act request to figure out why the Pentagon is so interested in the surfing habits of children.

N2H2 claims the data was aggregated, meaning it couldn't identify the surfing habits of individual students. Privacy advocates are skeptical. Jeff Chester, executive director of the Center for Media Education says the schools are "clueless" when it comes to knowledge of data collection. Jason Catlett, the president of Junkbusters, a privacy advocacy organization, says parents would need a degree in marketing and computer science to be able to keep up with the invasion of the data collectors. What parents need to know is that the child data-gathering steamroller is here: if not yet in your neighborhood school, it's on the way. Sometimes this is trumpeted as being a way for parents to have instant access to their kids' daily grades, attendance records, disciplinary reports, and so on. Just remember the Air Force cadets: when all that data is there ready to be zapped to parents, one mis-click zaps it to the world. Another point of concern, as in the Georgia case, is that student data allows access to parent data. There are also extended privacy issues: Forty years from now, when your daughter is a presidential candidate, she may not want data from her fourth-grade year to be out there on the Web. She may not want it out there even if her preferred vocation is hitchhiking to Patagonia.

A Federal law prohibits the collection or sale of a child's personal information without parental permission, but one can wonder how many parents read the small print. Or understand it. And if there is a privacy law, a number of parents are wondering why the schools don't ask permission to collect their children's SAT-9, CTB/McGraw-Hill, Riverside scores. With the evidence that schoolchildren are already being used as digital marketing fodder, one can only wonder what else is in store from the data warehouses.

Data warehouse is an up-and-coming term in ed-whiz-biz circles. Here's a promo statement from IBM Insight at School, an outfit that's off and running after a new cash cow:

> . . . our education specialists can design and implement a decision-making support system to help promote greater accountability and student achievement in your district. IBM Insight at School, IBM's K-12 data warehousing solution, will cleanse your school's data for accuracy and deliver information for easier interpretation and use, even over the Web.

IBM has a long history of not just selling its machines and walking away. It sticks around, anticipating the needs, and showing customers how to organize the data. As IBM explains on its Web site, "The amount of information that today's schools are required to collect can be overwhelming. But IBM's complete, packaged IBM Insight at School solution offers the technology, services, and training your district needs to help make the most of the following kinds of data: Student, Testing, Demographics, Transportation, Funding, Professional Development, and Human Resources.

"Decision makers can create mandated reports at the click of the button. With all the facts and historical data integrated, your district can make more efficient use of school resources and promote continuous student improvement."

Give that man a cigar. Lou Gerstner declares an education crisis, convincing his corporate and political cronies to join him in education summits. They lay out the ground rules requiring schools to collect enormous amounts of data. And then, voilà, IBM steps in to manage the data. Give him a case of cigars. (For more about data-driven decision making, see Chapter 5, The Global Economy Smokescreen and the Rest of the Story.)

## KIDS FIGHT BACK

In spring 2000, Annelise Schantz was the valedictorian at her high school graduation. Sitting on the stage as she delivered her valedictory address was hometown son Massachusetts Governor Cellucci, avid supporter of high-stakes tests. Annelise asked what separated her from number 2, 50, or 120? She said the assigned numbers reflected nothing about the true character of an individual. "Nothing about personality. Nothing about desire or will. Nothing about values or morals. Nothing about intelligence. Nothing about creativity. Nothing about heart."

Annelise detailed the abuses wrought by "the head honchos" who were determined to push standards and measures onto the school. "I doubt that a single one of these politicians has ever stopped to consider that we are not numbers. We are individuals. How dare they restrict us once more into useless categories of failing, proficient, advanced?" Annelise said, "The idea of MCAS testing is similar to putting a BAND-AID on a severed limb . . . We hear GPA, class rank, SAT, test grades, midterms, finals, scholastic achievement, but never once do we hear 'never mind the grade, think about the learning, think about activism, think about life.'"

Concluding her searing indictment of the system, Annelise said, "And so I stand here today and forever, and refuse to be defined as a number." Her fellow graduates gave her a standing ovation. Governor Cellucci sat silent on the stage.

In a *New Democracy* essay, "Take This Test and Shove It," John Spritzler describes the harsh crackdown against the MCAS boycott at Danvers High School. Seven students who refused to take the test were suspended for three days. One, Curt Doble, was falsely accused of making bomb threats. "Police went to Curt's home, told his mother to stop 'hiding her son,' barged in, handcuffed Curt, jailed him overnight, and set bail at $10,000 cash. The next day a judge declared there was no evidence and no probable cause for arrest, and wondered out loud how a warrant was issued in the first place."

Gene Sommerfeld, the parent of another of the Danvers test refusers, said, "I told them my son is not going to take the test when the next round begins. Why? Because now the father has learned from the son. I said, 'I know my 16-year-old son is just a piece of garbage in your eyes, but he's standing up to you and saying, 'I'm not going to take it.'" Sommerfield, a Ph.D. in chemistry, says, "It took a 16-year-old boy to make me understand. No form of punishment is acceptable, not suspension, not alternative service, not anything else. He had done no wrong, he cannot be punished."

Also in Massachusetts, the Student Coalition for Alternatives to the MCAS capitalized on the anagram possibilities of MCAS, and SCAM was born. They have a Web site with press releases, calls to action, and assorted information about the whys and hows of organizing a mass protest against the exam. Tim Kaldas, a student at Reading High, commented, "We have already lost one of our most enriching humanities courses to make way for world history prep." Imagine how much more cheated such students feel when, in the summer of 2001, the authorities also scrapped the world history test prep that bulldozed their humanities course.

SCAM organizers are responsible about pointing out the very real consequences of boycotting the tests, including facing suspension and receiving a zero on their school record. With regards to this latter penalty, SCAM points out:

> It is important to realize that a school record is different from a transcript.
>
> School records are not sent automatically to colleges or employers. For anyone to see them, you must give your written permission. Furthermore, most colleges are not even looking at the MCAS test . . . Even if colleges or employees do ask for the MCAS scores, many will also love to hear about informed, passionate, and persistent students who attempt to improve their educational system.

When 10 students at Chicago's prestigious Whitney Young High School deliberately failed the Illinois Goals Assessment Program, they ended up in newspapers around the country and on National Public Radio. As reported in *Substance*, the education resistance newspaper of record, after the protesters marched on the sidewalk outside school board headquarters and distributed an explanation of their protest to passersby, "Chicago police (who had been deployed against the protest in numbers exceeding the number of protesters) complimented them on their organization, intelligence, and politeness."

After surviving 12 years of traditional schooling, Bill Wetzel decided to postpone his entry into Cornell and bicycle around the country, visiting schools, talking to people. While narrowly losing a bid for a high school board of education post in New Jersey—against the past president of the board who had been a local teacher for 40 years—Bill launched the Power to the Youth network (www.youthpower.net) as a "spunky and creative tool for young people to become active school reformers in their local districts." A year later, in the summer of 2001, Bill decided to focus his efforts on standardized testing, and launched Students Against Testing (SAT). He sees standardized tests as "the most bold and directly counter-learning force in the schools today."

Students Against Testing, www.NoMoreTests.com, is a sophisticated site with an action gallery, reading/research section, quotes, links, merchandise, and a discussion board. The group has organized a number of protests in New York State. It offers practical information including:

- 101 Things to Do Besides Standardized Tests
- 10 Reasons to Oppose Standardized Tests
- Q&A About Testing

Here are a couple of questions from SAT's *The Best Standardized Test Ever*:

1. While a child takes a 12-hour exam, the child most likely feels:
   a) Tickled pretty by algebraic functions
   b) A strange sensation of nausea and near vomit
   c) Trapped in a never-ending tunnel of boxes and numbers
   d) The sheer discomfort of a plastic orange chair

2. The "Texas Miracle" proved that:
   a) Country music makes kids smarter
   b) All we need to do is kick out all the low scoring students
   c) Testing is the same as learning
   d) Y'all can't think for y'allselves

3. The scores of students most accurately reveal:
   a) Their parents' income
   b) Their ability to learn and explore the world
   c) The number of nose hairs they have
   d) How many doses of Prozac they were given the night before

## WHY IS THIS BEING DONE TO OUR KIDS?

Tests with nutty, abstruse, and otherwise impossible questions are at the core of education reform, which is at the core of the overall attack on working people in our society. For the past 25 years, workers have been subjected to speed-ups on the job, increased stress with reduced benefits. The bar is raised all the time, and when someone says "Jump!" they have to jump fast and high. Now the same strategies are being applied to young children in the schools. The tests are designed for massive failure rates and the goals are the same nationwide: declare schools lousy so you can have vouchers, assail teacher tenure, make education more stratified and competitive, and train students to know their place in a more unequal, less democratic society.

Students are supposed to fail the tests. That's part of the plan. In states where one can see the tests, everyone reports confusing, badly posed questions; questions inappropriate to the age of the child being tested; questions on material not even covered in class. The failure rate on the MCAS in Boston in 1999 was 70 percent. In Virginia, 98 percent of the school districts failed similar tests. And so on.

The looming threat of an impossible test provokes high dropout rates. By the senior year in Chicago public high schools, 41 percent of the class is missing. Since the initiation of the TAAS program in Texas, only 50 percent of the minority students have moved beyond grade nine.

In the words of education policy analyst and writer Anne Wheelock, "The tests are 'a set-up to tell you you're stupid.'" Instead of, as testocrats claim, encouraging students to take school seriously and become "graduates with skills," the test is pushing them to drop out in 10th grade. By the Massachusetts Department of Education's own estimates, 33 percent of Latino students, 25 percent of African-American students, and 10 percent of white students in the class of 2002 will drop out before graduating.

After talking with many students, Wheelock concludes, "Contrary to public rhetoric, MCAS is less likely to motivate students to work harder than to drive the most vulnerable away from school altogether. Nationwide, testocrats insist that the tests will motivate students to work harder. In practice, the most vulnerable are crushed by the tests. In increasing numbers, they decide it's better to avoid repeating the humiliation of failure than to keep showing up to school in hopes that they might pass one day. And when the test is the only thing that counts, when class grades, effort, and teacher recommendation don't count, it becomes increasingly difficult to tell them they are wrong."

The pressures are just as bad for younger children. Sherry Guzick says her daughter was "very concerned during the FCAT after she was told their scores are being compared with other kids in other states." So the weight of the school's reputation rests on the shoulders of one little girl. Sherry observes that this weighed heavily on her daughter. "The peer pressure and fear of exposure was upsetting to a private, introverted child."

Sherry continues, "My daughter was also very concerned when the teacher told them if they all scored a 4 or 5 on the writing test, they would have a pizza party. This makes the kids scoring a 3, which is, after all, the median, feel not only like failures, but that they were letting the class down."

Since when did "being average" become a dirty word?

Here's part of a letter from an Ohio parent to her state senator:

I am the parent of three children. I am very concerned with the way the OPT has taken over our school's entire curriculum. Teaching is no longer to individual students, but to a test.

My first exposure to the proficiency testing occurred two years ago when my daughter was in fourth grade. The entire year from September to June was a nightmare. My daughter had at least 2 to 3 hours of homework each night. Our entire family life revolved around helping her deal with her homework . . .

By February . . . my daughter suffered from frequent headaches, stomachaches, and sleepless nights. She was nine years old. At the request of our pediatrician, we took her for counseling to help her deal with the stress of the proficiency test. . . .

There comes a point when a parent must ask how much she owes her daughter to the state and when she must shout, "Enough!"

When Connor Murphy, a fifth grader in Minden, Nevada, boycotted the state's standardized test, the Douglas County School System named him "truant" and threatened his mother with jail. Connor asked his mother why his teacher taught the class about Patrick Henry and the American Revolution but wouldn't let him refuse to take the test.

"We have to practice what we preach," insists Michelle Trusty-Murphy, Connor's mother. "I don't want him to take a test I can't see. People don't understand how testing is used to control the curriculum and how that might connect very intimately to our democratic rights. I don't want to cede to the government such control over our children." She continues, "I'm not some whacko paranoid freak; I'm just one mom sounding the alarm."

Forced to sit for a makeup exam or be declared truant again, Connor drew a line through the answer column on three tests: the state's mandatory reading, writing, and math tests. He summed up the experience in a caption for a drawing he made, "Don't take the tests. Be a hero."

Members of the Debate Club at Bay High School in Panama City, Florida, researched high-stakes testing and organized a forum called "Grading Our Schools." They produced a video with a student band playing and singing "FCAT Day" to the tune of John Lennon's "Yesterday." Students made a trip to Tallahassee to talk to legislators about the FCAT and to invite them to the forum. No legislator attended.

Debate Club president Michaela Sprouse's guest column in the *News Herald* provoked a local citizen to write a letter to the editor. "If our public schools are producing students who research and write like Michaela, why are we disrupting the educational process for teachers and students?"

Some acts of resistance are quieter but no less profound. A sixth grader in Florida asked her teacher who she should write to if she wanted to share her thoughts about testing. The teacher says, "I was taken aback. This is a student who is generally quiet. And sixth graders aren't tested in our school. I told her there were several different options and I would find information for her. Then I asked her why she felt she needed to write about it."

The sixth grader replied that one of the poems the class had read recently—"Hangman" by Ogden, about World War II and the Holocaust—said that if you don't speak up when you can, you may not have a chance to do so. She said she didn't want to have to take tests for the rest of her time in school and so she'd better speak up.

Another sixth grader, this one in Ohio, suffered the yearlong drill as the teacher prepared the class for the proficiency tests. Her mother writes, "When she started asking questions about it, her teacher told her it wasn't the school but the state dictating the testing. She came home and surfed the Net, finding out that, by law, the schools must give the tests but that students could be exempted with a letter. The school about hit the ceiling when she walked in with Mary O'Brien's "Be A Hero" sheet that she printed off the Stop Ohio Proficiency Tests Web site. She refused to take the test, and they pressured and threatened her repeatedly with failing, being marked with unexcused absences, and so on. I phoned the State Department of Education, and they told me she did have to take it. Then I phoned back on another day, saying I was a teacher with a class full of children whose parents sent in notes saying they wouldn't allow the kids to be tested. The Department of Education then told me, 'They have that right!' They even faxed me a form about what districts need to do for students who do not take the test."

At Sherman Oaks Elementary School, principal Peggy Bryan took a stand, urging parents to let their second, third, and fourth graders boycott the SAT-9. "Schools should impart joy and the love of learning. But the current testing climate dims and numbs that sense of wonder because it pushes teachers to compress knowledge into a #2 pencil and fill-in-the-bubble Scantron sheets," she wrote to parents in a letter.

"At some point, we need to stop spending so many grueling hours of instructional time measuring and remeasuring children on tests of all shapes and sizes," Bryan continued. "You have the right to exempt your child. Write a note and give it to the teacher or bring it to the office." More than two-thirds of the parents did just that. By boycotting the exam, the school forfeited its chances to receive status bonus money for demonstrated scholastic achievement. But they made an important step to bringing joy back to their school.

Joy in schools: What a notion. But it's catching on.

# Bibliography

ACHIEVE. *A New Compact for Ohio's Schools: A Report to Ohio's Educational Policy Leaders*. (1999) Boston: Achieve.

_____. *Measuring Up: A Standards and Assessment Benchmarking Report for New Jersey*. (2000) Boston: Achieve.

ADAIR, JEFF. "MCAS Pressure Claiming Teachers." *Metrowest Daily News*. August 22, 2001.

ALLIANCE FOR CHILDHOOD. "High-Stakes Testing: A Statement of Concern and Call to Action." Alliance for Childhood.net. April 24, 2001.

ALLINGTON, RICHARD. *What Really Matters for Struggling Readers*. (2001) New York: Addison-Wesley Longman.

ANDERS, JANSON. "Web-Filter Data from Schools Put Up for Sale." *Wall Street Journal*. January 26, 2001.

ASIMOV, NANETTE. "Davis Feels Heat Over Student Depositions." *San Francisco Chronicle*. September 6, 2001.

_____. "Teachers Reject Test Score Bonuses." *San Francisco Chronicle*. August 2, 2001.

ASIMOV, NANETTE, and LANCE WILLIAMS. "Governor Davis vs School Kids. High-priced Legal Team Browbeats Youths about Shoddy Schools." *San Francisco Chronicle*. September 2, 2001.

ASSOCIATED PRESS. "High-Stakes Test Prep Robs the Three R's." *Cnnfyi.com*. April 17, 2001.

BACON, DAVID. "The Money in Testing." *Z-Magazine*. September 2000.

BEAM-CONROY, TEDDI. "Bamboozled by the Texas Miracle." *Rethinking Schools*. Fall 2001.

BENNETT, WILLIAM, CHESTER FINN, and JOHN T. CRIBB. *The Educated Child*. (2000) New York: Free Press.

BENNING, VICTORIA. "VA Parents Don't Trust Exam, Poll Finds." *Washington Post*. June 27, 2000.

BESZE, SUSAN. "Adults agree tests are challenging." *Denver Post*. March 1, 2000.

BIGELOW, BILL. "Social Studies Tests From Hell." *Rethinking Schools*. Spring 1999.

BLACKBOARD RESOURCE CENTER. "All Work and No Play: No More Recess." *Sarasota Herald-Tribune*. February 12, 2001.

BOLDEN, BARBARA K. "Should Standardized Tests Results Determine a Child's Future, Especially If the Test Is Not Designed for Individual Results?" *The Prince George's County Sentinel*. May 29, 2001.

BORSUK, ALAN J. "MPS Drops Standardized Tests for Second-Graders in Contentious Voting." *Milwaukee Journal Sentinel*. June 27, 2001.

BOUTWELL, CLINTON. Shell Game: *Corporate America's Agenda for Schools*. (1997) Bloomington, Indiana: Phi Delta Kappa.

BOYLE, DAVID. *In the Sum of Our Discontent: Why Numbers Make Us Irrational.* (2001) New York: Texere.

BRACEY, GERALD. "The Malevolent Tyranny of Algebra." *Education Week.* October 25, 2000.

_____. "High Stakes Testing." *Center for Education Research, Analysis, and Innovation.* December 5, 2000.

_____. *Setting the Record Straight.* (1997) Alexandria, Virginia: ASCD.

_____. "Failing Children—Twice." *Education Week.* June 16, 1999.

_____. "Poverty Issues Get Short Shrift." *USA Today.* November 8, 1999.

BRANDON, KAREN. "Test-prep Pressure Hits Grade Schools. Exam-Guide Industry Finds Younger Clients." *Chicago Tribune.* February 19, 2001.

BRAUER, DAVID. "Standardized Test Fails in Big Way, with a High Cost to Many Students." *Chicago Tribune.* August 14, 2000.

BRETT, JENNIFER. "Teachers Fear Taking Tests to Replace Thrill of Learning." *Atlanta Journal Constitution.* March 2, 2000.

THE BUSINESS ROUNDTABLE. *Continuing the Commitment: Essential Components of a Successful Education System.* (1995) www.brtable.org.

_____. *A Business Leader's Guide to Setting Academic Standards.* (1996) Washington, D.C.: The Business Roundtable.

_____. *Building Support for Tests that Count.* (1998) www.brtable.org.

_____. *Transforming Educational Policy: Addressing Ten Years of Progress in the States.* (1999) www.brtable.org.

_____. "The Business Roundtable Brings Employers to Capitol Hill to Make the Case for Education Reform." Press release. March 20, 2001.

_____. "The Business Roundtable Urges Quick Congressional Action to Support the President's Education Agenda." Press release. February 28, 2001.

_____. "The Business Roundtable Supports Annual Measures of Reading, Math Progress." Press release. February 23, 2001.

_____. "Nation's Business Leaders Aim to Elevate Teaching to Better-Rewarded, More-Demanding Profession." Press release. January 30, 2001.

CALIFORNIA DEPARTMENT OF EDUCATION. *1999 Academic Performance Reported for California Schools.* January 25, 2000. REL #00-5.

CAMERON, ANN. *More Stories Julian Tells.* (1989) New York: Random House.

CAMILLI, GREGORY, and KATRINA BULKLEY. "Critique of 'An Evaluation of the Florida A-Plus Accountability and School Choice Program.'" *Education Policy Analysis Archives.* March 4, 2001.

CAPUTO-PEARL, ALEX. "How the Stanford 9 Test Institutionalizes Unequal Education." *Los Angeles Times.* May 2, 1999.

CARLSON, DARREN K. "Nurses Remain at Top of Honest and Ethics Poll." *Gallup News Service.* November 27, 2000.

CHADDOCK, GAIL RUSSELL. "Corporate Ways Invade Schools." *Christian Science Monitor.* August 4, 2000.

CHAS, MURRAY. "Umpires Arguing Over Number of Balls and Strikes." *New York Times.* July 16, 2001.

CHEEVER, SUSAN. *As Good As I Could Be.* (2001) New York: Simon and Schuster.
and School Choice Program.'" *Education Policy Analysis Archives.* March 4, 2001.

COEYMAN, MARJORIE. "If These Are High Standards, We Don't Want Them." *Christian Science Monitor*. October 19, 1999.

COHEN, PATRICIA. "Oops, Sorry: Seems That My Pie Chart Is Half-Baked." *New York Times*. April 8, 2000.

COHN, EDWARD. "Selling Higher Test Scores." *The American Prospect*. October 23, 2000.

COMMON SENSE FOUNDATION and NORTH CAROLINA JUSTICE AND COMMUNITY DEVELOPMENT CENTER. *A Closer Look: A Parent's Guide to Standardized Testing in NC Schools*. No date.

CRUICE, VALERIE. "Seeing an Early Edge Into Elite Colleges." *New York Times*. May 28, 2000.

CUBAN, LARRY. "What Bad Reforms Won't Give Us Good Schools." *The American Prospect*. January 1, 2001.

_____. "How Systemic Reform Harms Urban Schools." *Education Week*. May 30, 2001.

DEWEY, JOHN. "My Pedagogic Creed." *The School Journal*. January 16, 1897.

DIBACCO, THOMAS V. "Umpires Right to Call Foul." *USA Today*. July 20, 2001.

DILLER, LAWRENCE. *Running on Ritalin*. (1998) New York: Bantam.

DODSON, CHARLIE G. "Standardized Testing Flunks Basic Education." *Los Angeles Times*. Letters. July 23, 2001.

DOYON, JUANITA. "Tests Are Harmful to Schools, Children. *Seattle Times*. Letters. August 17, 2000.

DRISCOLL, KATHI SCRIZZI. "Sticker Shock." *Cape Cod Times*. August 30, 2001.

EDELMAN, SUSAN. "Crews' 'Miracle' was a Fraud." *New York Post*. September 7, 1999.

EHRENREICH, BARBARA. *Nickel and Dimed*. (2001) New York: Henry Holt.

ELKIND, DAVID. *The Hurried Child*, 3rd Edition. (2001) Cambridge, Mass.: Perseus.

ELSNER, ALAN. "Bush's School Testing Plan Stirs Backlash." *Reuters Limited*. May 31, 2001.

ENGLISH, BELLA. "Winning at the Learning Game." *Boston Globe*. January 12, 2000.

ESQUIBEL, CURTIS. "8th Grade Students Have New Challenge This Fall." *Contra Costa Times*. August 11, 2001.

FARNSWORTH, MEGAN. "Schools: A High-Test Formula for Success." *Knight-Ridder/Tribune News Wire*. April 12, 2001.

FATSIS, STEFAN. *Word Freak*. (2001) Boston: Houghton Mifflin.

FERRECHIO, SUSAN. "Black History Events Lose Out to FCAT." *Miami Herald*. February 21, 2000.

FERRI, DANIEL. "Dancin' Circles." *Rethinking Schools*. Spring 1999.

FISCHER, KENT. "Florida Teachers Reject Bribe Money." *St. Petersburg Times*. October 25, 2000.

FISHER, MARC. "Mountain of Tests Slowly Crushing School Quality." *Washington Post*. May 8, 2001.

_____. "Schools Find Wrong Answer to Test Pressure." *Washington Post*. May 10, 2001.

FLETCHER, MICHAEL A. "As Stakes Rise, School Groups Put Exams to the Test. Critics Decry Heavy Reliance on Standardized Measures." *Washington Post*. July 9, 2001.

FOX, DENNIS. "The Corporate MCAS Agenda." *Brookline TAB*. August 17, 2000.
_____. "Corporate-sponsored Tests Aim to Standardize Our Kids." *New Democracy*. No date. newdemocracyworld.org.

FOX, JONATHAN. "Grilling Our Young." *Salon.com*. November 8, 1999.

FRAHM, ROBERT A. "A Tale of Two Teachers." *Hartford Courant*. June 21, 2001.

FULGHUM, ROBERT. *All I Really Need To Know I Learned in Kindergarten*. (1988) New York: Villard.

GARRISON, JESSICA. "Stanford 9 Drilling Puts Dent in Learning, Teachers Say." *Los Angeles Times*. January 14, 2001.
_____. "Struggling District Ponders 2nd Year of Kindergarten." *Los Angeles Times*. October 22, 2001.

GERSTNER, LOUIS V. with ROGER SEMERAD, DENIS DOYLE, and WILLIAM JOHNSTON. *Reinventing Education*. (1984) New York: Dutton.
_____. "1996 National Education Summit." Speech. March 26, 1996.
_____. National Press Club. Speech. March 27, 1997.
_____. "1999 Education Summit." Speech. September 30, 1999.

GLENN, DONNA. "Fourth-grade Tests Open to Third Graders." *The Columbus Dispatch*. March 12, 2001.

GOLDMAN, WILLIAM. *Adventures of the Screen Trade*. (1989) New York: Warner.

GOODNOUGH, ABBY. "Teaching By the Book, No Asides Allowed." *New York Times*. May 23, 2001.
_____. "School Board in New Dispute Over Testing." *New York Times*. June 9, 2001.
_____. "Strain of Fourth-Grade Tests Drives Off Veteran Teachers." *New York Times*. June 14, 2001.
_____. "'S' Is for Satisfactory, Not for Satisfied, on Teacher's Sentimental Journey." *New York Times*. July 1, 2001.
_____. "Summer School's Second Mixed Record." *New York Times*. August 21, 2001.

GORMAN, ANNA. "For Some Kindergartners, Vacation Becomes Academic." *Los Angeles Times*. July 10, 2000.
_____. "Reading by 9. A Philosophy that Doesn't Rush Pupils to Read." *Los Angeles Times*. October 18, 1999.

GROVES, MARTHA. "'Test Prep' moving into Primary Grades." *Los Angeles Times*. April 1, 2000.
_____. "2 Experts say Stanford 9 Test Has Many Flaws." *Los Angeles Times*. July 14, 2000.
_____. "Most 9th-Graders Fail High School Exit Exam." *Los Angeles Times*. June 8, 2001.
_____. "In the Classroom: For Teachers, So Much Text, So Little Time." *The Los Angeles Times*. June 27, 2001.
_____. "Kindergarten Is No Longer Child's Play." *Los Angeles Times*. July 11, 2001.

GUERRA, CARLOS. "Instead of Fixing Schools, Create Another Convincing Illusion." *San Antonio Express-News*. June 17, 2001.

HANEY, WALT. "The Myth of the Texas Miracle in Education." *Education Policy Analysis Archives*. August 19, 2000.

HARGROVE, THOMAS. "Testing Boycott Endorsed." *Scripts Howard News Service*. July 10, 2001.

HARRELL, DEBERA CARLTON. "Statewide Anxiety About WASL." *Seattle Post-Intelligence*. April 24, 2000.

HARTOCOLLIS, ANEMONA. "Results of New Reading Test Stir Debate." *New York Times*. June 11, 1999.

_____. "Summer School List May Include Many Students from Last Year." *New York Times*. June 7, 2001.

_____. "No More Test Boycotts, Scarsdale is Warned." *New York Times*. October 31, 2001.

HEGARTY, STEPHEN. "Mother Will Sue for FCAT Materials." *St. Petersburg Times*. November 9, 2001.

HEIM, THERESA. "Cramming for Kindergarten." *Salon.com*. September 6, 2000.

HENRIQUES, DIANA, and JACQUES STEINBERG. "Right Answer, Wrong Score: Test Flaws Take Toll." *New York Times*. May 20, 2001.

_____. When a Test Fails the School, Careers and Reputations Suffer." *New York Times*. May 21, 2001.

HILL, CLIFFORD, and ERIC LARSEN. *Children and Reading Tests*. (2001) Stamford, Connecticut: Ablex.

HOLLOWAY, LYNETTE. "Wrong Numbers Need Not Mean Summer School." *New York Times*. June 13, 2001.

HOLT, NANCY. "When Your Nine-Year-Old Asks for Some Wheels, Buy a Backpack." *Wall Street Journal*. August 24, 2001.

HOUTZ, JOLAYNE. "State's Big Exam Puts Pressure on Teachers, Students." *Seattle Times*. April 20, 2000.

HUBBARD, BENJAMIN L. "Measuring Failure. Is Testing the President's Low Road to School Privatization?" *TomPaine.com*. June 22, 2001.

HUFFINGTON, ARIANNA. "Betraying our children rather than reform our schools, Bush's test-centric education bill will lead to game-show-style teaching and unfairly categorize kids as failures." *Salon.com*. June 7, 2001.

HUGHES JOHN C. "Here We Go a WASLing with the Mary Pranksters." *The Daily World*. April 29, 2001.

HUNT, JUDI. "Anxiety About Test Boosts Sales of WASL Workbook." *Seattle Post-Intelligencer*. April 12, 2000.

HUNT, SPENCER, ANDREA TORTORA, and JENNIFER MROZOWSKI. "High Stakes Tests Raise Stress, Controversy." *Cincinnati Enquirer*. September 3, 2000.

IVINS, MOLLY. "Is Absolutely Everything for Sale in America?" *St. Louis Post-Dispatch*. July 19, 2000.

_____. "The Manufactured Public Schools Crisis." *Creators Syndicate*. September 2, 2000.

_____. "Bad Report Cards: Politicians Fail Our Schools." *Fort Worth Star-Telegram*. July 31, 2001.

JACKSON, DERRICK Z. "MCAS history test is not only silly, it's racist." *Boston Globe.* June 7, 2000.
_____. "A Lesson in Education." *Boston Globe.* June 15, 2001.
_____. "Would Bush Have Survived His Own Education Plan?" *Boston Globe.* June 20, 2001.
JOHNSON, DARRAGH. "Maryland, Virginia Standardized Tests Score High on Parent Anger." *Washington Post.* November 11, 2001.
JOHNSON, DIRK. "Many Schools Putting an End to Child's Play." *New York Times.* April 7, 1998.
JOINT COMMITTEE ON TESTING PRACTICES. *Code of Fair Testing Practices in Education.* (1988) Washington, D.C.: American Psychological Association.
JONES, ANDREA. "Grand Jury Blasts Gateway Exam." *Atlanta Journal Constitution.* March 31, 2001.
JONES, ROBERT A. "The Mysterious Stanford 9. California's New Scholastic Test Is Supposed to Evaluate Our Children, Our Schools, Our Teachers. So Why Are We Forbidden to Know Its Contents?" *Los Angeles Times.* March 5, 2000.
JUDD, ALAN, and KATHY BRISTER. "Barnes: Tell Me How HOPE Info Got Out." *Atlanta Journal Constitution.* July 25, 2001.
_____. "Hope Data Hit by Net Hackers." *Atlanta Journal Constitution.* August 2, 2001.
KANTROWITZ, BARBARA. "A Year in the Life." *Newsweek.* June 4, 2001.
KARP, STAN. "Bush Plan Fails Schools." *Rethinking Schools.* Spring 2001.
KASINDORF, MARTIN, and DEBBIE HOWLETT. "Summer Seen as Critical to Improving Schools." *USA Today.* July 17, 2001.
KASTNER, LINDSAY. "Stakes Are Raised on SOL Tests." *Times-Dispatch.* April 30, 2001.
KERR, JENNIFER. "New Study: Poverty Is Main Factor in Poor Test Scores." *Union-Tribune.* February 25, 2000.
KLEIN, STEPHEN P., LAURA S. HAMILTON, DANIEL F. MCCAFFREY, and BRIAN M. STECHER. "What Do Test Scores in Texas Tell Us?" (2000) Rand Education.
KOHN, ALFIE. "Confusing Harder with Better." *Education Week.* September 15, 1999.
_____. *The Case Against Standardized Testing: Raising the Scores, Ruining the Schools.* (2000) Portsmouth, New Hampshire: Heinemann.
_____. "Standardized Testing and Its Victims. *Education Week.* September 27, 2000.
_____. "Beware of the Standards, Not Just the Tests." *Education Week.* September 26, 2001.
KOLATA, GINA. "When Patients' Records Are Commodities." *New York Times.* November 15, 1995.
KOZOL, JONATHAN. "Industry's Whims Subjugate Student Needs." *School Administrator.* Web edition. www.aasa.org/publications/sa/1997-05/kozol.htm.
KRASHEN, STEPHEN. *Condemned without a Trial: Bogus Arguments Against Bilingual Education.* (1999) Portsmouth, New Hampshire: Heinemann.
KRONHOLZ, JUNE. "Business Groups Push Big Changes for Teachers." *Wall Street Journal.* January 31, 20001.
_____. "What Constitutes Failure? Education Bills Ponder Answer." *Wall Street Journal.* May 21, 2001.

LANE, MARK. "Addressing the Fun Deficit by the Slide." *Daytona Beach News-Journal.* June 15, 2001

LEVINE, BETH. "Say So." *Rosie.* September 2001.

LEONHARDY, GALEN. "Whither? Some Questions, Some Answers." In *Beyond Outcomes,* ed. Richard H. Haswell. (2001) Westport, CT: Ablex.

LEVY, JILL. "Bosses See No Link Between SAT Score, Business Success." *Los Angeles Times.* August 3, 2001.

LEWIS, PETER H. "How Fast Is Your System? That Depends on the Test." *New York Times.* September 10, 1998.

LINES, PATRICIA M. "Does WASL Pass the Test?" *Seattle Times.* September 15, 2000.

LUCAS, GREG. "'Abysmal' Exit Test Results for 9th-Graders." *San Francisco Chronicle.* June 7, 2001.

MCNAMARA, EILEEN. "Hard Sells Fails Test." *Boston Globe.* February 28, 2001.
_____. "Which Facts, What Truths." *Boston Globe.* July 25, 2001.

MANZO, KATHLEEN KENNEDY. "Protests Over State Testing Widespread." *Education Week.* May 16, 2001.

MARAN, MEREDITH. "The Perfect High: An Illinois Public School Admits the Gifted, Offers Prozac and Achieves Stunning Success. But Is It Fair?" *Salon.com.* January 24, 2001.

MARKEL, HOWARD. "When the Doctor Is Forced to Fire a Patient." *New York Times.* August 14, 2001.

MARTINEZ, BARBARA. "Care Guidelines Used by Insurers Face Scrutiny." *Wall Street Journal.* September 14, 2000.

MARTINEZ, MICHAEL. "Summer School the Biggest Ever." *Chicago Tribune.* June 20, 2001.

MATHEWS, JAY. "An Educational Melodrama Is Expanding." *Washington Post.* April 3, 2001.
_____. "Assessing Ability Versus Memorization." *Washington Post.* July 3, 2001.
_____. "Measuring Ways to Score Schools." *Washington Post.* July 17, 2001.
_____. "SOL Debate Reveals Bitter Division in Virginia. *Washington Post.* July 31, 2001.

MATHEWS, JAY, and VICTORIA BENNING. "VA Poll Gives SOLs Vote of No Confidence." *Washington Post.* September 11, 2000.

MAXLEY, STATE REP. GLEN. "Lies Can't Mask Bush's Bad Record on Texas Kids." *Houston Chronicle.* July 31, 2000.

MELTON R. H. "Virginia Pays $1 Million On TV Ads for SOL. *Washington Post.* October 6, 2000.

MICKELSON, ROSLYN ARLIN. "International Business Machinations: A Case Study of Corporate Involvement in Local Educational Reform." *Teachers College Record.* Spring 1999.

MORITA, JENNIFER K. "Marysville School's Test Rewards Have Some Parents Upset." *Sacramento Bee.* April 4, 2001.

MORRIS, BONNIE ROTHMAN, "School Testing Bandwagon Spawns Coaching Sites." *New York Times.* May 24, 2001.

MURPHY, SHARON. "'No-one Has Ever Grown Taller as a Result of Being Measured' Revisited: More Educational Measurement Lessons for Canadians."

In *The Erosion of Democracy in Education*, ed. John P. Portelli and R. Patrick Solomon. (2001) Calgary: Detselig Enterprises.

MYERS, K. C. "State Use of MCAS Exams 'Wrong.'" *Cape Cod Times*. May 22, 2001.

NEILL, MONTY. "High-Stakes Testing Flunks." *USA Today*. September 7, 1999.

NUSSBAUM, DEBRA. "Does School Testing Make the Grade?" *New York Times*. December 12, 1999.

OHANIAN, SUSAN. *One Size Fits Few: The Folly of Educational Standards*. (1999) Portsmouth, New Hampshire: Heinemann.

_____. "Goals 2000: What's in a Name?" *Phi Delta Kappan*. January 2000.

_____. *Caught in the Middle: Nonstandard Kids and a Killing Curriculum*. (2000) Portsmouth, New Hampshire: Heinemann.

_____. "You Say Stakeholder; I Say Robber Baron." *Language Arts*. November 2000.

O'HARA, DELIA. "How Much Is Too Much Homework?" Sun Times. August, 21, 2001.

OKEON, MOLLY R. "Scarsdale 8th-Graders May Skip State Tests." *Journal News*. April 11, 2001.

OLDON, LYNN. "Study Questions Reliability of Single-Year Test-Score Gains." *Education Week*. May 23, 2001.

OREL, STEVE. "Raising Standards By Pushing Students Out of School." *New Democracy*. March-June 2001.

ORFIELD, GARY, and JOHANNA WALD. "Testing. Testing. The High-Stakes Testing Mania Hurts Poor and Minority Students the Most." *The Nation*. July 5, 2000.

ORLICH, DON. "Education Reform and Limits to Student Achievement." *Phi Delta Kappan*. February 2000.

ORWELL, GEORGE. "Politics and the English Language." *Horizon*. April 1946.

OTTO, STEVE. "She's Taking the Battle to Z-Hills." *Tampa Tribune*. October 25, 2000.

PAGE, CLARENCE. "Parenting Makes Experts of Us All." *Jewish World Review*. May 22, 2001.

PAIGE, ROD. "Why We Must Have Testing." *Washington Post*. May 13, 2000.

PALM, JOHN. "WASL Is Trojan Horse for Social Control." *Seattle Times*. May 11, 2000.

PARDINGTON, SUZANNE. "Schools Learning Drill. Strict Houston Model Draws Much Attention." *Contra Costa Times*. February 11, 2001.

PASSY, CHARLES, and SARAH COLLINS. "End-of-Summer Rush For Supplies Begins." *Washington Post*. August 17, 2001.

PASTERNAK, JUDY. "Judgment Day approaches for poorly performing schools." *Los Angeles Times*. February 27, 2000.

PATRICK, KELLIE. "Palm Beach Teachers Quitting Their Jobs at Alarming Rate." *Sun-Sentinel*. March 1, 2000.

PERLSTEIN, LINDA. "Essay Test's Failings May Hold Back Maryland Students." *Washington Post*. June 15, 2001.

PHILLIPS, PAUL. "DOE Calculates Performance Standards . . . Incorrectly!" *New Democracy*. March-June 2001.

PIPKIN, GLORIA. "Glo, the Gov., and the Fourth Grade: E-Mail Dialogue." *Florida Coalition for Assessment Reform.* www.angelfire.com/fl4/fcar/page28.html.

POPPEN, JULIE. "Teacher Won't Give CSAP Test." *Rocky Mountain News.* January 27, 2001.

PORTER, JEFF. "Test Scores Don't Tell Whole Story of School Performance." *Arkansas Democrat-Gazette.* February 28, 2000.

PORTILLO, ERNESTO JR. "Schools Should Teach Thinking, Not How to Pass Standard Tests." *Arizona Star.* July 28, 2001.

POSTMAN, DAVID. "Letourneau Lands on WASL as Answer, Raising Questions." *Seattle Times.* May 4, 2001.

POWELL, MICHAEL. "In New York, Putting Down Their Pencils. Parent Rebellion Against Standardized Testing Strikes at Heart of Bush Plan." *Washington Post.* May 18, 2001.

QUACH, HANK KIM. "SABE Test More Closely Gauges Students' Progress." *Fresno Bee.* July 17, 1999.

QUAMMEN, DAVID. *Boilerplate Rhino.* (2001) New York: Touchstone.

QUINTANILLA, RAY. "Summer's No Break for City 3rd Graders." *Chicago Tribune.* June 12, 2001.

REICH, ROBERT, "One Size Doesn't Fit All." *The School Administrator.* March 2001.

ROBBINS, MEG. "The Failure of Testing." *Salon.com.* May 11, 2001.

ROTHACKER, JENNIFER WING. "Controversial in N.C., Tests Praised by Bush." *Charlotte Observer.* April 10, 2001.

ROTHSTEIN, RICHARD. *The Way We Were? The Myths and Realities of America's Student Achievement.* (1998) New York: The Century Foundation Press.

_____. "Lessons: How Tests Can Drop the Ball." *New York Times.* September 13, 2000.

_____. "The Blame Game. Are Public Schools Holding Back the Nation's Economy?" *The School Administrator.* March 2001.

_____. "Lessons: In the Kindergartens, A Misguided Push." *New York Times.* March 21, 2001.

_____. "Lessons: How to Ease the Burden of Homework for Families." *New York Times.* May 23, 2001.

_____. "Lessons: Test Here and There, Not Everywhere." *New York Times.* June 6, 2001.

_____. "Who Puts the Standards Into Standardized Tests?" *New York Times.* July 18, 2001.

_____. "Lessons: Food For Thought? In Many Cases, No." *New York Times.* August 1, 2001.

RURAL POLICY MATTERS. "Parents Saying No to High Stakes Testing." *Rural Policy Matters.* February 2001.

RUSSAKOFF, DALE. "A Tough Question for the Testers." *Washington Post.* February 10, 2001.

RUST, EDWARD. *No Turning Back: A Progress Report on the Business Roundtable.* (1999) www.brtable.org.

SACCHETTI, MARIA. "Nap, Play—and Take a Test." *Orange County Register*. April 8, 2000.

SACKS, PETER. *Standardized Minds: The High Price of America's Testing Culture and What We Can Do To Change It*. (1999) Cambridge, Mass: Perseus.

_____. "Predictable Losers in Testing Schemes." *The School Administrator*. December 2001.

SAGER, MICHELLE. "Could You Make the Grade?" *Tampa Tribune*. No date.

SAINT-EXUPÉRY, ANTOINE. *Le Petit Prince*. (2001) New York: Harcourt Brace and Company.

SALZER, JAMES. "Teachers Find Flaws in State Test's Science Part." *Arizona Daily Star*. June 3, 2001.

SANCHEZ, RICARDO. "Will State Tests Harm Latino Students?" *Seattle Times*. May 3, 2000.

SARASOHN, DAVID. "Oregon Student Testing: On the Level?" *Oregonian*. February 18, 2001.

SCHMIDT, GEORGE. "10,000 Students Pushed Out." *Substance*. October 2000.

SCHMIDT-NIELSEN, KNUT. *The Camel's Nose*. (1998) Washington D.C.: Island Press.

SCHRAG, PETER. "High Stakes Are for Tomatoes." *The Atlantic Monthly*. August 2000.

_____. "SAT 9 Days—California's Thriving Test-Prep Culture." *Sacramento Bee*. May 2, 2001.

SCHULTE, BRIGID. "Scores Led Montgomery to Scrap Exam." *Washington Post*. February 14, 2001.

SCOTT, JANNY. "Truths, Half-Truths, and the Census." *New York Times*. July 1, 2001.

SEATTLE POST-INTELLIGENCER STAFF. "Decoded State Test for 10th-graders Spells 'Letourneau.'" *Seattle Post-Intelligencer*. April 27, 2001.

SEYMOUR, LIZ. "SOL Tests Create New Dropouts. Frustrated Va. Teachers Switching Courses, Leaving Public School." *Washington Post*. July 17, 2001.

SHEA, CHRISTOPHER. "It's Come To This." *Teacher*. May 2000.

SILBERMAN, TODD. "A Fifth-Grade Pressure Cooker." *News Observer*. February 16, 2001.

SINHA, VANDANA. "Give Kids Recess, Virginia Beach Parents Urge." *Norfolk Virginia-Pilot*. March 21, 2000.

SLATER, JIM R. *Oklahoma Observer*. April 25, 2001.

SMILEY, JANE. *Horse Heaven*. (2000) New York: Knopf.

SMOLKIN, RACHEL. "With Assessment Tests, the Stakes Are High for Testers and Testees." *Post-Gazette*. August 27, 2000.

SPLETE, HEIDI. "Backpack Fitness: Rx for Heavy Class Loads." *Washington Post*. August 28, 2001.

STANLEY, THOMAS. *The Millionaire Mind*. (2000) Kansas City: Andrews McMeel.

STEINBERG, JACQUES. "Student Failure Causes States to Retool Testing Programs." *New York Times*. December 22, 2000.

STOEVER, DEL. "Who Grades the Essay on Standardized Tests? The Answer Might Surprise You." *School Board News*. March 23, 1999.

STONEWALL JACKSON HIGH SCHOOL. "2001 Summer Reading Program for Stonewall Jackson High School Students."

STRATMAN, DAVE. "A Call For Mass Refusal 2001." *New Democracy*. March-June 2001.

STRINE, FRED A. "Need a WASL Scapegoat? Blame the English Teacher." *Seattle Post-Intelligencer*. September 23, 2000.

STUTZ, TERRENCE, and MIKE JACKSON. "500 Schools Exceeded Class Limits. Dallas, Houston Have Majority of Overload." *Dallas Morning News*. July 29, 2001.

SWARTZ, MIMI. "TAASed Out." *Slate.com*. April 24, 2001.

SWOPE, KATHY, and BARBARA MINER, eds. *Failing Our Kids: Why the Testing Craze Won't Fix Our Schools*. (2000) Milwaukee: Rethinking Schools.

TOMSHO, ROBERT. "Heavy Tax Abatements Keep Firms in Toledo but Drain Education Coffers." *Wall Street Journal*. July 18, 2001.

TOSTO, PAUL. "Some Just Say No to Minnesota Exam." *Pioneer Press*. March 12, 2001.

TRUBETZ, AMY. *Haute Cuisine: How the French Invented the Culinary Profession*. (2001) Philadelphia: University of Pennsylvania Press.

TYLER, ANNE. *The Accidental Tourist*. (1985) New York: Knopf.

ULFERTS, ALISA. "Group Begins Campaign Against FCAT." *St. Petersburg Times*. July 31, 2001.

URBAN, HAL. "What Can a Flawed Test Tell Us, Anyway?" *Newsweek*. August 20, 2001.

VIADERO, DEBRA. "CTB Knew of Problems Earlier." *Education Week*. October 20, 1999.

VIADERO, DEBRA, and JULIE BLAIR. "Error Affects Test Results in Six States." *Education Week*. September 29, 1999.

WALSH-SARNECKI, PEGGY. "District Plan Angers Teachers: 12 Detroit Schools Need Reconstituting." *Detroit Free Press*. June 18, 2001.

WARTZMAN, RICK. "How Support Eroded for a Program Intended to 'End Starvation Wages.'" *Wall Street Journal*. July 19, 2001.

WELLSTONE, PAUL. *Conscience of a Liberal*. (2001) New York: Random House.

WELLSTONE, PAUL, and JONATHAN KOZOL. "What Tests Can't Fix." *New York Times*. March 13, 2001.

WELSH, JOHN. "Parents May Get More Access to Tests. Change Considered After Firm Botched Scores." *Saint Paul Pioneer Press*. August 2, 2000.

WELSH-HUGGINS, ANDREW. "Lawmakers rethinking views on proficiency-test mandates." *The Columbus Dispatch*. September 2, 2000.

WILDAVSKY, BEN. "The Question is: Are Tests Failing the Kids?" *US News and World Report*. May 21, 2001.

WILGOREN, JODI, and JACQUES STEINBERG. "Under Pressure: A Special Report; Even for Sixth Graders, College Looms." *New York Times*. July 3, 2000.

YARDLEY, JIM. "A Test Is Born." *New York Times*. April 9, 2000.

_____. "Critics Say A Focus on Test Scores Is Overshadowing Education in Texas." *New York Times*. October 30, 2000.

ZERNIKE, KATE. "As Homework Load Grows, One District Says 'Enough.'" *New York Times*. October 10, 2000

_____. "No Time for Napping in Today's Kindergarten." *New York Times*. October 23, 2000.

_____. "School Officials in Westchester Ask State to Suspend New Tests." *New York Times*. November 2, 2000.

_____. "Word for Word of Little Brain: Ritalin to the Rescue: A Children's Story for Our Times." *New York Times*. February 4, 2001.

_____. "Scarsdale Mothers Succeed in First Boycott of 8th-Grade Test." *New York Times*. May 4, 2001.

# Index